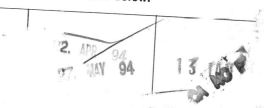

THE FUTURE OF VOLUNTARY ORGANISATIONS

REPORT OF THE WOLFENDEN COMMITTEE

THE FUTURE OF VOLUNTARY ORGANISATIONS

REPORT OF THE
WOLFENDEN COMMITTEE

Croom Helm London

© 1978 The Joseph Rowntree Memorial Trust and
Carnegie United Kingdom Trust
Croom Helm Ltd, 2—10 St John's Road, London SW11

British Library Cataloguing in Publication Data

The future of voluntary organisations.
   1. Volunteer workers in social service — Great
   Britain
   I. Wolfenden, John, *Baron Wolfenden*
   361.7'0941   HV245

   ISBN 0-85664-539-7
   ISBN 0-85664-660-1   Pbk

Printed in Great Britain by offset lithography by
Billing & Sons Ltd, Guildford, London and Worcester

CONTENTS

PREFACE

The Joseph Rowntree Memorial Trust and the Carnegie United Kingdom Trust appointed the following persons to be members of the Committee on Voluntary Organisations:

Chairman	Lord Wolfenden CBE
Members	Professor Anthony Bradley
	Miss Helen Brotherton OBE JP
	Mrs Gwyneth Evans OBE
	Professor Roger Hadley
	Mr David Jones OBE
	Miss Caroline Moorehead
	Dr Joyce Neill MB BChir
	Sir James Swaffield CBE RD
	Mr Lewis Waddilove OBE JP
Government Observer	Mr Tony Hart, Head of the Voluntary Services Unit, from 1st October 1974 to January 1975 when he was succeeded by Miss Margaret Clayton.
Secretary	Mr H. G. Croly CBE JP
Assistant Secretary	Mrs Sylvia Armour
Senior Research Officer	Mr Stephen Hatch

The Committee met on 31 occasions between 2nd October 1974 and 28th June 1977 and held two weekend conferences. In addition the Committee's Research Group met 15 times, and 93 sessions were held by small groups of Committee members and staff for receiving oral evidence.

1 OUR BACKGROUND AND APPROACH

We were appointed on 1 October 1974 by the Joseph Rowntree Memorial Trust and the Carnegie United Kingdom Trust to review the role and functions of voluntary organisations in the United Kingdom over the next twenty-five years.

We were recruited as members of the Committee by the two Trusts as persons, reasonably familiar with the field, who might be described as being sympathetic without being uncritical and critical without being unsympathetic. We come from many fields, from all parts of the United Kingdom; no one of us is carrying a banner, political, geographical or professional; we have served as individuals, not as representatives of any bodies or organisations.

In response to direct invitation from us and to our advertisements in the national Press we have received 320 submissions of written evidence.[1] Ninety-three interviews have been held, for the discussion of this evidence or for the purpose of benefiting from the experience of persons or groups with special knowledge. Some of these interviews have been conducted by the Committee as a whole, others by individual members of the Committee or its staff. Five members of the Committee were designated as a Research Group, to supervise the work of our Senior Research Officer, Mr Stephen Hatch, and his assistants. This work includes the 'locality studies' discussed in Chapter 3. Our Secretary, Mr H. G. Croly, and Assistant Secretary, Mrs Sylvia Armour, have carried a very heavy burden of arranging meetings, preparing papers and organising countless details, with unfailing efficiency, promptitude and cheerfulness.

There were two major reasons which prompted the Trusts to initiate such an enquiry. The first relates to their own activities. Since they spend almost the whole of their income in grants to what are broadly called 'voluntary organisations' or to individuals engaged in 'voluntary' activities, they thought that a review of the voluntary field might help them in their planning of the allocation of their funds over the next twenty-five years. The second reason was a more general one. It is some thirty years since the advent of what is comprehensively known as 'The Welfare State', which brought under statutory control and administration many of the activities which until that time had been conducted by voluntary agencies of one kind or another. (We use the word 'statutory' in a general sense to mean services provided by central or local government, and not in the narrower sense of something established by Act of Parliament.) Some of these statutory activities in the field of the social services were authoritatively examined by Lord Seebohm's Committee on Local Authority and Allied Personal Social Services.[2] But no comprehensive review had ever been made, so far as the Trusts were aware, of the effects on our whole national fabric of this fundamental change in the manner of meeting social needs. So it seemed that the time was ripe for some wide-ranging enquiry into the impact of the comparatively new statutory provisions on those areas where previously the burden had been carried by individuals or by groups coming together in voluntary association to deal with specific problems or needs. Certainly our enquiry did not originate in any suspicion of general incompetence, weakness, or inefficiency in what is sometimes called 'the voluntary movement'. On the contrary, the volume and vigour of voluntary activity make it a sufficiently important element in our national life to deserve a dispassionate and considered appraisal.

In writing this report we have tried to keep in mind four different classes of potential readers. First, there are the millions of our fellow citizens who might without disrespect be called the rank-and-file of the voluntary army. They make what contributions they can, in skills or money or time, to one or other of the voluntary organisations, and the organisations could not possibly carry on without them; but they would not claim to be leaders or experts. Secondly, there are those who hold positions of responsibility in the organisations, as administrators, field-workers or honorary officers. Much of what we say will be very familiar to them, and we have learnt a great deal from the evidence which individually and collectively they have submitted to us. Thirdly, there are the policy-makers, at national and local level, and the officials who advise them. We hope that they may find here some evidence of the voluntary contribution to the total picture. Fourthly, there are those who as social scientists have an academic, theoretical or research interest in the pattern of our national life. They may find the report as it stands inadequately based in fact and solid information. But we hope that the considerable volume of specialised material which has been amassed by our research group may be published separately later on; meanwhile, the appendices to the report provide some of the evidence for our conclusions.

We have tried to write as simply and straightforwardly as the subject allows. But inevitably there are possibilities of ambiguity and confusion in many of the words and phrases which are regularly used in discussing these topics. In our usage a voluntary organisation does not cease to be 'voluntary' if some of its members are paid or if it receives money from public funds, national or local. Nor does a 'volunteer' cease to be properly so described if he or she receives expenses or a mileage allowance. Nor is there a direct antithesis between 'voluntary' and 'professional'. It might be held to make for clarity if the word 'voluntary' were discarded and the word 'non-statutory' used instead. We have rejected this escape-route because we think that (a) it defines the 'voluntary' in too negative a way; (b) it suggests a rigid antithesis between the statutory and the voluntary; (c) since the boundaries of statutory provision are continually moving as legislation is enacted, the distinction as so expressed depends less on a difference of substance than on an accident of time and date; (d) 'non-statutory' does not exclude commercial provision, as we wish to do.

Our first problem was to decide what meaning we were to give to the words 'voluntary organisation'. A bewildering variety of activities falls within the untidy boundaries of the words as commonly used, as Lord Goodman's Committee of Inquiry on Charity Law and Voluntary Organisations found. The spectrum extends, for instance, from the National Council of Social Service, through the multifarious well-known national bodies which are members of it (e.g. Age Concern, National Association of Youth Clubs, Save the Children Fund), through regional or local branches or units of them, to small groups brought together in a town or village for particular and sometimes short-lived purposes. Accordingly, we began by consulting a very wide range of organisations. But as our work progressed it became clear that we should have to limit the scope of our enquiry in some way, so we adopted the self-imposed restrictions which we define later in this paragraph. In consequence, many of those whom we consulted will find that we make little or no reference to them in this report. These omissions are not to be taken as implying any value-judgements about the merit or importance of the work they are doing. Nor is our gratitude to them, for the information and help they have given us, in any way diminished. We simply had to draw boundaries somewhere. In another dimension, were we to include the churches, universities, trade unions, political parties? Our view was that we should not include them as such but that we should not exclude activities which they undertake or sponsor inside the fields which we have taken as our main concern. We decided that as a general guideline commonsense or common parlance must prevail over verbal consistency or logical precision, and that we would take as the centre or focus of

our review voluntary organisations dealing with the personal social
services and what is generally known as the 'environment'. We extended
our range outwards as far as time would reasonably permit and covered
a somewhat wider field in our research. By 'personal social services' we
mean, for the purposes of our report, services containing a social work
element and designed by our society to meet the needs of individuals
who are at a particular disadvantage in that society by reason of, for
instance, old age or physical handicap. If we were not to extend our
deliberations beyond the twenty-five-year time-span of our terms of
reference some such limitation seemed to us necessary, arbitrary as we
know it to be. Our hope is that our conclusions about this delimited
field of concentrated enquiry may prove to be capable of extension to
other areas.

Our concern is explicitly with organisations. Inevitably (and, as we
believe, rightly) we have given some consideration to the voluntary
principle itself, which leads individuals to band themselves together in
an organisation to embody a particular purpose or to express a
particular point of view; and our thoughts on this fundamental element
in our social structure are set out in Chapter 2. We have not attempted
any deep or detailed assessment of the contribution made by individual
volunteers, either within or outside the framework of the statutory
services. This is not from any lack of appreciation of the work they do;
on the contrary, the more we have learnt about it, the more we have
come to admire and respect it. And we are aware of the Report of the
Aves Committee of Enquiry into Voluntary Workers in the Social
Services and the present activities of the Volunteer Centre which
resulted from it. Similarly, we have made no quantitative assessment of
the simple care which is spontaneously and unobtrusively given every
day and night by neighbours to neighbours. Indeed, it is difficult to
assess, from its very unobtrusiveness; but we have no doubt that a
great deal more of it goes on than is commonly recognised.

We tried at the start to find some method of classifying or categor-
ising voluntary organisations, by size, history, form of administration,
nature of service provided, and so on. As our enquiry proceeded, we
found that different patterns of classification were useful for different
purposes. So we have not hesitated to use whichever seemed the most
illuminating one in a particular context. We recognise that this may
involve a risk of confusion; but in a field where, from the diversity of
the constituent elements, systematic rigour is not easy to achieve, we
have preferred that risk to the greater risk of distorting the facts for the
sake of an artificial tidiness.

We have not tried to prepare an encyclopedia or compendium of information about voluntary organisations. We have indeed assembled a good deal of factual information, partly from enquiries and research which we have ourselves initiated. But our concern, in accordance with our terms of reference, is primarily with the future, and our primary interest in facts is therefore to enable us to form a general picture of the present so that we might have a basis for looking into the future.

It was natural that most of our written evidence should come from organisations which were national in character and, more often than not, London based. We felt that to rely solely on that might well give us an incomplete and possibly misleading picture. We therefore arranged that our research staff should conduct several detailed enquiries in selected localities in various parts of the United Kingdom. These 'locality studies', as we came to call them, provided us with more detailed information from carefully selected and well-defined areas, and we record here our thanks to the thousands of people who have helped us in these enquiries. We are also indebted to National Opinion Polls Ltd for including in one of their surveys questions of specific relevance to our enquiry. We were aware too of the danger of undue emphasis, within the United Kingdom, on England in general and London in particular. So we arranged visits, each extending over several days, to Cardiff, Edinburgh and Belfast, in the course of which some of our members had conversations with representatives of a wide range of voluntary organisations working in these parts of the United Kingdom. For this same reason we visited Liverpool and some other major provincial centres, and, for purposes of comparison with a foreign country, the Netherlands (see Appendix 7).

All the time we have been conscious of one over-riding fact. What is generally known as 'the voluntary movement' is a living thing. New organisations are formed to meet newly-discerned needs. Others die. Yet others change their emphasis or venture into fresh fields. Relations with statutory authorities constantly change with new legislation or changes in administration. There is nothing static about the scene. This has meant that we have not been able to look at a timeless framed picture, but rather at a particular 'still' in a moving film. We have tried to stop the film at our appointed moment in time and to look as carefully as we can at our contemporary 'still'. This inevitably means that we are conditioned by the circumstances which at this moment surround us, economic stringencies, continuing inflation, national uncertainties about the future. We may therefore be giving undue weight to factors which may turn out, by the end of the twenty-five-year period we are asked to take under review, to have been transient; or conversely, we may have under-estimated factors which are only just now emerging. This is a disability which, writing when we do, we cannot avoid; but it is a point which we hope our readers will keep in mind.

Notes

1. Lists of respondents and a copy of the questionnaire to which they replied will be found in Appendix 1.
2. *Report of the Committee on Local Authority and Allied Personal Social Services* (1968).

2 THE VOLUNTARY SECTOR IN PERSPECTIVE

Voluntary action in Britain covers a myriad of different activities and is
undertaken from many different motives. It is not helpful to imply that
there is anything like a unified voluntary 'movement' with a common
philosophy guiding its work. Yet as a committee considering the role of
voluntary organisations we must necessarily make our own values clear
if we are to go beyond mere description.

We start by recognising two fundamental concerns: first, to encourage
the strengthening and extension of collective action to meet important
social needs in the provision of health care, housing, welfare, the
maintenance of minimum standards of income and the protection of
the environment; second, to ensure that this provision should be so
organised that it is consistent with maintaining a pluralistic system, that
is, a system in which power is spread over several political, social and
economic institutions and not concentrated in a few monolithic
structures. We therefore accept at the outset that voluntary organisations constitute only one of the means of meeting recognised social
needs. There are three other sectors or 'systems' concerned with
meeting these needs: the informal network of support provided by
family, friends and neighbours; the commercial or market system of
provision; and the statutory social services. Although in this report we
are strictly concerned with the voluntary sector, we must take some
account of the contribution of each of the other sectors, and of their
interaction with the voluntary sector, if we are to make recommendations which will be likely to strengthen collective action as a whole.
Further, this inter-relationship itself cannot be understood unless it is
seen in historical perspective.

We begin with a brief sketch of the development of voluntary
provision in Britain over the last two centuries, and its relation with
other kinds of help. We then examine in outline the current contribution of each of the four systems of meeting social need. In this way we
try to identify the range of roles which can most appropriately be
undertaken by the voluntary sector, and the nature of the interactions
with the other systems that is implied.

The Development of Voluntary Provision in Britain
The last two hundred years have seen profound changes in the provision

15

of social services. Behind these changes lie not simply the development
of an industrial society with the wealth, technology and organisational
skills on which sophisticated and comprehensive statutory services
could be constructed, but also major changes in social ideology and
structure. In summarising the principal developments in social
provisions over the last two hundred years it is possible to identify four
main phases.[1] The first, which we will call 'the last phase of paternalism', lasted until 1834. The second, which we will call 'the era of state
deterrence and voluntary expansion', covered the years 1834-1905.
The third, marked by the emergence of statutory social services,
occupied the next forty years. The final phase, which runs from 1945
to the present day, we describe as 'the consolidation of the welfare
state'.

The Last Phase of Paternalism

For most people the first resort in times of need two hundred years ago
was to family, friends and neighbours (what we have called the 'informal
system'). A commercial system existed too and those who could afford
it could buy the services of doctor; teacher, insurance company and so
on. But for the large majority, the only help available beyond the
informal system was from charity or the parish. Religion and social
service were closely intertwined throughout this period and well beyond
it into the twentieth century. Religious inspiration showed itself in
many kinds of philanthropy, including the provision of material
support, education and homes for the orphan, the crippled and the
elderly. But perhaps more important than religion was the traditional
bond of the aristocracy and gentry with those beneath them. The
paternalism and patronage which characterised class relationships in
much of the country were exercised not only on behalf of those in
work, through the protection of their wages. They operated also for the
destitute and sick, through the control of local charities and influence
on the management of Poor Law administration at parish level. The
challenge to the old order which developed towards the end of the
eighteenth century and in the early decades of the nineteenth century,
can be related both to the emergence of a new industrial and commercial class and to the 'abdication on the part of the governors'.[2] New
economic opportunities led the aristocracy and gentry to dismantle the
system of protection of wages and conditions of work and to attack the
old Poor Law. These changes were sanctioned by philosophers and
economists such as Smith and Bentham, who expounded the pernicious
effects of wage regulation, indiscriminate charity and poor relief on the

system of *laissez faire* and self-help which they believed was the prerequisite of prosperity and happiness.

The Era of State Deterrence and Voluntary Expansion (1834-1905)

The new views triumphed when the last main prop of the old system of protection, the Poor Law, was knocked away. The Poor Law Amendment Act of 1834 introduced a centrally controlled deterrent system of relief under which outdoor relief was drastically reduced, and many people in serious distress preferred to go without help rather than go into the workhouse. The new philosophy influenced many of those concerned with charity, and they sought to ensure that their policies of charitable giving were consistent with those underlying the administration of poor relief. The deserving poor had to be distinguished from the undeserving. The former could receive help to set them on their feet again but the latter must be left to the salutary experience of the workhouse. The culmination of attempts to rationalise charitable work on these lines was the founding of the Charity Organisation Society in 1869 with the aim of coordinating the activities in each area to prevent excessive help being given to any particular client, and to encourage the 'scientific' evaluation of each individual case.

By no means all voluntary activity was so heavily influenced by these self-help philosophies. Throughout the nineteenth century, and more particularly during the second half of it, many voluntary organisations were established to deal with a wide range of different categories of need, and helped people who otherwise would have had no other recourse but the Poor Law. For example, orphanages were opened by pioneers like Barnardo and Stephenson. Special organisations were established to help the blind, the deaf, the mentally defective, the crippled. Several of the churches set up organisations to undertake moral welfare work, and this was also a first concern of the new Salvation Army (founded in 1865). Settlements were established in London and many other large cities, following the example of Canon Barnett at Toynbee Hall (1884), to set up what we should now describe as community work projects.

Behind much of this new work was a very different understanding of the nature of the causes of social problems from that of Bentham and his colleagues. It was becoming increasingly clear, even before the pioneer studies of Booth (1891) and Rowntree (1901), that the conditions imposed by industrialisation were directly related to the widespread poverty, disease and ignorance among the people. In the 1880s, socialism, which had existed earlier in other forms such as

Owenism, was re-born under Marxist influence, and offered a comprehensive criticism of the existing society. From an unapologetically
working-class standpoint it singled out for attack such doctrines as
those of the Charity Organisation Society and the Poor Law, and
demanded radical reforms. More cautiously and painstakingly the new
Fabian Society (1885) began to pile up evidence for collective action as
the only solution to the problem of poverty.

The Emergence of Statutory Social Services

During its long period in opposition at the end of the century the
Liberal Party became conscious of changing attitudes to the causes of
poverty and related social problems. On return to power in 1905, the
Party embarked on a programme of legislation which, although initially
limited in scope, marked the beginning of a new epoch in the provision
of social services. Pensions, school meals, school medical services,
unemployment and health insurance for certain sections of the population, were all introduced outside the system of poor relief. Once the
principle of state involvement in ensuring minimum standards became
established, there followed a continuing extension of services to other
sections of the population and to new types of provision. In the inter-
war period the coverage of national insurance was extended to include
most of the working population, the State took over from the Poor
Law the responsibility for paying unemployment assistance and there
was public involvement on a large scale in housing. The Beveridge
Report in 1942, with its recommendations for a comprehensive
system of social security and its assumption of national provision for
health, education, housing and employment, was a logical culmination
of the process.

Throughout this period the voluntary sector continued to act as a
major provider of basic services. For example, voluntary hospitals
remained independent. Care of children and the handicapped relied
heavily on voluntary organisations. The new national insurance scheme
was administered in part by voluntary associations. There were even
some who felt that the voluntary sector should assume further major
responsibilities. In 1909 the majority report of the Royal Commission
on the Poor Law recommended that voluntary aid councils should be
set up in every county to parallel the public assistance authorities, and
should care for the needs of all those except the completely destitute.
The report was not acted on by the government of the day, but
attempts to coordinate voluntary effort at local level through Guilds of
Help and Councils of Voluntary Service became increasingly common.

In 1919 this movement found expression at national level in the establishment of the National Council of Social Service. The Council soon moved beyond coordination to direct action and became involved in helping to set up rural community councils and community centres and, when the slump came, sponsored unemployment clubs and other measures to help in the worst hit areas.

But the growing involvement of the state in the provision of social services made its impact. Voluntary organisations providing or sharing in the provision of basic services, such as the voluntary hospitals, were increasingly subject to criticism. Many agreed with Professor Simey when he wrote in 1937[3] that 'the solid framework of social administration must be provided by the State, which must also carry the burden of the "mass-production" services'. Simey went on to stress the importance of creating proper links between public and voluntary bodies to ensure that the work of the latter 'will be truly "supplementary" and not an unsatisfactory substitute for properly organised public services'. Voluntary organisations were increasingly finding themselves in the role the Webbs had proposed for them as an 'extension ladder' to the statutory services rather than the parallel but separate system which the Charity Organisation Society and its supporters had advocated.

The Consolidation of the Welfare State

The process of rationalising the hotch-potch of statutory provisions and establishing a comprehensive system of social services started with the first plans for a national health service and the passage of legislation for universal secondary education in 1944. The Labour Government of 1945-51 implemented most of the Beveridge proposals, the Poor Law was finally removed from the statute book, and the obligation of the State to provide basic social services to the citizen as of right was for the most part established.

The history of the voluntary sector over the last three decades has been dominated by the problems of adaptation to the new role of government. It is possible to distinguish two phases within this period. In the years immediately after the Second World War, some people expected that the establishment of a comprehensive system of social services would automatically lead to the withering away of voluntary action.[4] Others felt that while voluntary action might change its nature, it would continue to be of vital importance. Lord Beveridge, for example, detailed in his report, *Voluntary Action*[5] the ways in which he believed voluntary organisations would still be called on to help the old, children, the physically and mentally handicapped and others in need. But above all he stressed the importance of the moral contribution of the voluntary sector in 'making and keeping something other than the pursuit of gain as the dominant force in society'. This theme was taken up by others reviewing the future of voluntary action at this time. As Roger Wilson,[6] submitting evidence to Beveridge, put it, 'unpretentious neighbourliness is good in itself and there is a real danger that a society which thinks in terms of social planning may strike at the roots of spontaneous neighbourliness'. Wilson went on to stress the importance of the educative value of voluntary organisations and the training they give in social responsibility. The growth in state involvement in the social services, he concluded, in no way weakened 'the need for voluntary social responsibility in this country if the gap between "they" and the community as a whole is to be bridged . . .'.

Nevertheless, during the first fifteen to twenty years after the Second World War, the voluntary sector seems in some ways to have been marking time. Apart from the loss of the voluntary hospitals and much of the work of the Friendly Societies to the state sector, the pattern of provision seems to have remained much as it was at the end of the war. It was as though time was needed to absorb the substantial increase in state involvement in the social services and to assess its adequacy. However, from the late 1950s onwards we can see a number of significant developments in voluntary action. These included (a) the reorientation of some service organisations to differentiate their contribution from that of statutory agencies (e.g. the provision of specialist services, not available in the statutory sector, by Barnardo's and the Church of England Children's Society), (b) the rapid growth of pressure-group organisations, seeking to change government policy (e.g. Shelter, Disablement Income Group, Child Poverty Action Group), (c) the flowering of mutual-help groups in fields from preschool play to the drug addict and the single parent family, (d) the growth of coordinating bodies at local and national level, and (e) the increasing encouragement of voluntary organisations by local and central government, including most recently the Voluntary Services Unit, through grant-aid.

To summarise, in the development of social provision over the last two hundred years the pace was first set by the voluntary sector, and then by the State. The development of both indicates that the informal and commercial systems were no longer sufficient on their own to offer an acceptable minimum standard of provision. But it does not follow that either the commercial or the informal system had become redundant. It is true that the commercial system was weakened considerably as state provision outside the Poor Law was extended and its quality improved. But it continued to be of major importance in housing and of some significance in the welfare services, education and health care. The informal help of family, neighbours and others, although it was often weakened by upheaval resulting from urbanisation, the shifting location of industry, re-housing schemes, war and so on, continued throughout the period to provide most people with their main line of defence against many kinds of adversity.

In the environmental field the development of voluntary organisations followed a pattern initially closely akin to that in the social services. The Commons Preservation Society (now the Commons, Open Spaces and Footpaths Preservation Society) was founded in 1865 and fought the battles that preserved Hampstead Heath and many other open spaces in London from urban encroachment. The National Trust came into existence in 1895. In both organisations, and particularly in the person of Octavia Hill, there was a linked concern for conservation and for social improvement. Thereafter the social services moved ahead more quickly than the environmental services; and it was not until the development of town and country planning and the creation of the National Parks in the years immediately after the Second World War that a major extension of statutory responsibilities took place. The voluntary counterpart was the local amenity movement. This rapidly gathered momentum after the foundation of the Civic Trust in 1957, followed closely by the kindred movement for the conservation of wildlife and the countryside.

Our Fundamental Concerns

We must now explain rather more fully the fundamental concerns we outlined earlier so that we can establish a framework for examining, with the whole, the particular role of the voluntary sector. We referred there to two central concerns: the strengthening of collective action in meeting important social needs and the maintenance of a pluralistic pattern of institutions. On the first, we start from the premise that there are many areas of recognised social need where current levels of provision are inadequate. It can, of course, be said that it is of the very nature of the way in which social needs are defined that such criticisms will always be made, no matter how generous the standards achieved. But whatever position is taken on this question, we believe that each of the systems we have identified might be made more effective, even within the limits of existing resources; and it is clearly appropriate for us to consider in particular how the voluntary sector might contribute more in the future than it does today.

But our concern is not simply with making the maximum provision for meeting social needs. We are concerned also with how that provision is made. We believe that the social services, like government in general, are more effective where they and their administrative structures are open to public scrutiny and where alternatives to statutory provision are available. We accept and assert the value of the principal institutions of parliamentary democracy as they have evolved in this country, and we believe that they form the best available basis for government over the remaining years of the century. At the same time, we sympathise with the criticism that the existing pattern is not as responsive as it should be to the interests of the individual citizen. And we believe that if the pluralist framework is to survive there is need for a shift of power from the centre and for greater involvement of the individual citizen in the institutions and procedures of government, both national and local.

On this basis we see room in British society for each of the four systems of social helping which we have identified. We return later in our report to the relative roles of each of the different systems. At this point we should emphasise that in our view the contribution of each system should be measured not simply in terms of its effectiveness in meeting particular social needs but also in terms of its consequences for the fabric of society as a whole.

Four Systems of Meeting Social Need

1. The Informal System of Social Helping

The help and support that family, friends and neighbours give to each other is so much taken for granted that it often hardly enters into the discussion of the provision of social services. The relative neglect of this field by sociologists and social administrators means that we have very little exact knowledge about the factors which affect the weakness or the strength of informal support networks in different sectors of our society.

Such studies as have been made[7] suggest that the volume of informal help is very substantial, and imply that if for any reason such help ceased to be available an enormous burden would be placed on other systems of provision. The contribution of the informal system today would seem to be of three main kinds: (a) in the provision of care for the young and the weak, especially the sick, the handicapped and the elderly; (b) in the transfer of material resources, particularly between members of a family, from those with a surplus to those with a deficit, as with parental help to a newly married son or daughter in house purchase, or in the purchase of furniture; (c) in the provision of advice and psychological support as from the experienced to the inexperienced in matters such as child rearing, coping with crises such as desertion, divorce and widowhood.[8]

But there are important limits to what the informal system can do. First, it is not equipped to provide services which involve professional expertise and expensive plant and equipment. So while it might, for example, provide successfully in many instances for the care of the chronic sick, it cannot provide the necessary treatment for many acute complaints. Or again, while it may provide invaluable advice on how to handle the in-laws, it may not be able to produce the necessary information on social security regulations, rent acts, and the like. Second, while financial and material help may be transferred within the system, only in the richest strata of society will such transfers be adequate to meet all the heavy financial demands of long-term unemployment, sickness, homelessness and old age. Finally, the system by its very nature varies in its strength from time to time and from place to place.

To summarise, while there are many aspects of what we currently define as social need which the informal system cannot meet on its own, in other situations it is the prime source of help. There is every reason, in our view, to encourage the continued existence and strengthening of the system in the future. At present the other systems of social helping appear to relate to the informal system in a largely haphazard manner, sometimes strengthening and sometimes weakening it. There would seem to be a good case for both statutory and voluntary organisations to undertake more systematic evaluations of these inter-relationships and to develop policies which more consistently and deliberately support the informal system.

2. The Commercial System

To the most extreme exponent of the market economy the only appropriate alternative to the informal system of social helping would be a commercially-organised system. In fact it is theoretically possible to buy the whole range of social services on the open market — education, health, pensions, housing and social care. But at the present time only the very wealthiest members of society can afford to do so. For the large majority, apart from the once-in-a-lifetime expenditure on housing, the commercial sector provides nothing more than the possibility of topping up statutory provision (e.g. through the British United Provident Association, pensions schemes, extra tuition for school children). Further, it is very difficult to see how an individual's money can be used effectively to protect the environment on any substantial scale, except perhaps by those who are very wealthy. Schemes to extend the capacity of the ordinary consumer to use the commercial sector by issuing vouchers might, of course, be adopted during the next quarter century. Conceivably they could become widespread and might even be accepted as the main means of financing some sectors of the social services. The implications of such a move could be considerable for the voluntary sector, not least because in competition with commercial organisations it might attract many of the voucher payments itself. However, we think it unlikely that the many objections and obstacles to the voucher system will be overcome during this period, and we shall assume that the commercial sector as a means of providing the social needs with which we are concerned is unlikely to grow to any significant extent before the end of the century.

3. The Statutory System

The central place of the state in providing social services through national and local government agencies has become so firmly established that statutory provision is sometimes talked of as if it were the only form of social provision. Spending on social and environmental services has increased substantially in recent decades in both proportionate and absolute terms. In 1951 it was £2,271m or 38.9 per cent of all central and local government expenditure.[9] By 1975 it had risen to £29,161m or 53.5 per cent of such expenditure.[10] Both the scale and the growth of expenditure might be taken to be an expression of increasing confidence that the statutory system is the most appropriate vehicle for meeting social need. Yet there are grounds for questioning whether the statutory sector can continue to grow as it has over the last three decades, whether it should do so even if the resources were available, and whether even the existing allocation of resources between the statutory and non-statutory services is the most desirable one.

The system of statutory provision has a number of major advantages over the other systems. Most notably it offers the possibility of universal coverage, of sharing risks so that the minority who are in need can be supported by the majority who are not, of equity in treatment, of maintaining standards, of integrated planning and of control by the representatives of the electorate. But there are disadvantages too. In the

first place statutory provision is usually costly. The social services
employ a large work force (nearly two million in 1975). They rely for
the most part on full-time employees who, quite rightly, receive wages
or salaries comparable to those they would get in other employment.
They use expensive plant, particularly in health and education. The
present cut-back in public expenditure on the social services may be
temporary, but it has emphasised the huge size of the gap between the
supply of services and the ever increasing demand for them. Secondly,
given the size of the operations involved, most services are produced at
present through large-scale operations and are often virtually in a
monopoly position. They are subject to all the risks of bureaucracy,
inflexibility and resistance to innovation that similarly placed organisations in other sectors of society exhibit. Thirdly, and related to both
the preceding points, popular control of the organisations is difficult to
achieve. The size and complexity of most social service agencies make
them seem to users to be remote and impersonal. Users are seldom
invited to participate directly in agency affairs. More often than not the
persons who actually provide the services to individuals assume that the
relationship of professional to client is the only appropriate one. The
user who wants to change some aspect of agency policy or procedure is
advised to take his views to his political representative. Yet in reality the
gap between the elector and his representative is so large and difficult
to bridge, especially for the inexperienced or the timid, that for many
people such advice has little meaning. Even if contact can be made with
representatives in Parliament or local authority, and a sympathetic
response is assumed, the representative in his turn may have difficulty
in bringing about change in the well-defined bureaucracies he and his
colleagues are supposed to control. But as a rule, in a system of government such as our own, few representatives appear to come under much
direct pressure from their electors. It is far more likely that social
policies will be drawn up in Cabinet at national level or in party groups
at local level, in the light of much more diluted public views. Fourthly,
the system tends to act to deter direct public involvement in the actual
delivery of services. It does this in two ways: (a) by emphasising the
professional and bureaucratic aspects and procedures and failing to
encourage voluntary action in all but trivial or marginal aspects of the
work; (b) by creating and sustaining the paternalistic image of the state
as provider and the citizen as client.

These criticisms imply that there are major shortcomings in the
present system of statutory services, but we do not suggest that the only
way to improve the situation is by large-scale transfer resources from

the statutory to the other systems of meeting social need. We expect that the statutory services will continue to occupy something like their present dominant position over the next quarter-century and on the whole we regard it as desirable that they should do so, granted the need for major collective intervention if adequate social services are to be assured for the whole population. However, there are clearly grounds for examining the methods by which statutory services are provided and made accountable, and for considering how improvements could be introduced. The main responsibility for such initiatives must lie within the statutory system itself, but the voluntary sector, as we shall suggest, can also be a source of important pressures for change.

4. The Voluntary System

In our view the informal and statutory systems, taken together, constitute the principal means of meeting social needs in our society. In most of the areas of need with which we are concerned the commercial system remains marginal for the large majority of the population. Although the voluntary system, as we have shown, was once the chief form of collective action outside the Poor Law, it can now best be seen in terms of the ways in which it complements, supplements, extends and influences the informal and statutory systems. Beyond its contribution in these ways, however, we believe it should be evaluated in its role as one of the institutions in a pluralistic system of government and social structure. In subsequent chapters we review such evidence as we have been able to assemble on the scope and performance of the voluntary sector. Here we attempt only to identify some of the principal ways in which it has been suggested that the voluntary system can interrelate constructively with the informal and statutory systems.

The relationship of the voluntary and statutory systems In relation to the statutory system it would seem that the voluntary system may have three kinds of contribution to make. First, it may be able to extend the scope of existing provision. Second, it may be able to improve the standards of statutory provision. Finally, it may be able to offer services where little or nothing is available through the state.

Extending provision The voluntary sector can extend in a number of ways the services provided by the State. Traditionally, the voluntary organisation has been the setting for innovation. New methods of treatment, for example, have been developed in work with families and with delinquents. A second important way in which statutory services can be extended by the voluntary sector is by the provision of alternatives to statutory services, (e.g. residential care for children, the handicapped, the elderly, youth clubs, housing associations). These not only extend the quantity of provision but extend the choices available to users of the service. Thirdly, voluntary organisations can be said to extend the absolute amount of resources available to the social services by attracting people, ideas and material resources that would not have been attracted by statutory organisations. People are often more willing to give time, energy and money to a voluntary body devoted to a specific cause than to a statutory agency. Finally, voluntary organisations may offer direct support services to statutory bodies, as for example, does the WRVS in providing meals on wheels, hospital trolleys and so on, and as do the various organisations of 'friends' which have grown up to help residential homes, social service teams and hospitals.

Improving the quality of government provision. The quality of government provision may be improved by the voluntary sector's extension. Where an alternative can be offered to state provision, the statutory service is no longer in a monopoly position. Choice for the user means the right to turn down the statutory service, with implications for subsequent effort to improve the service and make it closer to what the user wants. A second way in which the monolithic aspects of statutory provision may be diluted by voluntary activity is where the voluntary organisation works closely with a statutory body and opportunities are afforded to members of the voluntary organisation to observe or infiltrate the statutory body (e.g. 'friends' in a hospital). The very presence of outsiders can prevent possible abuses of power and stimulate higher standards of provision. Thirdly, voluntary organisations, whether working with statutory services or not, are well placed to act as independent critics and pressure groups. Similarly they can become specialists in the range of statutory services available and offer disinterested advice to users on their rights.

Sole or principal provider. For various reasons some recognised social needs may attract little or no response from the state. For example, the need concerned may be rated as a low priority (as in the case of pre-school play) or as inappropriate for direct statutory involvement (as in the case of certain kinds of advice and counselling). In such fields the provision of service will depend mainly or exclusively on the voluntary sector.

Government planning and the voluntary sector. Some of the main
strengths of the voluntary sector can also constitute its weaknesses. The
voluntary organisation is the ideal medium for spontaneous, speedy and
autonomous action. But the same features mean that there is no
guarantee that voluntary effort will necessarily materialise where need
is greatest, that standards of service will be maintained, or that the
sector as a whole will operate in a coordinated manner. Where a
Council for Voluntary Service exists (we describe them in Chapter 6), it
may attempt to remedy these deficiencies but its ability to do so, given
the constraints on its authority and resources, is likely to be limited. It
would seem to us that in a political system such as ours, where the
ultimate responsibility for ensuring that formal provision is made to
meet social need rests with elected representatives, local and national
government must be ready to take on the task of compensating for
deficiencies in the pattern of provision. This means that there must be
national and local plans that include voluntary provision, and use the
means open to government, including grant-aiding and the direct
stimulation of new voluntary bodies, to influence the development of
the voluntary sector.

The relationship of the voluntary and informal systems. Ideally, it may
be suggested, the voluntary and informal systems should exist in a
symbiotic relationship. Certain kinds of voluntary organisations could
be expected to grow out of the informal system when it became
apparent that informal methods were no longer adequate to meet the
needs concerned. For example, informal arrangements for pre-school
children might lead to the formation of a playgroup, common action in
dealing with a landlord could result in the establishment of a tenants'
association, and so on. The voluntary organisation would seem better
adapted to such needs than some kind of statutory structure: voluntary
organisations can be established with a minimum of fuss and bother,
they can share much of the spontaneity and flexibility of informal
relationships, attract the support and loyalty of the groups affected,
and react quickly to changes in demand. In return, voluntary organisations may be able to provide support for existing informal networks
and even help create new networks where none exist. In Chapter 3 we
suggest a number of ways in which support can be provided: replacement, relief and reinforcement. The creation of new networks can be
instanced in terms of the varied work of organisations such as Task
Force (with the elderly), Cruse (with widows), and Gingerbread (with
one-parent families) where the formal organisation may be the means

by which isolated individuals can be linked with new informal networks.

The voluntary system and pluralism. Over and above the direct contribution of the voluntary system in meeting social needs, we must also consider the case made for its contribution to the pluralistic character of our political and social institutions. The principal benefits attributed to the voluntary sector in this sense relate mainly to its potential as a means of enabling widespread direct public participation. In the modern industrial state, dominated by large-scale political, economic and social institutions, most people have little opportunity to shape the society in which they live. The voluntary sector offers the possibility of direct involvement. In the space between the loosely structured informal system and the more strictly organised statutory system, people can use the medium of the voluntary organisation to join with others in devising means to meet their own needs, or those of others they wish to help. In consequence, those involved will not only feel less alienated from the society in which they live, but they will also be engaged in altering its nature both directly through the activities they undertake and, less directly, through the signals sent by these activities to the statutory system on the nature of shifts in public interests. In the process, those participating in the voluntary system often acquire experience and skills that enhance their capacity to contribute in roles they fill in other sectors of society.

The possible roles which we have identified for the voluntary sector in relation to the statutory and informal systems of social action cover a wide range of functions and suggest that it can make a substantial contribution to the overall system of social service provision in this country. We have also stressed its importance as a part of the pluralist society. In the following chapters we examine how far these functions appear to be realised in practice and in what ways they might be further developed in the last quarter of this century.

Notes

1. The historical section of this chapter draws on a number of sources including: Perkin, H., *The Origins of Modern English Society: 1780-1800*; Bruce, M., *The Coming of the Welfare State*; Rose, M. E., *The Relief of Poverty 1834-1914*; Hay, J. R., *The Origins of the Liberal Welfare Reforms 1906-1914*; Cole, G. D. H., 'Retrospect of the history of voluntary social action' in Bourdillon, A.F.C., *Voluntary Social Service*; Brasnett, M., *Voluntary Social Action*.

2. Perkin, ibid.
3. Simey, T. S., *Principles of Social Administration*, 1937.
4. Mess, H. A., *Voluntary Social Services since 1918*, 1947 (ch. 13, p. 204).
5. Lord Beveridge, *Voluntary Action*, 1948 (ch. 13, p. 322).
6. Wilson, Roger, 'The Future of Voluntary Social Work' in Lord Beveridge and A. F. Wells (eds), *The Evidence for Voluntary Action*, 1949.
7. Morris, Mary, *Voluntary Work in the Welfare State*, Appendix III: Voluntary Work in Bradford; Aves, Geraldine, *The Voluntary Worker in the Social Services*, Appendix 3; Bayley, M., *Mental Handicap and Community Care*, 1937; Shanas, E. *et al.*, *Old People in Three Industrial Societies*, 1968, ch. 5; Sainsbury, S., *Measuring Disability*, 1974.
8. Collins, A. H. and Pancoast, D. L., *Natural Helping Networks: A Strategy for Prevention*, National Association of Social Workers (US), 1976.
9. Social Trends 1974, Table 185.
10. Social Trends 1976, Table 13.5.

3 THE PRESENT PICTURE

When we started our enquiries into voluntary organisations, we were entering uncharted waters. Though the work of some voluntary organisations is very well known, hitherto hardly any information has been drawn together about the voluntary sector as a whole. When we began, it was hardly possible even to hazard a guess at the number of organisations and the scope of their activities, let alone to make qualitative judgements about the value of their contribution and what they ought to be doing in the future. Despite growing interest in the voluntary sector, the absence of systematic studies during the past twenty years is notable.

There are important reasons for this lack of knowledge. In the first place the voluntary sector, however one chooses to define it, lacks clear-cut boundaries. The array of organisations that needs to be considered is likely to change with each shake of the kaleidoscope according to the issues and problems with which one is concerned. For example, not all charities are voluntary organisations and not all voluntary organisations are charities. Likewise not all voluntary organisations use volunteers, and not all volunteers work for voluntary organisations, and so on. In the second place, wherever the boundaries are drawn, within them one will find a great variety of organisations. What, for example, has Dr Barnardo's in common with a local tenants' association? The former has a budget of nearly £8 million a year and employs full-time staff to provide a centrally administered professional child care service covering much of the country. In contrast, the typical tenants' association serves one housing estate only, relies entirely on voluntary effort, and its fortunes fluctuate sharply in response to local crises and enthusiasms. Thus in attempting to present a picture of the voluntary sector today, one has to tackle first of all the problem of identifying a coherent field to study.

As we suggested in Chapter 1, it is not particularly profitable to devote much effort to identifying a set of characteristics that serve to draw a sharply defined boundary round the voluntary sector. It is more fruitful to place the voluntary sector in a broad context by distinguishing it from the three other systems defined in the last chapter through which care for individuals and for the environment is provided – the informal, the statutory and the commercial. At many points on the

margins the dividing line between the four systems is blurred. For
example, much neighbourly care is entirely unorganised and informal,
and there is often not much to distinguish such activity from an
organised good neighbour scheme promoted in an informal way by a
voluntary organisation.

Similarly, there are some voluntary organisations not obviously very
different from statutory agencies. Housing associations have in recent
years evolved fast from what were purely voluntary beginnings. Now
practically all their resources come from a statutory body, the Housing
Corporation, or from rents paid by their tenants. With the exception of
a few organisations that have either not sought or not been granted
registration by the Housing Corporation, the work they do is closely
controlled by the Corporation on the basis of what are in effect
contractual agreements between the Corporation and individual
associations. Other voluntary organisations, like the Family Service
Units which provide intensive case work, enter into similarly close
relationships with statutory bodies. These relationships involve
clearly defined commitments to provide specified services, often
described as agency agreements, without however reaching the point
where they are under statutory control. We would regard as examples
of statutory control the appointment by a statutory authority of the
chief officer or a majority of the governing body. Local community
relations councils constitute an interesting hybrid case in this context.
Hitherto the salaries of the local community relations officers (CROs)
have been paid by the Community Relations Commission (CRC), a
statutory body, but the CRO has been accountable to the local
community relations council and appointed by the local community
relations council subject to the approval of the CRC. The position
may now alter as the CRC was recently merged with the Race
Relations Board to form the new Commission for Racial Equality.
Rural Community Councils (RCCs) are in a similar position *vis-à-vis* the
Development Commission. The WRVS is another hybrid case; its head
is appointed by the Home Secretary and its administrative expenses
come from the Home Office, but at the local level it is to most intents
and purposes one of several uniformed voluntary bodies.

The fact that an organisation is mentioned in or derives power from
a statute does not necessarily make it a statutory body. The National
Society for the Prevention of Cruelty to Children and the National
Trust are both independent voluntary organisations; but the power of
the NSPCC to bring proceeding before juvenile courts for the protection
of children derives from a statutory instrument based on Section 1 of

the Children and Young Persons Act 1969, while the constitution of the National Trust is enshrined in the National Trust Act 1971. On the statutory side of the dividing line are to be found some of the intermediary bodies we discuss in Chapter 7. The University Grants Committee was not established by statute but by a Treasury minute. Its members are appointed by the Secretary of State for Education and Science, which makes it a statutory body in our broad sense of the term. But it is in a more independent position than a branch of a government department which is directly accountable to Secretary of State and Parliament. Thus there is a continuum across which the dividing line between statutory and voluntary is more difficult to draw than might at first sight appear.

An organisation may also cross the boundary between the voluntary and commercial sectors. During the last century, the Friendly Societies counted as voluntary organisations although the members were paying for services through their subscriptions, since there was a large voluntary element in the running of the societies and members obtained more from their membership than simply insurance. Today there is still a mutual benefit element in that the organisations are not profit-making, but the voluntary element has disappeared and there is little to distinguish Friendly Societies from profit-making insurance companies. Playgroups exemplify a service where a boundary is blurred. Sometimes there is not much of a dividing line between a situation where a group of mothers come together and raise the resources to employ one of their number as a supervisor, from one where a mother charges a fee to other mothers to cover the cost of placing their children under her supervision. Homes caring for the elderly constitute a spectrum of organisations from those which derive none of their resources from payments made by residents out of their own pockets to those which do predominantly depend upon private fee paying. The latter we would count among the commercial sector, whether or not they were registered as charities. However any dividing line would certainly be difficult to draw, particularly since one would want to count among a home's resources all the help given voluntarily as well as items embodied in cash transactions.

Another distinction that should be drawn relates to an organisation's field of operations or the needs which it serves. As explained in Chapter 1 it was not necessary to circumscribe the Committee's deliberations by an exact definition since an organisation might be relevant in some contexts and not in others, and fixed boundaries could not be used to separate those organisations which should be discussed

from those which should not. However, for the purposes of our
research and for presenting summary figures a more exact definition
was necessary. Five main social services can be identified: social
security, health, education, the personal social services and housing.
Along with services dealing with the natural and the man-made
environment these are what we mean when we talk in general terms
about the social and environmental services. But the range of
organisations included in our research studies was somewhat
narrower than this though at the same time broader and more exactly
defined than that on which we concentrated in our discussion. For
research purposes we tried to cover all voluntary organisations active in
the field of responsibility of the Department of the Environment and
the Department of Health and Social Security. Certain organisations
related to the responsibilities of the Department of Education and
Science and the Home Office were also included in the research; those
concerned with youth and play, organisations like parent-teacher
associations and the Workers' Educational Association which could be
seen as a medium for community involvement in education, and bodies
working with offenders and ethnic minorities. This meant we did not
cover the arts or sport and recreation (except in connection with
services for children, the handicapped and the elderly) or schools,
colleges and other institutions for learning and education.

Accepting that there are no sharply defined boundaries within which
the voluntary sector lies, we thought we should try to obtain some
measure of its size. One criterion is income and expenditure. The
relevant data are discussed in Appendix 6A. It would appear that
altogether the income of charities in 1975 came to over £1,500 million.
This figure includes many organisations outside our field of research,
and there are some voluntary organisations that do not have charitable
status. But even after making a generous allowance for expenditure
devoted to religion, recreation, art, research and so on, we are still left
with the figure of around £1,000 million, or about 3 per cent of total
central and local government expenditure on social and environmental
services in 1975. Another criterion of the size of the voluntary sector is
the number of organisations. Some indication is given by the number of
charities registered with the Charity Commission: 120,000 in 1975. We
made no attempt to work out a figure for national organisations. At
the local level, Kenneth Newton, during his researches on local government in Birmingham, which has a population of 1 million, identified
over 4,000 different voluntary organisations active in the city, of which
nearly one thousand seemed to be within the Committee's field of

research.[1] Moreover, Newton suspected that there were more organisations that he had not been able to identify. In our locality studies (discussed more fully below) we identified within our field of research about three organisations per thousand persons in the two small towns (population under 5,000), two organisations per thousand in the two medium-sized towns (population about 50,000) and one per thousand in the town with a quarter of a million.

Perhaps the best measure of the size of the voluntary sector is the number of people active in it. In order to assess the quantity of voluntary work being done in the country, at our request National Opinion Polls Ltd included questions about voluntary work in a national survey carried out in September 1976. The results are reported more fully elsewhere,[2] but the main findings can most conveniently be summarised in the following table:

Table 3.1. Participation in Voluntary Work

	% reporting voluntary work in the previous	
	week	*12 months*
In the field of the social and environmental services:		
for voluntary organisations	5.7	10.2
for statutory organisations	0.8	1.9
for both or for organisations that could not be distinguished	1.0	1.6
	7.5	13.7
Outside the social and environmental services	1.6	2.9

On the basis of these figures it is possible to estimate for Great Britain roughly the volume of voluntary effort taking place through the medium of voluntary organisations. Altogether it seems that about 5 million individuals aged 16 or more undertake some voluntary work or other during the course of the year in fields with which this Committee is concerned. There is always a certain amount of unreliability in people's memories of their own activities, particularly when these activities concern their own credit. In order to minimise this, when asking about the amount of work actually done, we confined our attention to the previous week only. The answers indicate that those who had done voluntary work in that period claimed they had devoted on average about six hours to it. Translating this into figures for the population as a whole, it seems that somewhere in the

region of 16 million man hours are given each week. To provide a
comparative order of magnitude, in terms of hours worked, this is
roughly equivalent to 400,000 full-time workers. Of course, one cannot
translate voluntary work directly into paid work: for example, a
considerable part of the voluntary effort is devoted to fund-raising, and
many, though certainly not all, voluntary workers lack the skills of the
trained staff of the social services. Nevertheless, in order to provide an
order of magnitude it is worth noting that the number of full-time
employees in the social and environmental services comes to nearly
2 million. But the voluntary effort is not distributed in the same
proportions as the statutory employees. Some two thirds of the voluntary effort is devoted to fields served by the personal social services,
and here the local authorities employ only some 200,000 full-time staff,
or 10 per cent of all employees in the social and environmental services.

An important category of voluntary work was not covered by this
survey — work carried out *not* under the auspices of any organisation.
Such activity we count as part of the private informal sector. However,
it is significant that a study carried out in Bradford in 1967 found that
many more people participated in informal helping than in organised
voluntary work.[3] We also suspect that many people who participate
actively in voluntary organisations outside the social welfare and
environmental fields did not, in answering the survey question, count
this as 'voluntary work'. The table also shows the significant fact that
the voluntary sector mobilises much more organised voluntary work
than does the statutory sector.

We have not mentioned so far the number of paid staff working in
the voluntary sector. In 1975, the Personal Social Services Council
carried out a survey of voluntary organisation manpower, directing
their attention especially at paid employees in the personal social
services field.[4] The study was not quite complete in its coverage, but it
would appear that there were some 15,000-20,000 staff in the field
under consideration.

Taking volunteers and paid workers together, in the personal social
services the voluntary sector is clearly larger in terms of manpower than
the statutory sector. The same cannot be said of other need areas. Since
the creation of the National Health Service the size of the voluntary
sector in health has been small. The recent transfer of the Ambulance
and Family Planning Services to the NHS has meant further reductions
in the voluntary sector; but bordering on the personal social services
field there is considerable voluntary involvement in the care of the sick
and handicapped, in raising money for medical research and in first aid

services. In the field of social security the contribution of voluntary
organisations is nowadays small, being limited to pressure group
activity or to special categories such as the benevolent associations
concerned with ex-servicemen, actors, and so on. This contrasts with
the position in earlier centuries when the relief of poverty seems to have
attracted the main body of charitable activity. Housing differs from
other need areas in that although the number of dwellings owned by
voluntary organisations is only a tiny proportion of the whole, their
contribution to current housing production is much greater than their
share of total stock. Housing associations, for example, accounted for
10 per cent of new construction by the 'public sector' in 1975. It is
difficult to compare voluntary and statutory environmental services
since much of the statutory work is of a regulatory kind. However, the
National Trust plays the major part in preserving historic houses and
estates, and unspoilt coastal areas can be held inalienably only by that
body. The combined acreage of land of natural history interest held
by the National Trust, the RSPB and the Country Trusts exceeds that
of the nature reserves managed by the Nature Conservancy Council.
The Civic Trust and amenity societies have had a profound influence on
planning processes.

The Diversity of Organisations

There is such great diversity in the voluntary sector that it is difficult to
make any general observations about it. But it is of interest to look at
some aspects of this diversity. Perhaps the most obvious is size. In
terms of annual expenditure voluntary organisations range from the
National Trust, which spent over £9 million in 1975 (a figure greater
than that of many non-metropolitan district councils), to the multitude
of local organisations which consume no more than a few pounds a
year on expenses. Membership figures may vary from the three-quarters
of a million members of the Guides and Brownies together to the
hundred or less of many local organisations. A third measure of size is
the number of employees: Dr Barnardo's with some 2,500 employees of
all kinds must be one of the largest by this criterion.

A distinction of no less importance is whether a voluntary organisation relies predominantly on voluntary or paid staff. Many well-known
voluntary organisations like the Scouts, Guides, Red Cross and St John's
rely on a great mass of voluntary helpers. But we know of no organisation of large size which is entirely dependent on voluntary work, since
paid, usually full-time workers are needed for central administrative
tasks. Equally we are not aware of any voluntary organisation which

mobilises no voluntary effort at all. However, there is a large difference between organisations in which the main activities are carried out by voluntary workers, and others, for example, the Family Welfare Association in which they are run by professionals, the voluntary input being limited to participation in governing bodies and in supporting activities, notably fund raising.

The organisations named above are national. The coverage of some organisations is much more limited. Our locality studies suggest that although there are a fair number of purely local organisations, the proportion of local voluntary organisations that are not linked to national organisations in any way is small. Tenants and Residents' Associations and some of the ethnic organisations are usually local. Other types of organisation which are often without national affiliations are community action groups, clubs for the elderly and for the disabled, and the 'friends' of particular institutions. In these cases there is not infrequently an indirect link-up, as when a club for the elderly is affiliated to the local Age Concern. Though most voluntary organisations operating at a local level are part of a national network they are not all necessarily centrally controlled. The loosest type of network is exemplified by the local amenity movement. Local amenity societies do not belong to the Civic Trust, because the Trust has no members; but it does keep a register of local societies and circulates a newsletter to them in return for a subscription. It is our impression that the majority of local voluntary bodies belong to national networks whose links are not a great deal tighter than those of the amenity societies, in the sense that the number of conditions that a local branch has to meet in order to be admitted into membership of a national federation and allowed to use its name is limited. But some have more exacting requirements; for example the Samaritans, in keeping with the special character of the work they do, told us that they set the following conditions for their local branches:

Each local branch is independent in financing and most have registered as charities. The Branch must follow the Twenty Principles of the Samaritans and be governed, so far as work with clients is concerned, by a Director proposed by the Branch and recognised by the Council of Management. Each Branch, except the most new, pays a levy on its income for the purpose of the Samaritans' national and regional work.

The uniformed organisations tend to be more centralised, as do those organisations like the large child-care agencies which rely on professional staff and carry out most of their fund raising through the medium of their central organisation.

Another way of distinguishing voluntary organisations is by the nature of their intended beneficiaries. Four categories can be identified, but they are by no means mutually exclusive. Many organisations aim to help groups of people with special needs, for example the elderly and the homeless, who may be described as the clients of the organisation. Organisations of this kind have in the past attracted and still do attract the main body of voluntary effort at the local level. A second category, for example the Council for the Protection of Rural England and the National Council for Civil Liberties, are mainly concerned with the promotion of causes and with the public good in general rather than with particular categories of people. In recent years there has been a rapid growth of organisations of this type concerned with environmental issues. A third category consists of voluntary organisations in which the main beneficiaries are the members. For example, the British Association for the Hard of Hearing has some 8,000 members who suffer from 'acquired hearing loss' and are organised in local branches which act as social clubs. In other cases, members and beneficiaries do not coincide closely. Many but not all sufferers from multiple sclerosis belong to the Multiple Sclerosis Society, and the Society has many members who are not sufferers but provide voluntary help. Members may also constitute only a small proportion of those whom it is hoped will benefit from the organisation's activities. Mutual benefit societies are a fast growing group of voluntary organisations, particularly numerous and widespread being playgroups, tenants' associations, social clubs for the elderly and community action groups of one kind or another. A fourth category consists of organisations whose main beneficiaries are not individuals but other organisations. Local councils of voluntary service, which we discuss in Chapter 6, vary in the nature of their work, but many devote a substantial part of their efforts to supporting and facilitating the work of other organisations. Similarly, many local Age Concerns do as much by way of supporting their affiliated clubs for the elderly as by way of services delivered directly to individuals. Volunteer Bureaux can also be placed in this category.

There are also diversities in the decision-making structure of the organisations. The commonest pattern seems to be the federal system with an executive committee which is elected by and accountable to an annual general meeting of representatives of all affiliated branches. The branches themselves have their own committees which are appointed by and from individual members. Some voluntary organisations aim at a more direct form of democracy and, like the NCCL, choose their executive committees by a postal ballot of all members. Others, usually the older organisations, have a restricted category of members who appoint the executive committee. For example, the Royal National Lifeboat Institution has local branches, both fund raising and operational. Its Committee of Management is elected by the Annual General Meeting of Governors of the Institution. Governors are individuals who have given a once only donation of £60 or more, or make a subscription of not less than £10 per annum. A further category of voluntary organisations are not membership organisations at all, but have as a governing body a committee that renews itself by cooption. Organisations of this kind and also those with a more open membership, may ensure that particular interests are represented on their committee. Thus, where an organisation receives a grant from the local authority, one or more representatives of the local authority, either officers or councillors, may have a place on the Committee. Citizens' Advice Bureaux and Marriage Guidance Councils often exemplify this arrangement.

The formal structure for making decisions may be important if there is conflict in the organisation. It may also affect the view which local authorities and the public form of the legitimacy of the organisation, its responsiveness to the individuals it is aiming to serve and the extent to which the public is involved in its activities. However, the distribution of effective power as opposed to formal authority depends on other factors besides the organisation's constitution. In voluntary organisations the role of paid staff is particularly important in this context. When a competent full-time paid staff is juxtaposed with a governing body that meets only occasionally, and honorary officers who have many other calls on their time, the direction an organisation takes and its style of operations are likely to depend on the full-time staff. In giving evidence to us the representatives of one organisation spoke frankly about the problems that can arise when the staff want to move more quickly than the elected committee, and of the difficulty of reconciling democratic control with the need to make quick responses to new developments. The same sort of problems often exist in local authorities. Inspirational individuals also override formal structure. Many voluntary organisations owe their foundation to such people; indeed voluntary organisations today provide vivid examples of charismatic leadership, and of the problems of succession that arise when the charismatic leader dies or gets left behind by the development of the organisation.

Voluntary organisations can also be classified according to methods of operating and according to need area. Methods can be divided into the provision of direct services, giving support to other organisations (this category coincides with the fourth category of beneficiaries above) and acting as a pressure group, i.e. seeking to alter the policies and practices of other (usually statutory) organisations. Need areas can be divided up in different ways. There is some convenience in following the allocation of responsibilities within central and local government and this has been the practice adopted in analysing material prepared for us. But many voluntary organisations span different need areas and cut across the boundaries that divide the responsibilities of the statutory agencies. This enables them to provide an integrated service that may be difficult to mount in a statutory setting. Thus the Peter Bedford Project based in North London is concerned with people who are often described as 'single homeless'. Such people usually need employment as well as housing, and the Project provides both.

The Role of Voluntary Organisations in Relation to the Informal System

So far we have been discussing the nature of voluntary organisations. We next consider the kind of work they do first in relation to the activities of the informal sector and then of the statutory sector or systems as we called them in Chapter 2. In relation to the informal system, three roles deserve to be distinguished, and we define them as follows:

Replacement Some services are an alternative to care by family or neighbours and completely take their place. Such services involve long-term residential care, whether provided by statutory or voluntary agencies, and become necessary when family or neighbourly arrangements do not exist, have broken down or cannot cope.

Relief Some services do not permanently replace informal caring arrangements, but may do so temporarily or in limited respects. Short-term hospitalisation for the mentally ill is one example, as are day-care facilities for the handicapped and various forms of domiciliary care. Such relief services may augment and support informal arrangements by taking some of the burden from them, perhaps preventing them from breaking down under too heavy a load, but they do not positively strengthen informal caring.

Reinforcement This term describes services which do positively strengthen informal caring arrangements, whether by providing psychological support, developing extra skills and motivation or offering material resources. Playgroups that involve the mothers, aids and adaptations to the homes of physically handicapped people, good neighbour schemes, and much of the work of organisations of the parents of handicapped children exemplify services that fall into this category.

The classification above can be applied equally to the work of statutory and voluntary services, so from our point of view the interesting question is whether voluntary agencies are in any respect better fitted than statutory agencies to fill these roles. A prominent characteristic of replacement and relief services is the large amount of resources required to run them, because most depend on full-time staff and some on substantial capital investment in buildings or equipment. This points towards statutory responsibility or, within the voluntary sector, to larger organisations. The latter in fact provide between 10 and 20 per cent of residential care for both children and the elderly. Voluntary organisations doing relief services are more diverse. A majority of meals on wheels are still delivered by volunteers, most of them members of the WRVS; while many churches, settlements and other voluntary bodies run social clubs and day centres for the elderly and the handicapped.

Reinforcement services are much more dependent on voluntary organisations because most of them require the involvement of families and neighbours and by virtue of their autonomy voluntary organisations are more likely to secure voluntary commitment. However the statutory side is also involved and the statutory provisions such as attendance allowances are of great importance. The advantages of caring for people in the community rather than in institutions are now well understood. But without good reinforcement services care in the community may simply place an intolerable burden on families. Volunteer and mutual benefit organisations particularly have a crucial part to play in bridging the gap between the individual and the statutory services, a point which is not everywhere adequately recognised by the statutory services.

In collaboration with the Family Fund Research Team we were able to send a questionnaire to a sample of parents who had applied to the Fund for financial help for their handicapped children. A full report on the findings is being published elsewhere[5] but the main points deserve mention here since they concern voluntary organisations in their reinforcement role. About half the respondents belonged to an organisation for handicapped children, and a majority of the non-members said they would like to belong. Seven out of ten members found membership 'very worthwhile'. The most valued aspects of membership were the opportunities to share problems and to obtain information and advice. Direct services available from the organisations came lower down the list.

Before the Second World War almost the only organisations for people with specific handicaps or diseases were those for the blind and deaf. There are now a great many. The largest particularly concerned with children are the National Society for Mentally Handicapped Children, the Spastics Society and the Association for Spina Bifida and Hydrocephalus (ASBAH). Their growth can be described as a major post welfare state development. Part of their work, mainly at the national level, consists of providing specialist expertise, pioneering new services and putting pressure on government. Our survey shows that at the local level the children's organisations are essentially mutual aid associations for the parents, which help them to cope with the heavy responsibility of caring for a handicapped child, and provide a different kind of support from that available from the statutory services.

The Role of Voluntary Organisations in Relation to the Statutory System

A voluntary organisation can act in the following ways in relation to the statutory system:

As a pressure group seeking changes in the policy and provision of other organisations.

As the pioneer of new services with the intention that if successful they should be adopted more widely either by statutory or by voluntary agencies.

As the provider of services complementary or additional or alternative to statutory services.

As the sole provider of services.

The meanings of complementary, additional and alternative require elucidation. A complementary service is different in kind from that provided by a statutory agency. A good example is neighbourhood visiting schemes; the visiting of the elderly by neighbours on a voluntary basis cannot fully replace or be replaced by a visit from a paid social worker. However efficient the visiting scheme, elderly people 'at risk' still need to be on a social worker's case load and conversely, however frequent a social worker's visits, a paid worker cannot 'befriend' in the same way as a volunteer. This is not to say that complementary services of this kind do not or cannot replace each other to some extent, but in so far as they are different in kind they cannot be deemed alternatives or additions. Many services provided by self-help groups and volunteers fall into this category, often acting in the reinforcement role discussed above.

There may be little apparent difference between additional and alternative roles. However a useful distinction is lost by conflating them. If there are alternative services the recipient may be given one or the other, but not both. Thus voluntary and statutory children's homes are alternatives in the sense that the child cannot at the same time be in more than one home. If there are additional services the recipient may receive services of the same kind from both the statutory and the voluntary source. For example, in cases of child abuse, social service departments and the National Society for the Prevention of Cruelty to Children are in some respects additional to each other. Similarly charitable funds directed towards the relief of poverty or medical research are generally additional to the statutory provision. The term supplementary is sometimes used rather than additional. We have avoided it since in common parlance complementary and supplementary do not have clearly distinguished meanings.

The distinction between additional and alternative is based on the consumer's perspective. To a statutory agency, such as a local social services department with overall responsibility for levels of provision, the distinction between the two roles may have little significance since both represent additions to statutory provision. Thus the consequences of their presence (or disappearance) for the level of resources the statutory organisation has to deploy are likely to be the same. But this will not be so from the point of view of the consumer, since the presence of alternative services offers an element of choice. Analysing the situation from the consumer's point of view also raises problems of classification, since there are services which may be perceived by some consumers as alternatives in that they use one or the other but not both, while other consumers may use both. To take the example of day centres for the elderly, some elderly people may attend only one and see statutory and voluntary centres as alternatives. Other elderly people may attend several centres both statutory and voluntary, which means that for them the voluntary provision could be complementary or additional. In contrast, residential establishments are unambiguously alternatives since, from the nature of this service, a consumer can only live in one at a time. Where there is ambiguity the problem of classification is simplified by saying that a service becomes an alternative one as soon as a significant proportion of consumers treat it as such.

The extent to which provision by voluntary organisations at present makes a choice available to consumers of the social services that would otherwise be absent is not easily assessed. In the case of some consumers, for example children taken into care or the mentally handicapped, it does not make sense to think of a consumer exercising a deliberate choice. Decisions are made on his behalf. Provision by voluntary organisations can only extend the range of services to which he may be allocated, though this itself may be valuable. In other situations a service, whether voluntary or statutory, may be a natural monopoly. One would not want to suggest that two agencies should provide meals on wheels in the same area in order that a choice may be offered. Nor would one wish to advocate the duplication of such expensive facilities as hospitals simply so as to offer a choice. In other situations choice already exists within the statutory sector: up to a point patients can choose their general practitioner; subject to geographical accessibility most local education authorities provide for some element of parental choice in allocating children to schools; and there is wide choice for students entering higher education. The extension of choice directly attributable to voluntary provision is limited to a few fields. Housing associations (where their allocation policies are not completely controlled by a local authority), youth clubs, playgroups, day centres, advice centres and residential care are all services where, subject sometimes to geographical limitations on access, voluntary organisations do significantly augment the choice available to consumers, or to those acting on their behalf. We took the view that the alternative role of voluntary organisations was a valuable one. What the tidy minded administrator might regard as duplication or overlap can often be defended if it enables the consumer to exercise a choice, and thereby an influence on the character of the services provided for him.

Looking at the country as a whole, it is difficult to find a set of needs being met wholly by voluntary organisations which are thereby the sole providers. The Royal National Lifeboat Institution provides a unique service, but the helicopters which also take part in rescue at sea are provided by the armed services: in this way the RNLI and the armed services are complementary to each other. However, when one looks at particular localities, voluntary organisations frequently find themselves in the position of sole providers. In many areas, the WRVS is the sole provider of meals on wheels and in some places a voluntary youth club or day centre for the elderly may be the only one available. The provision of accommodation for the single homeless is another field where not infrequently voluntary organisations are on their own, and where if one takes the country as a whole the voluntary sector is certainly the main provider. All women's refuges are run by voluntary organisations, although some battered women may be housed in homeless families' accommodation provided by local authorities and may receive other forms of support from statutory social services.

Another contribution which voluntary organisations make, acting in both their complementary and alternative roles, is to provide a service more specialised than may be available from statutory agencies. For example, the Family Welfare Association and Family Service Units mobilise a special set of skills in their intensive casework services. The constant pressures facing an area team in a social services department make it difficult to set aside the necessary staff time and develop the necessary expertise required to provide an equivalent service. FSU suggested to us that 'many local authority social services departments are increasingly aware of the fact that they cannot offer either long-term support or shorter intensive care to families with multiple problems. Our pattern of development has been and will be of small units which can offer a flexible and personal style of work.' With other voluntary organisations the specialist element may lie more in the nature of the needs being met than in the skills being deployed though there is usually a combination of both. For example, the Spastics Society has done a lot to develop training facilities for spastics as well as creating much greater public awareness of their problems. The generic approach embodied in the reorganisation of the personal social services has increased the scope for specialist agencies which operate outside the social services department and usually on a national basis. One particular expression of specialisation is in unpopular causes. To quote FSU again: 'FSU's work is with the most disadvantaged families and they come as a fairly low priority to local authority departments, i.e. the handicapped and the elderly attract more sympathy, support and are more "important" politically.' Offenders, addicts and gypsies are other unpopular groups which the voluntary sector has been active in helping.

The role of voluntary organisations in pioneering many of the services that were subsequently incorporated in the welfare state is well

recognised. There is also widespread recognition that pioneering continues to be a valuable role of the voluntary sector. Possibly the best
known recent development in social provision is the growth of refuges
for battered wives which gained its impetus from Chiswick Women's
Aid. This organisation identified and dramatised a hitherto scarcely
recognised need, and devised in the form of a refuge a way of meeting
it. Since then women's refuges have spread rapidly, mostly as a result of
spontaneous local initiatives and mostly adopting philosophy and
methods somewhat different from Chiswick's. A pioneering organisation directed at the needs of a different group of women is Cruse. Its
efforts to secure greater recognition of the needs of widows and
supporting services for them are being carried out in a lower key and are
less well known. Another field in which voluntary organisations are now
doing pioneering work is the provision of accommodation for single
people. Patchwork is an organisation active in the London area that was
visited by members of the Committee. It now has a number of houses,
mostly short-life, in which it has established living arrangements with a
communal element, seeking to include a minority of people with special
needs. In a wider context, it can be seen as one among a number of
organisations endeavouring to develop a social framework for everyday
living outside the nuclear family.

We have mentioned so far organisations which can be described as
doing pioneering work today. But most existing voluntary organisations
began their lives as the pioneers of some service or other, and have
subsequently become the providers of that service in a more routine
way. It is an interesting question how far voluntary organisations
continue to act in a pioneering role once their opening phase is over.
Just like statutory agencies, established voluntary organisations
continue to extend the range of needs they are meeting, and improve
and develop the services they provide. But the established organisation,
because of all its existing commitments, is not usually the one that
makes the great leap forward. Particularly if exclusively identified with
one particular need or type of service it runs the risk of resting on its
laurels.

So far we have discussed pioneering at the national level. Most new
developments in social and environmental services at the local level can
be seen as the extension of a service existing in a similar form somewhere else in the country. Developments usually arise partly out of an
awareness of what is happening elsewhere and completely new developments are scarce. If one defines narrowly what constitutes a pioneering
activity, the role of voluntary organisations as pioneers may seem

limited. Alternatively, if one thinks in terms of new developments generally, the role of voluntary organisations is much greater. Perhaps we should emphasise the role of voluntary organisations as a source of new initiatives. New organisations are constantly being formed. As our three main locality studies showed, between 20 per cent and 30 per cent of the organisations about which we obtained information in each town had come into existence between 1970 and 1976. In our view the role of voluntary organisations as a medium through which people can come together to take initiatives, whether long- or short-term ones, is of inestimable value.

So far this discussion of the role of voluntary organisations has been concerned with organisations that themselves provide services. When a voluntary organisation acts as a pressure group it is concerned with the services provided by other agencies. Not all organisations which seek changes in the policies and provisions of other agencies would wish to be designated as pressure groups. The word 'pressure' has different meanings to different people. There are all sorts of ways of exerting pressure, from gentle persuasion behind the scenes through campaigning in the media to direct action of one kind or another. Organisations such as the National Council for Civil Liberties, the Child Poverty Action Group, the Disablement Income Group and Friends of the Earth explicitly identify their role as that of pressure groups. It is, however, interesting to note that the Wales Council for the Disabled in giving oral evidence to us said that they regarded themselves as 'advocates or watchdogs rather than a militant pressure group'. They might on occasion support protest groups of one sort or another, but on the whole their object was to win the confidence of the authorities and this meant making their case to and working closely with statutory and voluntary bodies. The British Trust for Conservation Volunteers made much the same point when they said that 'the message is sometimes more effectively conveyed to certain members of the public by skilled hard work than by political or pressure group activities'. Also concerned with the environment is the Dartmoor Preservation Association which led the successful campaign against the proposed reservoir at Swincombe. Perhaps the importance of the pressure group role was best made to us in evidence from Oxfam, who is their written evidence said

> we recognise that to make an impact on the tremendous needs which exist in developing countries, enormous sums such as can only be supplied by Government and supra national bodies are necessary . . . We believe that Oxfam and other organisations have an important

function to draw the attention of the public to the needs which exist overseas and some of the unfair practices which have developed in relationships with commercial organisations in different countries.

There is another service of which voluntary organisations are the main providers that is distinct from but related to the pressure group role. This is advice to and advocacy on behalf of individuals. The main organisation in this field is the Citizens' Advice Bureaux (CABx), a general service which began under the auspices of the NCSS during the war. In recent years it has continued to expand. In addition there has been a growth of specialist advisory services dealing with housing, welfare rights and legal and consumer matters. The relationship between casework for individuals and wider ranging pressure group activities is a delicate one for organisations in this field. The representatives of the CABx said they did not wish to be regarded as a pressure group, but preferred to influence matters by persuasion and to be seen to be impartial. SHAC (Shelter Housing Aid Centre), on the other hand, explained that it now attached more importance to seeking improvements in the services offered by local authorities, 'as we are very much aware that many families in need do not approach us for help, and also that when we succeed in helping one particular family – perhaps by pleading their case with their local authority – it can be to the detriment of another family that we do not know'. The Child Poverty Action Group (CPAG) stressed the wider significance of casework: 'the Citizens' Rights Office is not just a casework agency but provides the Group with a constant flow of information about what is happening to poor people'. A related development has been the growth of advice centres operating at a neighbourhood level, often in association with community projects. Local authorities run some of these services themselves, but a great many of the problems on which individuals require advice arise from the activities of public authorities. Often they feel it is essential to obtain this from an independent source. Hence voluntary organisations are rightly the main providers in this field.

Some Local Evidence

Most of the discussion so far has been concerned with voluntary organisations as seen from a national standpoint, and except for the NOP data the information presented has been illustrative rather than synoptic. As such it reflects the nature of the written and oral evidence obtained by the Committee, which came mainly from the headquarters of national organisations. In order to complement the picture obtained from the evidence, we initiated a number of pieces of research which are described in Appendix 2. What we called the locality studies formed the largest item in the research programme. Their aim was to obtain as complete a picture as possible of voluntary organisations in particular areas. Research was done in five towns described here under pseudonyms: *Forgeham* is a Midlands industrial town. It constitutes a metropolitan district with a quarter of a million population. *Anglebridge* is a town of over 50,000 within commuting distance of London. With its surrounding rural area and dormitory villages, it comprises a non-metropolitan district. *Kirkforth* is a Northern, industrial, administrative and education centre with a population almost as large as Anglebridge. It makes up about half of a non-metropolitan district. We also studied two small towns with populations under 5,000 — *Drumnockie* in the lowlands of Scotland and *Stanhampton* in the West Country. The former is industrial, the latter non-industrial. In addition, research was commissioned on two neighbourhoods in Glasgow, the purpose being to increase our data from Scotland and to yield information about the activities of voluntary organisations in particularly deprived areas. These two neighbourhoods are also discussed under pseudonyms: *Craigwood*, a 'problem' post-war estate on the edge of the city, and *Levernshiel*, an inner city residential area consisting mostly of inter-war council tenements, each with a population of about 20,000.

Drumnockie and Stanhampton illustrate the voluntary sector at its most basic and widespread. In both towns the largest number of organisations is concerned with children and young people — seven out of eleven in Drumnockie and seven out of fourteen in Stanhampton, ranging from playgroups through Scouts and Guides to a youth club. Next come organisations for the elderly: in Drumnockie these consist of a WRVS meals on wheels service and two clubs for the elderly; in Stanhampton as well as the WRVS meals on wheels and one club for the elderly, there is a Red Cross visiting service, an Abbeyfield Society and the 'friends' of an old persons' home. The third significant field for voluntary involvement is the environment. In Stanhampton there is a strong amenity society of quite recent origin, which kept a vigilant watch on planning applications, preserved footpaths and milestones and was restoring a medieval dovecot. In Drumnockie there is no equivalent organisation, but at the time of our enquiries a community council was in the process of being formed, and though one cannot forecast exactly what direction the community council will take, it is possible that it may include among its functions some of those carried out by an amenity society. There are in addition social organisations for women, in Stanhampton an ex-servicemen's organisation (the Royal British Legion) and a number of fund-raising branches of national agencies. Despite the wide geographic and social distance between the two small towns the broad similarity in the pattern of voluntary activity is notable. However, Stanhampton is the more middle-class town: it does have a greater variety of organisations, and in the Abbeyfield Society it has the only voluntary organisation in the two towns with a full-time employee.

When one turns to the larger towns, Anglebridge, Forgeham and Kirkforth, the number of organisations catering for children and young people and the elderly is multiplied several times. In addition, there are many other fields in which the voluntary sector is active, often responding to needs of a very specific nature. Foremost in terms of numbers of organisations are those that cater for people with particular diseases or handicaps. Most of these organisations came into existence during the last two decades. The pattern varies to some extent from town to town and we were particularly impressed by the strength of the organisations in Anglebridge catering for the disabled and seeking to integrate them with the rest of society. Similar in character, though fewer in number (four organisations in each town) are the associations active in the mental health and handicap field. Also notable are the Hospital Friends which attract a lot of voluntary support, and organisations for single parents, of which Gingerbread is the most active.

Each of the three towns has a Citizens' Advice Bureau and a Marriage Guidance Council. They all employ part-time staff and are partially dependent on local authority grants. The Samaritans also have branches in each town, but only in Anglebridge do they receive any local authority financial support. The YMCA is another voluntary organisation present in each town, and in each town it employs one full-time worker. Otherwise the strength of voluntary youth provision varies considerably between the towns, depending partly on statutory willingness to provide financial support for voluntary clubs. Also variable between the towns is the level of activity in housing and the environment. Each town has a recently established refuge for battered women (though these refuges differ considerably from each other). In Anglebridge and Kirkforth there are no tenants' associations, and in Kirkforth there is not an active local housing association. Each town has a hostel for offenders, though the one in Anglebridge is only just beginning. Another category with special needs are the single homeless; a shelter for them exists in Forgeham and another has recently been

established in Anglebridge. Environmental issues are actively pursued
by the civic societies in each town, supplemented by an uneven
scattering of residents' and community associations.

So far we have considered the three larger towns together, but
Forgeham is much bigger than the other two and has a set of needs and
problems far less evident in the other towns. In particular, 7.5 per cent
of Forgeham's population was born in the New Commonwealth and we
identified eighteen organisations which were concerned with the needs
of the various minorities which comprise this population. These range
from primarily religious organisations, often with associated social and
recreational activities, to those mainly concerned to provide a service.
In the nineteenth century many voluntary organisations came into
existence in order to further the beliefs or protect the values of
particular religious denominations. The ethnic organisations can be seen
as a latter day expression of the same impulse.

Another organisation with no counterpart in the other two towns
was an outpost of the Young Volunteer Force Foundation. Though it
started off as an agency for recruiting and placing volunteers, most of
the efforts of its staff have been devoted to community projects, one
being located in a housing action area, and another being a rights and
advice centre on a problem estate. Pioneering ventures catering
especially for the ethnic minorities include two hostels for homeless
black youths and an advice centre. There is, too, a youth club with
which is associated a counselling service for young people with problems of all kinds. These are perhaps the most noteworthy voluntary
organisations in Forgeham which are doing pioneering work directed at
categories of people with special needs. Most of the organisations so far
discussed have been volunteer organisations; these Forgeham organisations are dependent to a very large extent on grants and can be described as specialist agencies.

It is difficult to present a bird's-eye view of such a diverse array of
organisations. Table 3.2 attempts to do this by summarising the number
of organisations working in different fields and giving the total number
of people working for voluntary organisations.

The weakness of this tabular presentation is that it does not say anything about the volume or quality of work done by the various
organisations; and of course it only covers those organisations which we
were able to identify. There are certainly other organisations, but apart
from parent-teacher associations, we do not think these are very strong
or numerous. As regards the amount of work done, we asked the
organisations how many people were actively involved in their activities

Table 3.2. Voluntary Organisations in Three Towns

(a) *Number of organisations by need area*

	Angle-bridge	Forgeham	Kirkforth
Physical handicap	21	25	19
Mental health & handicap	4	4	4
Children excluding playgroups	4	7	10
Playgroups	27	65	5
Elderly excluding social clubs	3	5	7
Social & luncheon clubs for the elderly	18	56	8
Hospitals & health	7	8	4
Single parents	2	4	1
Housing including special hostels	4	20*	2
Environment	7	3	5
Miscellaneous	15	42**	17
TOTAL	112	239	82

(b) *Number of people working for voluntary organisations*

	Angle-bridge	Forgeham	Kirkforth
Active volunteers (not membership)	2,500	4,000	2,000
Paid staff: full-time	10	28	13
part-time	20	15	26

(c) *Total Population* — 60,000 | 265,000 | 50,000

*including 14 tenants' associations
**including 18 ethnic organisations and 14 community associations

and whether they had any paid staff, whether part-time or full-time. Answers to the questions about the number of volunteers must be treated with caution, both as regards what our informants claimed and because we did not obtain information about all the organisations we identified. However when we had completed our sums, we came out with the round figures shown in Table 3.2. These do at least give some idea of the order of magnitude of the voluntary sector in the three towns. One significant category of organisations has been left out of the discussion so far: established charities with local operational branches. Kirkforth has a training centre and a children's home run by voluntary organisations, each with a large number of paid staff. In Forgeham, there is also a children's home, but in Anglebridge there are no such organisations.

In terms of population, the two Glasgow neighbourhoods, Craigwood and Levernshiel, came in between our small- and medium-sized towns. The studies we commissioned were concerned with local organisations, so they do not cover Glasgow-wide organisations with which local

Table 3.3. Voluntary Organisations in the Two Neighbourhoods in
          Glasgow

	Craigwood	Levernshiel
Physical handicap	0	0
Mental health & handicap	2	0
Children & youth (excluding playgroups)	10	10
Playgroups	3	1
Elderly (excluding social clubs)	0	2
Social & luncheon clubs for the elderly	4	8
Hospitals & health	0	0
Single parents	1	0
Housing & environment	5	6
Miscellaneous	3	3
	28	30

residents may have had some association. Thus organisations, like those
for the handicapped, which are concerned with very specialised needs,
do not seem to occur. As Table 3.3 shows there is, as in the two small
towns, a predominance of organisations caring for children and the
elderly.

The two mental health organisations mentioned in Table 3.3 are
Alcoholics Anonymous and Alanon (for the relations of alcoholics).
Gingerbread is the organisation for single parents, and most of the
organisations in the housing and environmental field are tenants'
associations and action groups. Under the heading miscellaneous comes
a community newspaper in each area, a group organising a local festival
in Levernshiel and in Craigwood a coordinating group mostly made up
of professional workers.

We were particularly interested in any differences there might be
between the pattern of voluntary activity in these two deprived areas as
compared with the other two towns that we studied. In terms of the
number of different organisations, when one makes an allowance for the
exclusion of Glasgow-wide organisations without a presence in the two
neighbourhoods, there does not seem to be a great deal of difference.
However, there were some differences in the character of the organisations. It seems that in both neighbourhoods, active leadership in the
community depended on a small number of people: some of these were
local residents, often people with strongly held left-wing political
beliefs, and others were professionals, like teachers and priests, who
might or might not be resident in the area and whose involvement was
part of or an extension of their work. In Levernshiel one such

professional was a community development officer appointed by the
local authority. Another difference lay in the apparently rather
precarious nature of many of the Craigwood and Levernshiel organisations: all our studies showed that many voluntary organisations were of
very recent origin, but in the towns other than Glasgow we had the
impression that more of the organisations were firmly bedded in their
local communities. Related to this there are differences in aims and
methods: in Craigwood and Levernshiel there seem to be proportion-
ately more organisations acting predominantly as pressure groups, and
fewer organisations concentrating on providing services for others. This
was an understandable response to social and environmental conditions
in the two neighbourhoods.

A category of organisations that has not yet been discussed is the
one whose main beneficiaries are other organisations — these are the
intermediary bodies we discuss more fully later in Chapters 6 and 7. In
Kirkforth there was a Council of Voluntary Service and a Volunteer
Bureau with part-time staff. But at the time of our enquiry it seemed
that more was being done by the statutory side in mobilising the
voluntary sector than by the voluntary sector itself. There was an active
community development officer based in the local social services
department's office, and one of the hospitals had a lively volunteer
organiser. In Anglebridge more developmental and coordinating activity
was coming from within the voluntary sector itself. The local Age
Concern was active among organisations in that field, and the local
County Community Council, though covering a very much wider area
than the town itself, did relate some of its activities to Anglebridge
specifically, including the Volunteer Bureau. There was also a Standing
Conference on Voluntary Organisations independent of the Community
Council. The Social Services Department, as in Kirkforth, was interested
in promoting voluntary effort, but its liaison officer was concentrating
on the development of local visiting schemes and play activities and
was not seeking to marshal the voluntary sector as a whole. Forgeham
is unusual for a town of its size in not having a Council of Voluntary
Service. The local authority has a special consultative committee
through which it communicates with voluntary organisations, and a
senior officer in the Social Services Department acted as a contact
point for voluntary organisations. However, no local authority
employee devoted a large part of his time to relations with the
voluntary sector. The local Age Concern and the Community Relations
Council are both well established in their own fields, and efforts were
being made to bring together organisations concerned with counselling.

However for a town of its size the voluntary sector in Forgeham seemed weak and there must be an untapped potential for further development. In Glasgow the intermediary bodies operate generally at a city-wide level and they fall outside the terms of our enquiry into two neighbourhoods. However, in each neighbourhood there had quite recently been formed a committee of professional workers and local residents which was concerned with initiating action on the problems of the area and represented a coming together of the external and indigenous leadership, with the initiative coming from the former. This is an instance of the spread of community work during the past ten years.

Another way of taking a synoptic look at the contribution of the voluntary sector is to examine one type of provision as a whole. The Day Care Research Project at the National Institute of Social Work kindly allowed us access to their preliminary data on day-care units. Voluntary organisations were responsible for one in four of the units they surveyed. The extent of the voluntary contribution varied greatly from one local authority to another according to local tradition, historical accidents, current local authority policies and other factors difficult to identify. Voluntary organisations most often provided day units for the elderly followed by those for the physically handicapped. Few voluntary units were intended for the mentally handicapped and the mentally ill. Voluntary units made much more use of volunteers than those run by local authorities and health authorities and seemed more informal and closer to the communities from which their users came. In so far as broad differences could be distinguished, this was the main one. But it should also be noted that most of the small handful of units that were quite clearly playing a pioneering role were voluntary ones.

The Distribution of Voluntary Activity

One criterion by which any arrangements for providing social welfare need to be judged is whether resources are directed to where the needs are greatest. The kind of people usually described as middle class are more disposed to belong to voluntary associations than manual workers and their families.[6] Our NOP survey confirmed this fact: 30 per cent of those classified by the interviewer as AB (i.e. people employed in higher or intermediate managerial, administrative and professional jobs) reported participation in voluntary work compared to 9 per cent of those classified as DE (i.e. semi-skilled and unskilled manual workers, state pensioners, etc.). By contrast, it should be noted that the Bradford Survey found the propensity to give help in an informal, unorganised way was much more evenly distributed over the social classes.[3] Some voluntary organisations have a very strong middle-class flavour: amenity societies are an obvious example, but there are organisations like tenants' associations with a much more working-class character. Others are neutral. For instance our study of applicants to the Family Fund showed that social class made only a small difference to whether the parents of handicapped children belonged to or held office in organisations for such children. Thus 22 per cent of applicants to the Family Fund, 25 per cent of members of voluntary organisations for handicapped children and 30 per cent of the officers of such organisations came from non-manual families. Evidently the problems of rearing a handicapped child transcend distinctions of class and status. It is also significant, though, that despite the absence of a strong class bias only about half the parents surveyed belonged to any one of these organisations.

In pointing out that as a whole middle-class people take more part in organised activities concerned with the social and environmental services, we are not suggesting any criticism of individual voluntary organisations. But this observation does have implications for the voluntary sector as a whole. First, as far as mutual benefit organisations are concerned, uneven social participation may mean that some groups benefit more than others, at any rate in the absence of deliberate efforts to counteract this tendency. Second, in so far as organisations serving others are concerned, some areas will be less well endowed than others. The point concerning mutual benefit organisations was well illustrated by preschool playgroups in Forgeham. The local Pre-school Playgroups Association had made most headway in the town's more desirable suburbs, and we were told that the playgroups which had come into existence in the more deprived areas had found it 'not quite their cup of tea' and did not get from the PPA the kind of help that was appropriate to their circumstances. In response to this situation the local authority playgroup adviser was concentrating most of her resources in the deprived areas and was not giving the PPA the help it expected.

The tendency for there to be an uneven geographical distribution of voluntary organisations is exemplified by the Child Poverty Action Group (CPAG). The location of its branches correlates highly with the presence of universities, particularly those with departments of social administration, but not with data indicative of the presence of families with low incomes. CPAG probably makes its main impact through the influence of its headquarters organisation on central government.

Nevertheless, the underlying point is a valid one. In order to examine the extent of this kind of disjunction, we made an analysis by computer of the location of the branches of twenty-two national organisations. The most significant point to emerge was the large difference between the frequency of voluntary organisation branches in some types of town as compared to others. The type of town most richly endowed with voluntary organisations was what we described as the 'old county town', places like Bath, Exeter, Oxford and Reading. On average the ten towns in this category had 1.26 branches per 10,000 population. In contrast, the sixteen towns like Barnsley, Sheffield, and Sunderland that came into the category 'traditional centres of heavy industry and manufacturing' had an average of only 0.44 branches per 10,000 population. But it was not a matter of a simple social class gradient since a group of places like Esher and Solihull, which we described as exclusive residential towns, also had a small number of branches, perhaps because they were served by branches in nearby metropolitan centres. Seaside towns like Blackpool, Bournemouth and Southend formed a distinct group that scored highly in terms of voluntary organisations. Thus some social and geographical contexts seem to provide a much more fertile soil for voluntary organisations than others.

We also used our NOP data to examine the distribution of voluntary effort over different need areas. Four categories attracted the greater part of the attention: of those who had done some voluntary work in the previous week, 36 per cent had helped the elderly, 21 per cent schools and youth, 15 per cent the physically handicapped and 12 per cent children and families. A few people (12 per cent) had helped more than one category and caution should be used in interpreting such small sample figures, but the low level of attention for other types of need such as mental handicap (5 per cent) and mental illness (nil) is noteworthy.

This finding conveys an important point about the nature of the voluntary sector, or at any rate about that part of it dependent on voluntary effort. It is of its essence unplanned and spontaneous, and it will not necessarily of itself allocate its energies in accordance with abstract criteria of need or equity. Its resources are not deployed in the way that a beneficient deity or social planner, taking all factors into account, would wish. This applies not only to distribution between geographical areas but also to distribution between need areas: thus the number of volunteers working with the mentally ill is tiny in relation to those helping the elderly or the physically handicapped. We did not examine variation in the quality of the services provided by voluntary organisations, but we suspect that with the exception of the established charities relying on paid staff, an equivalent unevenness exists in this respect also. However, it should be noted that much of the support given over the past decade by local authorities and trusts to community development in one form or another can be seen as attempts to rectify the maldistribution of voluntary organisations by using specialist agencies to generate additional mutual benefit organisations.

Summary and Conclusions

The following points from this review of the present situation deserve emphasis:

(a) Whether measured by man-hours or by expenditure, in the fields with which we are concerned, the voluntary sector is much smaller that the statutory, except in the personal social services where, taking the efforts of voluntary and paid workers together, the input of the voluntary sector is the greater.

(b) There is widespread voluntary involvement in caring for the elderly, for children and for the handicapped. Some of this amounts to filling gaps in statutory provision, but much of it is different in kind from statutory provision, either because the beneficiaries are involved in mutual aid or because the voluntary helper can sometimes develop relationships not possible for paid professionals.

(c) In relation to the informal system of caring, the special contribution of the voluntary sector consists of filling or bridging the gaps between the individual and the statutory services, through the medium of organised arrangements for mutual aid and neighbourly care and by transmitting from one side to the other knowledge about unmet needs and available resources.

(d) In some cases the voluntary sector provides alternative services which offer the consumer, or those acting on the consumer's behalf, a choice. The frequency with which a choice is available by virtue of voluntary provision should not be exaggerated, but the additional source of diversity is significant. Often the voluntary alternative takes the form of more specialised provision.

(e) The pioneering role remains an important one for the voluntary sector. Specialist agencies, financially dependent upon grants and working with stigmatised, unpopular groups were often to be found in this role. More widely, voluntary organisations are the instruments through which a host of independent initiatives are brought into effect, only a few of which would from a national perspective be thought of as pioneering.

(f) At the local level, voluntary organisations which concentrate on a pressure group role occur mainly in the environment field. Others serve to communicate the needs of particular groups to the public authorities without seeing themselves or being seen as pressure groups. Outside the environmental field, explicit recognition of the importance of seeking to influence official policy is to be found more frequently at the national level.

(g) Voluntary organisations are the main providers of advice and advocacy services. Where the performance of statutory agencies is what is at issue the consumer will need the support of an independent organisation.

(h) In addition to the specific roles played by the voluntary sector in relation to the other care providing sectors, wider functions served by it in relation to society in general should not be overlooked. As well as providing a vehicle for the expression of care and concern on the part of local community life, it is the medium through which religious, ethnic and other minorities can, in the field of social provision, sustain their own identities.

(i) In summarising the positive contribution of the voluntary sector it would be wrong to ignore its main limitation. This is its unevenness. Its very diversity and specificity, and the small size of the financial resources at its command, mean that the voluntary sector is less able than the statutory to remedy mismatches between needs and resources that become evident when an over-view of social provision is taken.

Notes

1. Kenneth Newton, *Second City Politics*, 1976.
2. *New Society*, 7 April 1977.
3. Morris, Mary, *Voluntary Work in the Welfare State*, p. 969
4. Webb, Adrian; Day, Lesley; Weller, Douglas, *Voluntary Social Service Manpower Resources*, Personal Social Services Council, September 1976.
5. In a forthcoming issue of *Child Care, Health and Development*.
6. For example see Goldthorpe, J. H., *et al.*, *The Affluent Worker in the Class Structure*, 1969, pp. 93-4.

4 CENTRAL GOVERNMENT AND THE VOLUNTARY SECTOR

In our second chapter we have given some account of the influences which have affected voluntarism in the past and the reasons why we ourselves believe in what we have called 'pluralism', the principle that the State and the voluntary sector should be partners. Two recent Prime Ministers, Mr Heath in 1971 and Mr Harold Wilson (as he then was) in 1975, have stressed in addresses to the National Council of Social Service the importance they attached to the encouragement of the voluntary sector. The general attitude of the government towards voluntary organisations was also set out in a speech in the House of Lords on 25 June 1975 by Lord Harris, at that time the Minister of State at the Home Office with special responsibility for voluntary services. He denied the view that the development of the welfare state reduced the need for voluntary service, pointing out that the statutory services were under more pressure than at any time since the Second World War and that if the lifeline provided by many dedicated volunteers were cut, many of the most underprivileged in society would be the first to suffer. In this and other Ministerial speeches it has been stressed that there is a need for voluntary services complementary to those provided by the State and that a society in which all needs were met by the State would be a less civilised and humane one. References have been made to the importance of the pioneering role of the voluntary organisations in identifying needs and demonstrating how to meet them; to the need for greater involvement in the community and more emphasis on mutual help; and to the increased opportunity for self-fulfilment open to individuals concerned with voluntary work. The government has therefore given general encouragement to the voluntary sector. We comment later on some aspects of its policies in practice.

It may be of interest to quote also the views of some others. In his book *Politics in Practice*,[1] Lord Windlesham, who was Minister of State at the Home Office and later Lord Privy Seal in Mr Heath's Government, says: 'There is nothing new in government, central as well as local, joining with voluntary organisations in the pursuit of a variety of commonly accepted social aims. Indeed the process by which social aims become commonly accepted results from a cross-fertilisation between official and unofficial thought and action.' Later he adds,

Whatever the expectations which accompanied the birth of the
welfare state a quarter of a century ago, there is no doubt that the
need for volunteers and voluntary organisations in the social services
is as great as ever. As the services provided by the State have expanded, new needs have been disclosed and old needs have stubborn-
ly remained unmet. There is now a general recognition that it cannot
all be done by professional administrators and experts, however dedicated and skilled. Today in Britain, state and voluntary social services co-exist side by side. They are complementary and should be,
as they usually are, cooperative.

A Labour backbencher, Mr Bruce Douglas-Mann MP, former Vice-Chair-
man of the National Council of Social Service, speaking in the House of
Commons debate on voluntary organisations on 8 July 1975 said

my attitude [i.e. towards voluntary organisations] has changed during
the last few years. I believed ten years ago that the role of voluntary
organisations was somewhat superfluous in a properly organised
society. I felt the Government and local authorities should be taking
on a great majority of the responsibilities fulfilled by voluntary
organisations. But I have subsequently changed my view. The extent
to which voluntary organisations provide flexibility in an area where
Government operations have to be conducted within fairly rigid
rules provides opportunities to remedy many ills which otherwise
would remain unmet.

Thus it appears that the pluralist philosophy is generally accepted by
both major political parties.

At the start of our enquiry the government were good enough to
appoint an observer to assist us in our work. Our first observer was Mr
Tony Hart, Head of the Voluntary Services Unit. After the first few
months of our enquiry he was transferred to a different post, and was
succeeded by Miss Margaret Clayton, who has been our observer for
all but three or four months of our deliberations. One of the many tasks
which she carried out for us was to consult government departments
with whom the Voluntary Services Unit deals and to provide a paper
giving their general views. This paper, entitled 'Government Departments
and Voluntary Organisations', is of such importance that we reproduce
it in full in Appendix 4 of the report with grateful recognition. In the
next few paragraphs we summarise some of the major points in the paper
and we give our own views and comments at the end of the chapter.

Some Major Points in the Government Evidence

The Voluntary Services Unit

The belief that voluntary organisations have a significant role to play in the United Kingdom is exemplified by the setting up under the previous (Conservative) administration and the continuation under the Labour Government, of the Voluntary Services Unit. It has four main functions. First, it acts as a link between voluntary organisations and government departments, giving advice to the former as to their best points of contact within departments and alerting the latter to the possible effects upon voluntary organisations of certain major policy proposals, legislation and government directives. Secondly, it provides a useful focal point for the diverse departmental interests within Whitehall relating to the voluntary sector. For this purpose the Unit has within each major government department a Liaison Officer at Assistant Secretary level. The third function is to encourage voluntary organisations to co-operate with each other and to stimulate the use of volunteers where this can appropriately be done by central government. (In practice the latter part of the third function has largely been delegated to the Volunteer Centre which was established in 1973 and whose function, although of great importance, we do not discuss here because it is not of direct concern to us in view of our terms of reference.) Finally, VSU acts as a financier of last resort within government, with limited funds available to assist national organisations or projects whose work spans the interest of several different departments. Its funds may also be used in exceptional cases to support innovatory local projects from which lessons of national relevance can be learned and to maintain organisations working in areas of high social priority where alternative funds will definitely be available within a short time.

Departmental Policies

Voluntary organisations generally deal within departments with whatever division or branch is relevant to their work. Some departments, notably the Department of Health and Social Security and the Health Division of the Scottish Home and Health Department, have a central point of reference within the department and sometimes a point of origin for general policy information. The point of reference is particularly useful for organisations which span the interests of more than one branch or division of a department, but such arrangements are not common and are probably only necessary in the larger and more complex departments. Responsibility for dealing with voluntary organisations

generally rests therefore at divisional or branch level. Generally, no one
Minster within any one department has a specific responsibility for
matters concerning voluntary organisations except in the Department
of Health and Social Security, where responsibility lies with the
Minister of State (Health), and in the Home Office, where the Home
Secretary has a general coordinating interest and one Minister of State
has a particular concern for those organisations which fall within the
terms of reference of the VSU.

Reasons for Government Support

Broadly speaking, government support to voluntary organisations can
be divided into three main categories. The first is where voluntary provision is considered preferable because, for instance, the number in
need is not great enough to justify special statutory provision, as with
specialist provision for unusual physical handicap, or where services
are needed for those who might generally be thought to be anti-
authoritarian, such as ex-offenders, alcoholics and drug addicts; or
where advice is given on certain personal problems or on difficulties
with statutory bodies. The second category covers cases where the
voluntary organisation can provide a desirable alternative to statutory
provision or a desirable degree of choice; of this, the best example
is probably in the area of housing. The third field is the extension and
supplementation of statutory services by voluntary effort, of which an
outstanding example is the WRVS. It is useful to distinguish these
categories, but they are not mutually exclusive and it is often difficult
to determine within which of them the work of an organisation falls;
but taken together they account for the great majority of voluntary
organisations which are supported by central government. (Fuller
details will be found in paragraphs 8-17 of the government evidence in
Appendix 4.)

The Use of Statutory Agencies

Departmental policy is not always implemented directly by the department but sometimes by way of a statutory agency set up to pursue
particular government policies and usually given power to make grants
to voluntary organisations in pursuance of these policies. (This subject
is considered more fully in Chapter 7.)

The Absence of Specific Government Policies

The government evidence explains that as policy towards voluntary
organisations is generally decided in the context of the particular area

in which they work, it would be difficult to have a more specific overall government policy towards them than that described in the first paragraph of this chapter. It is argued that the lack of overall specific policies is probably advantageous to voluntary organisations because it allows for a more flexible response to the needs of the voluntary sector than would be possible if there were general rules about the kind of organisation which could be encouraged. One of the functions of the Voluntary Services Unit, which it is only just beginning to fulfil, is to identify situations where consistency of approach might be beneficial to all concerned and, where appropriate, to encourage departments to work towards a common policy.

Finance

Governments operate within the strict principles and rules for the provision and expenditure of public money, and departments proceed in accordance with their recognised functions and responsibilities within the resources made available to them. As most voluntary organisations are dealt with by a division or branch of the particular departments most relevant to their work, composite departmental 'bids' or 'estimates' are not common except in those departments which have one central point of contact. If departments should decide, as a matter of general policy, to support voluntary rather than statutory services, there would, in theory, be nothing to prevent them from doing so. But departments have certain statutory responsibilities which must be met from the total amount of money made available to them, and only limited funds are left over for help to voluntary organisations other than those which are simply acting on an agency basis to fulfil statutory duties. Financial restraints therefore more often determine specific departmental policies than do departmental policies determine the availability of funds. It is the availability of funds which is the decisive factor, after applying the normal stringent criteria of merit and need which must be met, before a grant can be made.

Duration of Grants

Availability of funds has a considerable influence on the duration of grants, which are usually made for one year at a time subject to annual review. Strictly speaking grants can be made only on an annual basis because they are always subject to Parliament voting the necessary funds, but many organisations are offered slightly more security by being offered three-year grants, subject to Parliament voting the necessary funds and to the satisfactory fulfilment of any conditions of grant. Generally speaking, where the need for an organisation's services continues, renewal of annual grant is found to be more or less automatic, and the annual review is then primarily for the purpose of altering the amounts needed in the light of inflation or improvement of services because of an increase in the scale of an organisation. This policy, however, carries the danger that departmental funds may become totally and automatically committed to on-going grants year after year, with the result that new organisations, with useful and coherent aims or new projects put up by organisations, cannot be funded. For this reason, more thorough reviews are often held at periodic intervals so that departments may satisfy themselves that serious attempts have been made to find money from alternative sources, that the need still exists, that the work is still in line with government policy and that the service given is still of value.

Application for Grant

The attitude of most departments to voluntary organisations is generally speaking responsive rather than positive. That is to say, they generally react to demand rather than actively plan for the involvement of voluntary organisations in pursuance of any particular policy, though there are a few exceptions. When funds are limited, it is obviously difficult to invite applications from all comers, and there is even greater difficulty in selecting particular organisations to undertake work for government departments on an agency basis. Sometimes national agencies, such as the National Association for the Care and Resettlement of Offenders, and national coordinating agencies, such as the National Council for Voluntary Youth Services, can assist, but the agency itself may not be universally accepted by, or representative of, all voluntary organisations operating in similar fields. On the whole therefore most departments find that only in the area of research is it practicable to commission work from voluntary organisations. Most departments do advise on the availability of funds and on how applications can be made, often by means of widely distributed circulars. They also issue forms or guidance notes, or allow officials or advisers to meet organisations and offer personal help and advice. The information requested by departments varies considerably: most will ask an applicant organisation to supply certain background financial details, for example, what other sources of support it has and what other applications for funds have been made; some ask formally for copies of the organisation's constitution or the composition of the board of trustees or management committee; while others make enquiries about the structure, standing and constitution of

the organisation only if informal enquiries raise doubts or questions.
When it receives applications VSU, because it is concerned primarily
with applications which either span the interest of several departments
or fall between them all, has to consult all departments likely to be
concerned.

Criteria for Funding

Departments apply a large variety of criteria to determine which voluntary organisations should be supported. The first is that the organisation
is working to a policy in accordance with the department's own policy.
Then most departments stress that the services provided must be cost-
effective; managerial competence and the avoidance of duplication and
overlap are also regarded as important. A government funded organisation is usually expected to be clear in its objectives and to demonstrate
an ability to carry out successfully the work for which it is being funded.
If the case is one where the voluntary image or style is valued in itself,
then relevant criteria are applied, for instance, the extent of community
participation and whether the applicants are representative of the local
community. Departmental funding is usually related to the provision
of specific services; and voluntary organisations which are basically
orientated towards research, campaigning or pressure activities are, on
the whole, less likely to obtain government funds. Central government
departments usually support national rather than local organisations,
though occasionally local projects may be supported if they are innovatory and may be of national significance, and the government evidence
shows that there are a few exceptions for particular reasons (paragraph
31 of Appendix 4). In general, central departments give money for the
administration of national voluntary organisations and only to a limited
extent for local work. They rarely support project work, mainly because
this is traditionally the area in which trusts and foundations operate.
The reluctance of the government to fund local work does not necessarily apply to the statutory agencies which make grants to voluntary
organisations in pursuance of government policy.

Conditions of Grant

How far departments keep a check on organisations to which grants
have been made depends largely on the nature of the grant. If it represents only a small percentage of the income of the organisation, it is
quite likely that the only condition will be that an annual report and
audited accounts should be submitted and any grant unspent at the end
of the year should be returned. Where a particular project is being

funded, it may be made subject to inspection by a government inspec-
tor (as would often be the case for premises such as hostels or workshops, whether or not in receipt of government grant) and there is
increasing recognition among departments of the need to establish some
valid way of assessing the effectiveness and value of projects supported
by public money. A number of grants for specific projects are now made
on the condition that some form of independent monitoring or evaluation be undertaken. This is a difficult matter to arrange, and the most
common situation is for departments to assess the projects themselves
by informal contact, reliance on professional advisers, and the informal
views of those with whom the project has the closest contact. If the
grant made to a voluntary organisation represents a substantial proportion of its income, it is regarded as a 'controlled fringe body' and becomes subject to detailed examination of the salaries and conditions of
employment of the staff.

Influence and Control

The government evidence explains that it is very difficult to generalise
about the extent to which the receipt of a government grant by a voluntary organisation means that it becomes subject to government influence
and control. The very fact that government money may be available if
an organisation pursues one activity rather than another may have an
influence on the organisation's decision but this would normally be only
at the margin. It is unlikely that any voluntary organisation would
change its activities simply in order to obtain government funding, but
if it has been given a government grant on the understanding that it will
continue to follow a certain line of action, there may well be an
influence, even though indirect, on the extent to which it modifies or
alters that action. Departmental observers or assessors are usually
appointed not as a condition of grant but by agreement between the
voluntary organisation and the funding department, often at the request
of the former. Though they may influence the organisation by advice
and information, they are not there in order to exercise control. The
element of control becomes obtrusive only when the department has to
approve pay and grading structure with consequent monitoring of grading standard, and agree salary levels and conditions of service. Apart
from these cases however the government evidence states that in general
the amount of influence or control exercised by departments over
voluntary organisations to which grants are made is remarkably
small.

Consultation

The last section of the government evidence stresses the importance of liaison and consultation between departments and voluntary organisations. Where departments and organisations have a relationship through funding, contact between them on an informal basis may be almost as close and continuous as between departments themselves; although informal consultations are more common, there are cases of formal arrangements. It is not difficult to arrange formal consultation in those fields in which there are large national organisations with standing, knowledge and experience accepted in both the statutory and the voluntary worlds. But in most cases the situation is not so clear and a department may lay itself open to embarrassment and criticism where it enters into formal consultation with one or a group of organisations and appears to exclude other organisations which feel that they too have a right to be involved. For this reason informal consultations tend to be preferred to formal ones. In some areas of work there are coordinating agencies (which we have called 'intermediary bodies' and which are discussed in Chapters 6 and 7) which may be used, but there are disadvantages in this also as the agencies' claim to be representative may not necessarily be valid. They may be putting forward their own opinion or the majority opinion to the exclusion of equally valid minority views. In spite of these difficulties it is generally true to say that where departments and voluntary organisations are operating in the same field of work there is a fair degree of liaison and consultation. This is not true in cases where problems common to all voluntary organisations are concerned. One of the Voluntary Services Unit's functions is to try to identify such issues and to ensure that the voluntary sector's general interest is taken into account. This also involves the major national intermediary bodies such as the National Council of Social Service.

Before giving our views on points of the government evidence it may be useful to refer briefly to the actual figures of government grant aiding. We discuss finance, including grants from central government to voluntary organisations, in Chapter 9. But it is an important part of the background to our general discussion in this chapter to note that the volume of grants made by central government has steadily been increasing. It is difficult to obtain accurate figures before the financial year 1974/75, but the total given in that year, £19 million, certainly represents a substantial increase on earlier years. Since then the rate of increase has continued at well above the level of inflation and the total sum for 1976/77 is about double that for 1974/75.

The Setting Up of the Voluntary Services Unit

The government's desire to encourage the voluntary sector is demonstrated by the setting up of the Voluntary Services Unit. An account is given in Chapter 3 of Lord Windlesham's book to which we referred earlier. He explains that in planning the government's relationships with the voluntary sector three possible models of internal organisation were considered: either one of the central departments (Treasury, Civil Service Department or Cabinet Office) should assume responsibility for most, if not all, government involvement with the voluntary sector; or one of the major functional departments should act as lead department, taking the initiative in fostering voluntary endeavour and coordinating responsibilities, but at the same time leaving existing departmental responsibilities untouched; or some kind of quasi-independent public body should be established, possibly on the lines of the Arts Council, to develop the voluntary sector and channel public funds to voluntary organisations. After considering the three possibilities, the government decided to designate a Minister of State at the Home Office as Minister with special responsibility for coordinating the government's interest in the field of voluntary social services, saying that it was not the intention to supersede the existing close links between individual organisations and the government departments with which they dealt, but to have a direct point of contact between the government and voluntary organisations on matters which affected them all. The Minister of State was to become responsible for coordinating activity within Whitehall and providing a direct point of contact between the government and the voluntary organisations on matters which affected them all. He was also to deal with matters falling outside the recognised field of any one department.

Lord Windlesham then describes how the Home Office's new responsibility fitted easily into the departmental structure and in particular with the interests and general approach of the Community Programmes Department. He notes later that

the effectiveness of the Ministerial coordinator was impaired by the fact that he was outside the Cabinet, and so junior to, and not closely in touch with, those Ministers in charge of Departments such as Education and Science, and Health and Social Security, which had considerable interests in various forms of voluntary endeavour. The additional funds were also under departmental control, and therefore the Home Office Minister of State had little independent power in the all important matter of grant aiding particular activities or organisations from public funds.

Later it was decided that the coordinating Minister should have some
direct control over funds, in order that promising and worthwhile
developments in voluntary service could be supported without having
to persuade another department to find the money. It was also agreed
that there should be a specialised unit formed under a full-time
official with whom the voluntary movement could identify. This was
the Voluntary Services Unit, which was first established in the Civil
Service Department but has since been moved back to the Home Office.

Some Conclusions and Reflections

VSU's functions, described earlier in this chapter, of being a focal point
for diverse departmental interests within Whitehall and of being
financier for 'across-the-board' projects, inevitably raise the question of
its position and powers within the government machine. We would
agree that the coordinating role does require VSU to have some direct
control over funds, not only for the reason given by Lord Windlesham,
but also because it gives to VSU a standing of its own and consequently
some power to make its voice heard in exercising the coordinating role.
But we wonder whether VSU is rightly placed within a major spending
department as at present or whether it should be independent of them,
though not necessarily under the Civil Service Department as before.
To be in a large department brings the advantage of the general support
which that department provides. Among relevant departments the coordinating role is probably best exercised by the Home Office, which
has in the past pioneered many new projects before passing them over
to other departments; it thus has a tradition of coordinating in matters
in which it is concerned. The counter-argument is that any Minister and
his officials will inevitably be influenced by their own departmental
policies, so that if the VSU is in a major spending department, it is
likely over a time to be biased in favour of organisations and projects of
particular concern to that department. There is also the added danger,
particularly in times of economic restraint, that VSU's funds may be
cut as part of economies in the overall department budget, whereas we
consider it essential that they should be clearly seen as an interdepart-
mental resource.

These are the obvious practical difficulties in having the VSU in a
major spending department. A less obvious, but in our view more important, reason for a separate Unit is the need for departmental responsibility for individual voluntary organisations to be established wherever

possible. It is a great advantage to have some way of funding organisations which are generally approved of by government but fall within
the responsibility of no particular department. But it seems to us that
this can become a disadvantage if departments use the VSU as a way of
evading the question of departmental responsibility so that the work of
the organisation is never seen as related to any particular government
policy. It makes sense for the VSU to have a continuing commitment to
organisations such as the WRVS, the NCSS or the Volunteer Centre
because of its responsibility for the encouragement of volunteers and of
its interest in cooperation between voluntary organisations. Except
where the specific responsibilities of the VSU are concerned, however,
or where there may be a special reason for not wishing a particular
organisation to be funded by any individual department, we consider
that VSU funding should be regarded as a temporary measure pending
the allocation of departmental responsibility. This is partly to ensure
that there is a continuing ability for the VSU to fund development
work, but mainly because we believe that if the work of an organisation is considered to be of such value as to justify government funding
for anything other than an experimental period, it should be of sufficient significance to justify consideration of its development within the
context of particular departmental policies. We believe that this can
only be done if one department acepts responsibility. It may well be
difficult, however, for a particular part of one spending department to
persuade another spending department to assume new financial responsibilities. It therefore seems to us that a Minister with no departmental
interests would be in the best position to suggest an appropriate allocation of responsibility without being accused of undue bias, and that to
have sufficient authority to press his suggestions he must be of Cabinet
rank.

Another question is whether VSU is better placed within government
or should become an intermediary body or statutory agency to which
we referred earlier in this chapter. We deal with national intermediary
bodies as a subject on their own in Chapter 7 and here only discuss the
subject from the viewpoint of the VSU itself. In general terms a unit
which is part of government and directly responsible to a Minister is in
a strong position to persuade the government to take a positive line over
any issue, particularly if the Minister is of Cabinet rank (though, as we
have said, if it is within a large department, the unit itself and the
Minister may be subject to a degree of departmental influence). An
intermediary body outside the government machine keeps its independence, but unless it has a very strong chairman who has access to

Ministers, it may not have as much influence as it would wish on government policy. Certainly the staff of the intermediary body will have less power to influence civil servants than they would have if they were part of the government machine. We therefore feel that VSU is rightly placed within the government structure. There is perhaps a danger that VSU as part of the governmental structure could be saddled with a greatly increased load. This could take a number of different forms, such as giving to VSU a very large grant-giving function or perhaps involving it in some way in an 'Urban Development Commission' role. We are not arguing the case for or against such suggestions in themselves. As far as VSU is concerned, however, we believe it to be essential to its relationships with the voluntary sector generally that it should remain small in numbers of staff and easily accessible and should continue to be seen as independent of strict departmental control. To integrate it closely into the government machine would in our view undermine its usefulness.

The government evidence comes to the conclusion that in relation to the voluntary sector it would be difficult to have any overall government policy applying uniformly to all departments. The Ministerial speeches quoted at the beginning of this chapter are evidence of a general desire for partnership with the voluntary sector. But departments differ from each other in their functions and in their opportunities for collaboration with voluntary organisations: and from its diversity and complexity the voluntary sector would not fit easily or tidily into a uniform overall policy. On balance we agree that too strong a central direction of individual departments would weaken existing links between the departments and the relevant voluntary bodies. We should regret this, because we see reciprocal benefit in each department working closely with voluntary organisations in its own sphere. But short of a rigid uniformity there are steps which could be taken by the government as a whole. For instance, the government could urge each individual department to develop and apply its own positive policy towards the voluntary sector, ensuring that departmental structure and machinery were adequate and appropriate; they could include, in the funding of particular innovations like the Job Creation Programme or the Urban Aid Programme, a proposal or even a requirement that some proportion of the resources be allotted to voluntary organisations; they could give financial support to the voluntary sector at local level, subject to the usual proviso of local authority concurrence. In these ways the government would be demonstrating in practical terms the value which they place on the voluntary sector; and they would probably save money.

There is one further point which we feel bound to make. As we look forward over the next twenty-five years we cannot see any likelihood that public expenditure on the social and environmental services will continue to grow as fast as it has done during the last quarter of a century. Nor can we see any likelihood of a diminution in the rate at which additional services will be expected and demanded. In the past there has been a tendency to think and act as though the answer to social problems is for the state to assume direct responsibility and provide resources for the extension or intensification of statutory services. We believe that this assumption is only partially valid and that there is an urgent need to look afresh at the whole present pattern of social and environmental services and their organisation. We are not thinking simply of a redistribution of activities between the statutory and the voluntary sectors. What we are proposing is the development of a new long-term strategy, by a new examination of the potential contributions of the statutory, voluntary and informal sectors, and their interrelationship. In our view this examination is likely to point to the need for a substantial extension of the last two sectors. We believe a major reappraisal of this kind should be given a high priority by the government and by the relevant institutions of the voluntary sector. In particular this is a call for a governmental initiative of a new kind, based on an explicit recognition of the contribution which the voluntary organisations, both corporately and individually, are in a position to make. They should be challenged to make it.

Note

1. Lord Windlesham, *Politics in Practice*, 1975, ch. 2.

5 LOCAL AUTHORITIES AND THE VOLUNTARY SECTOR

Local government has, since the establishment of the welfare state, played an increasingly large part in the life of very many organisations. We therefore thought it useful to take a general look at the attitudes and practices of local authorities towards the voluntary sector. It may, however, be helpful to the general reader first to explain briefly how local government itself is organised.

Local Government since Reorganisation

The London Government Act 1963, The Local Government Act 1972 and the Local Government (Scotland) Act 1973 between them reorganised local government in Great Britain. Counties and districts in England and Wales, which have what the Local Government Act 1972 calls 'principal councils', are as follows: 6 metropolitan counties and 36 metropolitan districts in England; 47 non-metropolitan counties and 333 districts in England and Wales; the Greater London Council with the City of London and the 32 London Boroughs. Scotland has 9 regions and 53 districts. There are also all-purpose authorities consisting of the three island authorities in Scotland and the Isles of Scilly. There are some 7,200 parish councils in England with 800 community councils in Wales, and the statutory community councils in Scotland.

The variations between principal councils in functions and other characteristics are set out in detail elsewhere.[1] For present purposes they may be summarised as follows. In the English metropolitan counties, district councils have responsibilities for personal social services, education and housing; county councils basically have strategic responsibilities; arts and recreation are divided. In the non-metropolitan counties in England and Wales, responsibility for personal social services and education lies with the county councils, housing with the district councils, arts and recreation again being divided. London differs from the metropolitan counties mainly in that education in the Inner London boroughs is the responsibility of the ILEA (which comprises the members of the GLC for Inner London and representatives of the Inner London boroughs) and the GLC has considerable responsibility in the field of housing. In Scotland responsibility for education and social work lies with the regional councils; the district councils administer housing and recreational services. The three island councils have roughly speaking the powers of both region and district.

Throughout Great Britain health is now the responsibility of the area health authorities and is not a local government function. Since many local voluntary organisations are active in the health field it deserves a little attention here. As a source of funds the NHS does not make a major contribution to the voluntary sector: in 1974/75 total grants from the fourteen regional health authorities in England to voluntary organisations came to less than £200,000. However, during the past decade there has been a growing recognition of the part which volunteers can play in the NHS. This has found expression in the circular 'Voluntary Help and the New Health Authorities' issued by the DHSS in April 1974 and in the appointment by hospitals of persons usually described as Voluntary Services Organisers whose numbers had risen to nearly 300 by 1975. Their main concern is often the direct recruitment of volunteers without the mediation of a voluntary organisation, but in many areas they work closely with voluntary organisations like Hospital Friends and the Red Cross. There are also the Community Health Councils which have been set up in order to represent the views of the consumer. There are 229 of them in England and Wales, each covering a health district. A third of their members have to be nominated by voluntary organisations. They represent a new form of relationship between statutory and voluntary sectors.

Mention should also be made of the neighbourhood councils that are coming into existence in some of the larger English and Welsh towns. They are not statutory bodies, but resemble the Scottish community councils, which do have a statutory basis, in having neither powers nor access to public funds as of right. These various local councils together with the statutory parish councils provide a means of decentralisation and an opportunity for the views of local people to be represented. Neighbourhood councils are in our sense of the term voluntary organisations, but in their functions of representing people and providing a limited range of services at the local level there is little to distinguish them from their statutory counterparts.

The system in Northern Ireland differs from that in Great Britain in several important ways. Since October 1975, there has been a single-tier system of local government under which twenty-six district councils have replaced the former two-tier system. These district councils have greatly reduced responsibilities as health and the personal social services are the responsibility of four area boards under the Department of Health and Social Services; education is the responsibility of five Education and Library Boards under the Department of Education; roads and water, etc. come under the Department of Environment and Housing. There are also District committees intended to represent the consumer and to act as watch dogs.

The Local Government Acts are not the only factors which have greatly changed the position of local authorities in Great Britain. The Social Work (Scotland) Act 1968 and the Local Authority Social Services Act 1970, which followed the publication of the Report of the Seebohm Committee, led to the creation of the social work and social services departments and in brief brought into operation the generalist approach to social work. In some cases this coincided with increased workloads and a shortage of professionally qualified staff. For a variety of reasons the new local authorities also tended to establish strong policy committees linking more closely the different decision-making committees and needing the appointment of a chief executive officer heading a management team of officers. The aim has been to create a united policy for the whole authority coordinating the work of the different committees.

The new system of local government brought in by the different Acts led to a complete restructuring of all but one of the local authority associations. In England and Wales there are now four national associations: the Association of County Councils which represents non-metropolitan counties in England and Wales; the Association of Metropolitan Authorities, whose members are the metropolitan counties, the metropolitan districts, the Greater London Council and the London boroughs; the Association of District Councils, looking after the interests of non-metropolitan districts; and the National Association of Local Councils (which has changed little except in title) acting for parishes in England, communities in Wales and town councils (where they exist) in both England and Wales. Additionally the London Boroughs Association deals with the London-wide aspects of borough services. In Scotland the opportunity of reorganisation was taken to combine the four separate local authority associations which previously existed into the new Convention of Scottish Local Authorities. In Northern Ireland there is the Association of Local Authorities which came into being in November 1973 and has all the District Councils as members. We have had the opportunity of having discussions with or receiving evidence from most of these bodies.

In our discussions with a number of local authority and other associations we have raised the question of their dealings with voluntary organisations. In general terms they stress that local government, as its very name suggests, means control by elected members who must make their policies and take their decisions in the light of local needs and circumstances and their own electoral policies; and that any measures of centralisation or standardisation of policies which might take more away from the local element is something to be resisted. We have noted that in line with this view the Layfield Committee reported that despite a desire by both central and local government to increase local responsibility for decision-making, there had been a continuing drift towards central responsibility. They refered to the weakening of local accountability being brought about in part by the government's concern with the total of local government expenditure. They also referred to the drift towards centralisation being even greater in Scotland than in England and Wales. Though the Layfield Committee was concerned with local finance, we believe that these points are not irrelevant to our present enquiry and we say more later about the general tendency to centralise. In the next few paragraphs we summarise the views of local authority associations and some other associations as expressed to us.

Some Views Expressed by Local Authority and other Associations

The Association of County Councils pointed to two underlying principles governing relationships between the public and voluntary sectors: that of public accountability for carrying out statutory duties which in a democracy can only be exercised by elected members; and that of involving outside individuals, as volunteers, and outside independent organisations in the provision of services. The Association supported both these principles. Where county councils had either statutory duties or powers it was, of course, naturally up to the elected members to decide whether they should provide services directly or by the use of voluntary organisations. However, most county councils use voluntary organisations, some quite extensively. Difficulties could, naturally, arise when members were asked to provide money for organisations whose role was to act as a pressure group on the council. On the other hand, many voluntary organisations combined a pressure-group function with that of providing services, and such organisations were accepted by local authorities. Although in theory it was probably easier to accept a critical role on the part of Councils for Voluntary Service (which we consider in the next chapter) than of individual organisations, the Association were not aware of any evidence that this consideration was a deterrent to most voluntary organisations. Some authorities, of course, held the view that on the whole it was better to use the statutory services and only to turn to the voluntary sector if there were no one else; this view was less widely held today than a few years ago. Many now felt that there were some jobs which volunteers or voluntary organisations could do better than the statutory side and that what one needed was a partnership and ability to judge which tasks could most suitably be performed by each side. Partnership in these terms with voluntary organisations is effectively practised by many local education authorities in their youth and community service provision. On the whole the Association accepted what we describe as pluralism since on this basis there is a role for both the statutory and the voluntary sectors. They added that since the emergence of the generic social service departments there was probably a greater awareness of the needs of the community, thus confirming the argument in the Seebohm Report for the fullest possible community involvement. Perhaps a part of the role of local authorities and in particular the social services departments was the general education of the community in becoming aware of needs and how to meet them. It was much easier to deal with the so-called 'unpopular causes' if there was a good working partnership between statutory and voluntary sides.

The Association of Metropolitan Authorities said that the role of local authorities towards voluntary organisations should essentially be that of providing guidance, coordination and some assistance. They felt that local government as a whole could help organisations by making clear the criteria for aiding voluntary activities and quoted as an example the criteria which had been agreed by the London boroughs. Some of their authorities divided voluntary organisations into four broad categories: those providing a coordination service (e.g. Councils for Voluntary Service); those providing direct services; those providing services which complement existing local authority provision, such as services for the deaf; and promotional or pressure-group types of organisation. There was naturally a great difference of view on grant-aiding the different types of organisation, but certainly many were reluctant to support the promotional or critical type. Some held that the best way of supporting voluntary organisations lay in helping them to become more efficient by providing financial support for staff and management, a cause which had little popular appeal, thereby freeing the organisation from some of the time spent in fund raising. Their member authorities probably looked to voluntary organisations principally as providers of services; few would particularly feel that they had a duty to support them as part of their duty to the community. Nevertheless, organisations of the community type, such as tenants' associations, are growing in importance.

The Association felt that even though the attitudes of individual local authorities might vary it was now generally recognised that voluntary organisations do have an important role to play in the life of the local community. The Association does not on the whole offer guidance on grant-aiding to their member authorities, but if a national organisation's central administration depends on a subsidy and it also provides a service locally, then a recommendation may be made to member authorities for a certain level of support; for example, the National Children's Bureau and the Disabled Living Foundation are treated in this way. Assistance is also given in such matters as charges for residents in accommodation of the type used by many authorities, where it may be agreed that the treasurer of one particular authority shall negotiate standard charges on behalf of all.

The Association of District Councils, whose member districts vary in population from something under 20,000 to over 400,000, said that it was the essence of local government that each authority should make its own decisions in the light of its own local conditions and that to give them a duty to encourage voluntary organisations would act against this principle. It was much better for them and, in their view, for voluntary organisations themselves, for districts to work behind the scenes, to help voluntary organisations discreetly but not attempt to direct. Some tasks they felt could be better done by the voluntary side than the statutory and they gave examples of Meals on Wheels and Marriage Guidance. There were also some things better done by the statutory side, particularly if expensive skilled workers were required. But they made the interesting point that sometimes a service using professional staff could be so costly and demanding in standards that it was beyond the resources available and it might therefore be better to have some sort of service provided by the voluntary sector, even of a lower standard, than to have nothing at all. The impression they had through their members was of a general feeling of sympathy with voluntary organisations and a desire to help and support them. As an Association, however, they gave no general guidance to their members about grant-aiding nor had they ever undertaken any survey of what was done by their members. They could, however, say that where voluntary organisations were grant-aided it was nearly always done 'without strings'. There were occasions when a councillor or an officer would be invited to take part in the council or governing body of the organisation and so keep in touch.

The National Association of Local Councils saw the encouragement of voluntary effort as morally desirable and also a convenient arrangement since a great deal of administration, particularly in the rural areas, is done voluntarily. They mentioned an interesting difference in view towards voluntary organisations; in the South, and away from the larger towns everywhere, the tendency is for their member local councils to encourage voluntary organisations to undertake work; whereas in the North, and in the areas near the large towns all over the country, the Council itself tends to do the job. On the question of which activities could be left to voluntary organisations, the Association explained it was not possible to generalise since everything depended upon resources and local attitudes. Sometimes the statutory authority had to take the decision to step in because a voluntary organisation might collapse, possibly after a change in leadership; sometimes the problem was financial.

The London Boroughs Association referred to their powers under the Greater London Council (General Powers) Act 1970 to authorise contributions to the funds of voluntary organisations, provided that three-quarters of the boroughs agree, and provided that the total does not exceed 1/20th penny rate for London as a whole. In using these powers the London Boroughs Association define a voluntary organisation as one providing a service which could by statute be provided by one of their constituent local authorities; so that all bodies supported by them provide a service which the boroughs could themselves undertake if they wished. The general policy is to contribute only to those voluntary organisations which provide services for the whole of London and not to those whose activities cover only part of London or which are nation-wide. Grants are not limited to those organisations concerned with personal social services and have been made, for example, to the Greater London Arts Association. In discussing the Community Development Project the London Boroughs Association raised with us difficulties which had already come to our notice over support to critical groups or action groups. In their view these groups raised the question of whether small groups making particular demands for their own members, possibly irrespective of the requirement of the community at large, could expect to be assisted, as opposed to those which operate on a wide basis providing a service for the large part of the community. They drew to our attention the danger of articulate small groups, representing very few people, tending to rival the function of local government without being in any way accountable to the people. Grant-aiding to voluntary organisations involved an element of monitoring and a local authority

could not just hand over money but must, they thought, accept
some responsibility for seeing that the organisation was properly run as
well as seeing that funds were not misappropriated. In the LBA a Grants
Working Party also looked at the effectiveness of a voluntary organisation, i.e. whether in fact the organisation is able to do the job for which
it is set up. This was done by having full discussions with the organisation's representatives: this included staffing questions, job specifications
and so on. But the officers of the LBA could not carry out a detailed
and continuous supervision of individual organisations.

The Convention of Scottish Local Authorities told us that they have a
positive policy towards the voluntary sector and believe in the principle
of partnership between statutory agencies and voluntary organisations.
Grant-aiding of national voluntary organisations is done by means of a
special subcommittee of the Convention Policy Committee. It makes
recommendations annually on which voluntary organisations should be
supported by its member authorities, in the form of suggesting the
monetary support to be granted per 1,000 of population in the authorities. The recommendations are advisory not mandatory but in practice they are nearly always followed. Smaller organisations of a local
character are directly dependent upon their own local authority and are
not covered by this scheme, and the scheme in no way inhibits local
authorities from giving grants to these smaller organisations. The list of
the organisations supported in 1975 shows that the same tendency
exists in Scotland as in England and Wales, that is, of giving support
mainly to the service-providing organisations.

The Association of Local Authorities of Northern Ireland said that the
main duties of district councils in Northern Ireland are environmental
health, recreational and community facilities, and building regulations
to which has been added, by arrangement with the Department of
Education, certain important aspects of community work. Local
authorities have agreed to take responsibility to foster the voluntary
sector; it is the duty of individual councils to make provision for leisure
activities and they have power to make contributions towards voluntary
organisations to this end. There are differences between districts, as in
other parts of the United Kingdom, but there tends to be a common
policy towards grant-aiding voluntary organisations; this follows from a
report of a joint working party which was set up by the Department of
Education and the Association of Local Authorities covering community sporting and recreational provision. Although the Department of

Education pays 75 per cent of all approved grants made by district councils to voluntary organisations, a substantial portion of all grant-aid to voluntary organisations comes from district councils. There is a difference in the type of voluntary organisation which is supported by district councils in Northern Ireland because of the different responsibilities of these bodies from those of their counterparts in Britain, but a considerable degree of assistance is provided.

During the period of direct rule there are no members of a Northern Ireland Parliament and district councillors tend therefore to be consulted by voluntary organisations and others on aspects which concern the whole of the Province.

The Association of Directors of Social Service stressed to us the importance of avoiding too much planned development of the voluntary sector because this could lead to the creation of something like a parallel bureaucracy and thus inhibit the spontaneity which is a strength of the voluntary side. They explained the value of the voluntary side's alternative role; statutory services do not have a monopoly nor do they have the resources to provide a range of options; yet people have a right to reasonable choice; perhaps therefore the statutory side should define its own role more clearly as acting positively to mobilise community effort, though still providing a safety net for the more intractable problems. Local authorities have neither the money nor the other resources to provide all the services which the volume of legislation has imposed on them as duties or for which they have been given wide powers (as for example under the Chronically Sick and Disabled Persons Act 1970), but they can help to mobilise whatever resources are available and where they think it necessary, encourage the voluntary sector in particular tasks. Like the Association of District Councils, the Association's representatives referred to the curious and widespread problem that standards have risen so high in some cases that a local authority cannot afford to run a service at all, whereas a voluntary organisation is not compelled to provide buildings or staffing levels to the same standards; it can therefore attempt to provide some service (a good example is Women's Aid Centres). The Association thought that there was some indication that voluntary organisations can usually provide a cheaper parallel service, but if there are comparable standards of service, staffing and conditions of employment, costs may be very similar. On pressure groups the Association mentioned the risk of paying attention to those that shout loudest and neglecting the less popular groups which may have little public sympathy and perhaps therefore need special attention by local authorities.

The Society of Local Authority Chief Executives first referred to the
historical pattern of voluntary organisations pioneering schemes and the
statutory services then taking over once the ideas were established: a
pattern which still existed, as one could see from the voluntary effort
in such matters as helping autistic children, battered wives, one-parent
families. They referred also to the rapid increase in community neighbourhood groups such as tenants' associations. It seemed likely that this
tendency would continue and that however many needs were met by the
statutory side, others would always arise and provide opportunities for
the voluntary sector. One of the most important advantages of the
voluntary organisation is its ability to take risks and to be able to make
mistakes that would cause grave problems for local authorities. Local
government attitudes, they felt, naturally varied: there are those who
take the view that the state should do all, and those who disagree, so
there is no agreement in the country as a whole about the part to be
played by voluntary effort. But they stressed to us that there is an
even greater need now for community effort because of obvious gaps,
such as lack of community development in many council estates. It may
have been the case that professional staff of local authorities have during the initial expansion years of the new social service departments
been somewhat disdainful of the role of voluntary organisations. The
present tight controls of expenditure, however, are leading to a new attitude of welcoming the help of voluntary organisations. It is possible that
there may be a new relationship between the two sectors in which the
statutory bodies will be saying, in effect, 'this is all we can do with our
resources and the rest is up to you'. If local government were to take
in future a more positive approach to voluntary effort than in the past,
the stimulus should come from within itself. There could be political
difficulties involved, particularly over approaching the newer pressure
groups who could be described as a self-elected alternative democracy.
Yet it might well be worthwhile to establish working relationships with
them. Monitoring of voluntary organisations is a difficulty, since there
are great limitations in evaluating the cost-effectiveness of human service, and this applies as much to local authorities themselves as to the
voluntary sector. Some obvious things can be done, such as checking
the accounts and balance sheets, but it is very hard to be systematic
in assessing voluntary organisations though it is possible to produce a
check list of questions which ought to be asked before giving or renew-
ing a grant. Finally the Society representatives referred to a point also
made to us by a number of organisations who gave evidence: the high
cost of transport and the problem this causes to volunteers and volunt-

ary organisations especially in rural areas.

Local Authority Attitudes – General Considerations

In Chapter 1 we mentioned our difficulty in defining what is or is not a voluntary organisation and how we decided to limit the scope of our enquiry. Although we do not include local authorities for our purposes as part of the voluntary sector, there is a sense in which they, particularly local councils, can be regarded as closely akin to it. In talking to us, representatives of the National Association of Local Councils said that the local council itself had 'the emblem' of a voluntary organisation in that in many cases there is only one paid official, the clerk, the rest of the work being done by volunteers. It is therefore not surprising that local government like the voluntary sector (as defined in our terms) includes units of all sizes and shapes and great varieties of opinion. As local government is the expression of democracy at various levels there are bound to be differences of view and great varieties of practices and attitudes towards the voluntary sector. It would have been impossible within the time at our disposal to attempt a complete survey of all these different practices and attitudes and we doubt whether it would be worthwhile even if we had done so. What we have done is to examine a number of studies which were made available to us and to carry out some direct enquiries of our own besides using the material which emerged from the locality studies mentioned earlier.

Although we could find no overall pattern governing the relationships between local government and the voluntary sector, there are some basic considerations which affect these relationships. The first is that differences of general approach to the voluntary sector are far wider in local government than they are in central government. Central government, as we have seen, officially accepts the principle of partnership with the voluntary sector though there may be criticisms of the application of this principle in practice. It is different in local government. In some local authorities, councillors and officers on the whole welcome the voluntary sector and feel that there is a need, though not a statutory duty, to give all possible help to its expression as being for the general good of the community. There is a contrary view which in its most extreme form holds that local authorities should not grant-aid or cooperate with voluntary organisations because of the belief that bodies which are not publicly accountable should not have power to give or withhold crucial services or to dispense funds affecting people's lives: but this view is seldom encountered today. There are obviously great varieties of opinions held between these two extremes.

The second basic consideration, closely allied to the first, is that councillors may sometimes question the validity of the arguments put forward by representatives of voluntary organisations on the grounds that they may be self-appointed or elected or appointed by their own members. But some voluntary organisations have officers elected by the residents of their area and others represent a very large number of people, though differently constituted from the electorate. In contrast it might be noted that some councillors are elected by only a very small proportion of the electorate, and that some councils are entirely in the hand of one party so that there is little or no overt opposition or criticism in the council chamber. The counter-argument is that the electorate has at least had the opportunity of expressing its opinion, even though it may not have made full use of that opportunity. Whatever the rights and wrongs of these arguments, they can lead to tension between the statutory and voluntary sectors and especially between councillors and members of very small community-based organisations. This can be aggravated if the latter are led by people who are not electors in the area concerned. Attitudes are not constant and vary greatly with the personalities concerned and occasionally with a particular moment; for example the imminence of an election and its result can obviously affect the general attitudes of the councillors.

There is another basic consideration of a different kind. We have spoken earlier in this chapter of the measures of reorganisation which have recently taken place. A very great strain on councillors, senior officers and local authority employees generally was caused by the centralisation of the social services departments and then by the far-reaching changes in local government described earlier. Some of the difficulties which have been brought to our attention by those who have given evidence to us have been accentuated because we have taken our evidence at a time when the effects of the changes were still being felt. The point was made very clearly to us in some of our locality studies, where voluntary organisations were still finding difficulty in relating to the new local authorities because of the changes in boundaries and administrative centres and because in some cases the headquarters of the new large authority is far away. There are other cases where the voluntary organisation has not been able, perhaps because of shortage of manpower or money, to change its organisation to fit in with the new regions and counties. In Northern Ireland the combination of the reorganisation of local government and the loss of the Northern Ireland Parliament leading to direct rule from Westminster, has meant that lines of communication between voluntary organisations and local government have undergone several recent changes and can sometimes be difficult to discover.

The general impression we have received is that local authority relationships with those voluntary organisations which provide services are rather different from their relationships with voluntary organisations of other types. No doubt individual local authorities view voluntary organisations in many different ways, some welcoming them for their own sake, some accepting them readily because they supply a need which the local authority can meet either not at all or only in part, and perhaps some accepting them for the same reasons, though a little reluctantly, with the hope that they may be able to provide a full statutory service as soon as possible. Among service-providing organisations those which raise their own money or do the work mainly or wholly with unpaid volunteers may have fewer difficulties in relating to local authorities than have those which depend on grants. One can however in general terms infer that the relationship between the local authorities and the service-providing organisations normally involves a straightforward decision of an almost commercial kind — whether the local authority wishes to buy the services and can afford them or not.

With other organisations of many different types — whether they provide for the general well-being of the population, administrative services, a resource centre or act in the role of critic — the variation in attitude is, as one would expect, very much greater. Apart from payments for services rendered (e.g. accommodation in voluntarily run homes or on a meals service), grants towards administrative or organisational expenses of voluntary organisations tend to be very small in terms of the relevant departmental budgets, even though some of them may well be the lifeline of particular societies. One fairly recent study pointed out that at the most generous such grants amounted to only 2 per cent of the social services department budget of a county and 5 per cent of a London borough, and remarked on 'the very large number of small donations to a great variety of societies and causes, local or national, which read something like a private subscription list'. One of our own locality studies showed that a local authority in 1975, apart from payments for services, gave £74,000 out of a £20m budget to voluntary organisations. As we show in Appendix 6, some local authorities are much more generous.

Except where well developed forms of partnership between statutory and voluntary providers exist, as, for example, in the youth and community services in some places, the amount of the contribution to non-service-providing organisations will usually be dependent upon a subjective judgement made by some committee or individual. Though sometimes the authority may have councillors on the management committee of the organisation concerned who may make comprehensive reports, in other cases there is little evidence available to local authorities to enable them to make objective assessments of the current values of particular organisations, still less of their possibilities for the future. One of the local authority associations remarked that though a voluntary organisation can start by doing a job cheaply, it may well become more expensive as time goes on, and, if heavy capital costs have been involved, the local authority cannot in practice then take over the service itself. Some local authorities are also, perhaps understandably, somewhat suspicious of organisations set up as a pioneering venture with funds for a limited period, as they fear that when the funds are exhausted they may come under pressure to continue the work, whatever may be their views of its merits, and this at a time when money is so short that they may have to cut some of their own existing or projected tasks.

Some Views Expressed by Voluntary Organisations

Many voluntary organisations commented to us about their relationships with the statutory side and in particular with local authorities. There were a number of pleas for a greater recognition of the need to preserve the voluntary element as part of our society and also to make explicit terms for granting financial aid. As the British Red Cross Society put it in their evidence to us:

> There has been general recognition by successive governments of the value to the State of the voluntary and charitable movement, partly because it relieves the State of responsibility for many of the functions which it would otherwise be forced to provide. . . The acceptance by the State of some degree of financial responsibility for the support of voluntary effort is already evident but it would be helpful if the Government could make a clear declaration of the criteria within which financial aid could be expected by a voluntary organisation, and of the procedures by which such aid should be sought.

Though this extract in fact refers to central government it is, in our view, equally applicable to local government. A number of organisations providing services for the weaker members of society pointed to the need for greater assistance, as they were in fact carrying out a task which would otherwise have been placed on the local authority. For example, in speaking to us the Cheshire Homes representative said that the capital cost of constructing their homes was their own responsibility, and maintenance that of local authorities, but there could be differences of interpretation in practice about what constituted maintenance.

The voluntary sector was prepared to be critical of itself and to be generally constructive. For example, the Scottish Council for Spastics observed to us that 'there is no reason to suppose that relationships with statutory bodies will not remain excellent always provided that the voluntary agency demonstrates efficiency and responsibility in its work'. Rotary International referred to the great value which could be obtained if 'the statutory bodies could be brought to a greater awareness of the part the voluntary bodies can play, and if in their turn the voluntary bodies could gain a greater understanding of the problems facing the statutory bodies, particularly at local level'. An interesting point was made by the Stevenage Council for Voluntary Service, which referred to the possibility of endangering relationships with the statutory bodies if Councils for Voluntary Service supported pressure groups, as this might have the effect of local authorities reducing the grant. We conclude this very brief look into the evidence on this point by quoting the Secretary of the Wakefield Metropolitan District Council who remarked that 'one of the things that should be said is that it is time that voluntary organisations combined to produce a Seebohm-type reorganisation of their own', and he referred to the disadvantages of overlapping and duplication of function in the voluntary sector and the occasional difficulties of getting local voluntary organisations with the same interest at heart to cooperate to meet the needs which they are striving to serve.

Relationships between Local Authorities and Voluntary Organisations

It may be of interest to look briefly at views of some others on relationships between local authorities and voluntary organisations. In his booklet, *Bargain or Barricade*,[2] Giles Darvill summarises the attitudes of social service departments towards the volunteer programmes and this has some relevance also to voluntary organisations. In light-hearted terms he classifies the categories as: 'the abstention attitude', where professional and voluntary services function separately; 'the call-girl attitude' which looks upon voluntary organisations as a shameful but necessary convenience; the most common of all, 'the suburban attitude', in which the department requires polite, obedient, cheap and respectful service from voluntary workers; the 'King Henry VIII attitude', by which volunteers are encouraged to experiment and lose their heads if their experiments are not successful; and finally, 'the intimate enemy atti-

tude' in which there is conflict but it is brought out into the open and
regarded as healthy. Dr Cousins, in his study[3] on voluntary organisations and local government in South London, discusses the relationship
of voluntary organisations with official council committees and subcommittees and distinguishes five broad categories:

> a) those groups which worked closely with the council departments
> and which were in contact with officers frequently, although they
> also furnished many coopted members for council committees;
> b) those groups which were in receipt of council aid (financial or
> otherwise), and which in general did not oppose the council publicly.
> Officers, and less often, councillors were contacted by these groups,
> the relations being good; c) those groups which commonly found
> themselves in conflict with the council, but which confined them-
> selves to using orthodox means of influence when contacting the
> council; d) those groups which often found themselves in conflict
> with the council and which pursued this opposition, in general by
> using more extreme methods — petitions and demonstrations for
> example; e) those many groups which only contacted the council
> infrequently, and then purely as a matter of routine — booking halls
> or hiring equipment for example. Any contacts were with junior
> staff.

This leads us to the question of relationships and how they are
achieved. Much depends upon the category of need which is under consideration. Local authorities are on the whole well used to assisting
organisations in the categories of personal social services, education and
youth work, arts and recreation. They are becoming increasingly concerned with those in what may be called broadly the environmental
field. They are less accustomed to organisations which deal with rights
and advice, other than CAB. They are often understandably a little
doubtful of those who adopt the role of critic. Voluntary organisations
themselves in seeking to influence local authorities, whether it be to
obtain funds or to modify their attitudes, may use a variety of ways.
Sometimes it may be through cooption on to a council committee,
though this method is more usually available to the intermediary bodies
such as Councils for Voluntary Service or to the large established bodies
because of the mere factor of numbers. Sometimes contacts are made
with council members or with officers, the latter often being thought
to be more fruitful as being the more permanent. Another way is for
local councillors or chief officers to be invited either to join the board

of management or to become assessors to the voluntary organisation supported by grant. There are also cases in which a member of a voluntary organisation is an elected member of the local authority and can in this way bring influence to bear.

Local authorities themselves use a variety of methods for handling their own business with voluntary organisations. They may handle it through a single committee, through a group of officers under the Chief Executive or the Social Services Department, or they may allow each department to deal on its own. Too much coordination by the local authority may tend to act against the interest of voluntary organisations. If there is no coordinating body within the local authority, this may create difficulties for an organisation which is generalist in character. There are different methods also in the external side of the business. Some local authorities deal with voluntary intermediary bodies such as a Council for Voluntary Service (often called Council of Social Service) as, in their terms, representing the voluntary sector in their area. Others prefer to appoint their own voluntary service coordinator (to use the term adopted in 'Pivot', a report of the working party chaired by Geraldine Aves), who deals direct with voluntary organisations and does not use the Council for Voluntary Service. Much depends on the general view taken by the authority on the subject of community development and the means by which it should be fostered.

All sorts of methods can be used. None the less we have obtained a picture of difficulties experienced by voluntary organisations in their relationships with local authorities. The difficulties related mainly to finance and the duration of grants, but we also have an impression that many organisations, especially the smaller ones at local level, find it hard to obtain the information they need about the statutory side and its working in general, as well as the more particular details about the criteria to be met in order to qualify for grant-aiding. Our own direct enquiries included some authorities which have worked out a clear policy towards the voluntary sector. Of these, two, Islington and East Sussex, which we discuss in the next few paragraphs, provide contrasting examples.

Some Examples of Local Authority Relationships with the Voluntary Sector

Islington is a London borough which faces the problems characteristic of an inner city area. Its level of grant-aid to voluntary organisations is higher than that of any other local authority known to us. Including funds distributed under Urban Aid, in 1976/77 grants to voluntary

organisations totalled £1.24m or over £7 per head of the population.
The figures exclude fees and charges. Of these over half, or £5 per head
of population were made under the auspices of the Social Services Committee. The Council's policy towards voluntary organisations has to be
placed into the wider context of the active encouragement it has given
to public participation since 1971. It sees voluntary organisations as an
essential medium for the involvement of the public as critics and partners in the provision of services. After five years of rapid growth a
special review of support for voluntary organisations was completed in
1976. This enunciated a policy of encouraging and assisting voluntary
organisations to contribute towards the attainment of the Council's
objectives, particularly on the grounds that:

(i) Voluntary organisations are sometimes able to be more flexible
than the services provided by the Council and respond more directly
and quickly to demands made upon them; (ii) in some cases they
may well be more acceptable to the recipient than more official help;
(iii) Voluntary organisations may be more cost effective from a
Council point of view either because: (a) they may have access to
national or other sources of funds; or (b) a large amount of the costs
of voluntary organisations may, in fact, be met from the time and
energy of volunteers; (iv) Voluntary organisations are one form of
public participation and in some cases give a more active involvement
in their management to the people using their services than can the
Council. . . .

Each Committee grant-aiding voluntary organisations was requested to
formulate its own policy, subject to the following criteria:

(a) Whether the voluntary organisation is supplying a need in a
'priority' area, (b) whether the voluntary organisation provides a
specialist service which the Council does not supply, (c) whether the
nature of the activity offered demands that it be independent of the
Council, (d) whether the organisation is 'participant operated',
(e) whether the voluntary organisation is offering an activity hitherto
not recognised as contributing to the objective, (f) whether the
voluntary organisation has the necessary management and administrative expertise to support its activities.

A carefully developed procedure exists for making and considering
applications for grant-aid. An extensive application form has to be com-

pleted. When the application is considered by a committee, representatives of the applying organisation are invited to be present and are given an opportunity to take part in the discussion if the committee is minded to alter what has been proposed.

As well as providing grant-aid through its various committees, Islington also supports voluntary organisations by the appointment of staff with particular responsibilities in this field. Four of the ten social service area teams have a community worker; the Social Services, Recreation and Housing Departments have a central liaison officer; and the Planning Department has two liaison officers. Unlike some of the other liaison officers, the Social Service liaison officer gives nearly all her time to work with voluntary organisations and takes part in departmental policy-making.

East Sussex is an authority responsible for a population mostly located in south coast resorts or in reasonably prosperous rural areas. Its policy for voluntary organisations has been developed mainly through the medium of its Social Services Committee. Its level of grant-aid to voluntary organisations (£0.2 per capita through the Social Services Committee and £0.4 per capita in total) is not far from the national average. However it has given more attention to community development than most counties. Each of the Social Service area teams has a community worker attached to it, and the future of community work in the county has been the subject of a recently published discussion document. Care has been taken to establish contact points for voluntary organisations: each voluntary organisation has a liaison officer designated from among the staff of the department.

The Social Services Committee has a subcommittee for grants to voluntary organisations, which was responsible for a recent survey of voluntary organisations in the country. As the introduction to the ensuing report states:

> In July 1975 the Subcommittee on voluntary organisations first met and agreed to undertake a survey of all organisations receiving annual grants from the East Sussex Social Services Committee. The Subcommittee were aware that most of the grants incurred were inherited at local government reorganisation in 1974 and no formal review had taken place of all such grants paid. Futhermore in the light of both restrictions on local authority expenditure and an increasing emphasis on the need for more community care the Subcommittee decided to undertake this review of grant-aid in conjunction with an evaluation of the contribution of voluntary organisations to the total pro-

vision of social services for the people of East Sussex. It had become clear that the Social Services Committee needed some form of established criteria or policy towards grant-aiding voluntary organisations. Expenditure on grants to voluntary organisations in 1975/76 amounted to £118,700. With restrictions on spending, some kind of priority setting task was also required which would reflect the Committee's commitment to a policy of partnership with voluntary organisations which seeks to provide integrated and coordinated social services to the people of East Sussex.

The subcommittee had already established criteria for grant-aiding. The main ones were:

The extent to which the stated aims and activities of the organisations are consistent with the aims and activities of this Committee and the extent to which any variations can be utilised to explore and innovate new areas of work.

The extent to which the grant-aid application reflects public, political and professional concern for the appropriate cause.

The extent to which the applicant organisation can demonstrate its ability to: (a) Share, coordinate and liaise its activities with other relevant bodies. (b) Be a part of interlocking services for groups organised on a locality basis, as opposed to being an isolated service for narrowly defined client group(s). (c) Develop new areas of innovatory work in response to changing circumstances. (d) Maximise the use of voluntary as opposed to paid assistance in its work. (e) Meet priority social services needs in the locality it serves within East Sussex.

The review of voluntary organisations in East Sussex identified a number of aspects of the voluntary sector that deserved attention. There was a lack of coordination between organisations serving the same needs, unevenness in the quantity and quality of services in different geographical areas, and in some cases, the review suggested, an excessive expenditure on administrative overheads. In the view of the East Sussex Social Services Committee it would be important, in negotiating future grants to voluntary organisations, to look for ways of filling gaps, co-ordinating between voluntary organisations, and ensuring that voluntary organisations provided services clearly complementary to those of the local authority. The Social Services Committee defines its policy as one of partnership with voluntary organisations, and is evidently seeking to establish an integrated and coordinated pattern of provision by fitting the voluntary sector into the framework established by the statutory services.

Both Islington and East Sussex have therefore developed explicit policies in different ways, the former with the emphasis on public participation, the latter with the rational allocation of resources mainly in mind. Before discussing the implications, the example of a third local authority deserves a brief mention. Camden is nearly as generous as its neighbour Islington in the level of financial support it provides for voluntary organisations – £1.1 million which is equivalent to £6 per capita as opposed to over £7 in Islington. Most of this money is disbursed through a special subcommittee of the Policy and Resources Committee, according to criteria which in terms of the efficacy of the organisation, whether the work to be done is innovatory and the mobilisation of voluntary effort, are very similar to East Sussex and Islington. However, there is less emphasis on integration with council policies.

The main feature of actual grants awarded is the large sum (about £400,000) received by the Camden Council of Social Service, in respect of a great variety of work it undertakes, some of which in Islington is carried out by council officers. In contrast £27,000 was earmarked for Islington CSS in 1976 and a substantially reduced amount in 1977/78. Camden's support for voluntary organisations dates from the formation of the borough in 1964, and is an expression of a belief in public involvement. However Camden's approach is more *laissez faire* than Islington's. Its criteria for grant aid are narrower in scope and it has no officers given responsibility for liaison and coordination with voluntary organisations: rather these functions rest much more with the CSS.

Some Reflections and Conclusions

We believe it to be generally accepted that statutory bodies have the ultimate responsibility for planning and provision of social services and for looking at the needs of the areas they serve as a whole; and that voluntary action is one means of helping to meet such needs. There is among many local authorities a general recognition of the desirability of community development and of the role of the voluntary sector in this context. The Association of County Councils mentioned this point to us and referred to the arguments in the Seebohm Report (to quote from paragraphs 480-483):

Community development in this country is seen as a process whereby local groups are assisted to clarify and express their needs and objectives and to take collective action to attempt to meet them. It emphasises the involvement of the people themselves in determining and meeting their own needs . . . it has been urged that one of the important functions of voluntary organisations should be to ensure a high degree of consumer participation and to help the spontaneous development of neighbourhood interests and activities in meeting needs. We entirely support this view, but consider that such work should be undertaken by the local authority social service department as well as by voluntary organisations. . . . A clear responsibility then should be placed upon the social service department for developing conditions favourable to community identity and activity.

Although the Association of Metropolitan Authorities thought that their members on the whole would not feel that they ought to support the voluntary sector as part of their duty to the community, yet they emphasised that it was necessary to make clear the criteria for grant-aiding voluntary activity and they quoted the example of the London Boroughs Association. The Directors of Social Service stressed to us the need for the statutory side to act positively to mobilise community effort, and the Society of Local Authority Chief Executives pointed to the need for community effort though for rather different reasons. What seems to emerge from all this is that there is a growing sense of the need for the statutory side to encourage the voluntary sector not simply for the service it provides, and certainly not solely because the statutory side lacks resources, though both these factors are important.

This tendency to recognise the value of the voluntary sector is not yet matched in most local authorities by the adoption of explicit policies. We are not suggesting that there should be a single uniform policy which would cover all authorities throughout the United Kingdom. This is obviously impracticable and would in any case go right against the whole principle of local responsibility. But we do suggest that each individual authority should develop its own policy, and we have given two examples in this chapter of local authorities which have done this. The development of a policy requires first of all a clarification on the part of the local authority of the ways in which voluntary organisations can contribute to the welfare of the community. From this the local authority can work out its views about the need for and objectives of local authority support. We have seen how Islington puts the emphasis on public involvement, and East Sussex on rational resource allocation. Another possible emphasis is to give first place to the mobilisation of voluntary effort. Whatever philosophy the local authority adopts, unless it be a completely negative one, its implementation will require a variety of practical steps. Prominent among these are criteria and machinery for grant-aiding. In addition it seems to us important for the local authority to be fully informed of the nature of existing voluntary organisations, and one important detail is to see that there is an up-to-date register of local voluntary organisations kept by the voluntary sector itself or by the local authority. There should be readily identifiable contacts for voluntary organisations in the authority and if possible individual officers designated as liaison officers for particular need areas. The voluntary sector should be able to understand easily how to obtain information about the local authority and its policies. Also the local authority could on occasions take the initiative to encourage the development of voluntary organisations to provide services or carry out activities which are needed but not in existence.

A word of warning is necessary here. The local authority is bound to have a powerful influence over the voluntary sector through the kinds of encouragement and cooperation it offers and through the allocation of resources, whether in cash, premises or services. But in our view it is most important that influence should not slip into control. Autonomy is of the essence of the voluntary sector, and if a feeling should grow up that organisations working with the local authority have become a subservient part of the established machine, no doubt in the course of time new voluntary organisations would arise outside the controlled ones to reassert the voluntary spirit. But in the meantime much harm might have resulted.

Although we have said that each local authority should make its own policy towards the voluntary sector, this general principle is subject to one qualification. The machinery adopted by the London Boroughs Association makes it possible to levy all the boroughs to raise funds for voluntary organisations which provide services for the whole of London. It seems to us that similar machinery, if it were available, in the metropolitan counties and perhaps elsewhere, would be of value to the local authorities as well as to voluntary organisations.

We have had much evidence on a subject which we have come to describe as 'unpopular causes' and it may be convenient to discuss it briefly here. We are referring to the well-known fact that it is difficult to raise money for such matters as administration, headquarters expenses and the like and that services provided for many people such as mentally handicapped adults, drug addicts, ex-prisoners and other

groups often seem to attract less support from the public than do
children and the elderly. One society, for example, mentioned that
among the sufferers with whom they deal, the appeal of children is very
much stronger than that of adults. In this general field we have encountered two different attitudes. The first is that if a cause is unpopular,
this is a reflection of public opinion and the local authority should
therefore not support it but leave it to the voluntary sector. The second
view is diametrically opposite. It is that the voluntary sector cannot be
expected to be a general provider and that causes which are difficult
from the point of view of fund-raising and recruiting volunteers should
for this reason alone be the responsibility of the statutory sector. There
is no tidy solution which can resolve these conflicting views. We know
that many local authorities do recognise that fund-raising is a waste of
staff time for voluntary organisations and a distraction from their main
purpose, and the more unpopular the cause the more time and effort
are needed. We believe that if a local authority does have a positive
policy towards the voluntary sector, including a good knowledge of its
capabilities, the point about unpopular causes is one which must be considered in forming that policy. It would not wish the voluntary sector
to dissipate its resources by having to pay undue attention to fund-raising. To be dependent upon the public for a certain degree of support is,
however, a good discipline for the voluntary sector itself and we are not
suggesting that 100 per cent grant-aiding, even if funds permitted,
would be desirable.

Another difficult question which came up often in our conversations
with local authority associations and others was that of supporting
organisations which are themselves critical of the statutory side. Basically this is a simple human problem: the critic has never been a popular
figure from the days of the Old Testament prophets to the present. The
lot of the critical organisation may be easier if it is producing some form
of service so that it can be seen by local authorities and the public
generally to be doing things as well as criticising others. It may also carry
more weight if it can show that it has a large membership particularly
among the local electorate and if it supports its causes with the evidence
of having done its homework. Even so there will still be difficulties. The
local authority must, as we were told, be concerned with the danger of
paying too much attention to articulate, small groups representing very
few people and trying to rival the function of local government without
being themselves accountable. And we were also told that there is a
danger of paying attention to groups that shout the loudest, neglecting
those which are less popular. But in general we agree with the point put

to us by the Society of Local Authority Chief Executives that it is well worth trying to establish working relationships with these kinds of organisations. These relationships will be much easier to achieve if there is already some form of working partnership between the statutory and the voluntary sides based on a positive policy and easily understandable machinery to implement it.

We have suggested that local authorities should have a positive policy towards the voluntary sector. But we are not advocating that they should be compelled to support voluntary organisations, either by the allocation of a fixed proportion of expenditure to them, or by some operation of the Rate Support Grant involving an obligation to earmark a stated percentage to grant-aiding voluntary organisations. These devices seem to us to be too inflexible to take account of the great variety which exists among local authorities and voluntary organisations. We have however suggested that local authorities should see that there is suitable machinery to enable the statutory and voluntary sectors to work together efficiently. We also suggest, as we did in Chapter 4 when considering central government, that the part the voluntary sector can play should normally be considered whenever a new programme or a major extension to an existing programme is planned.

Section 137 of the Local Government Act 1972 and Section 83 of the Local Government (Scotland) Act 1973 deal with the general power of local authorities to incur expenditure for certain purposes not otherwise authorised. Those local authorities which wish to help the voluntary sector seem to find that this section gives them the powers they need to do so. Other local authorities, we are informed, say this section does not give them enough power to help voluntary organisations. It is not for us to interpret the law. We suggest however that government and the local authority associations might study this matter and see whether they can give guidance to local authorities and also whether there is a need for conferring more clearly defined powers on local authorities. If so, time for the necessary legislation should be made in the Parliamentary programme. Legislation however may well not be necessary and in any case action need not await it.

Notes

1. *Report of the Committee of Enquiry on Local Government Finance* (the Layfield Committee) Annex 9.
2. Darvill, G., *Bargain or Barricade?*, The Volunteer Centre, 1975.
3. Cousins, P. F., Voluntary Organisations and Local Government in Three South London Boroughs, *Public Administration,* Vol. 54, 1976.

6 LOCAL INTERMEDIARY BODIES

Definitions

In any consideration of the relationships between government and the voluntary sector one soon encounters the so-called 'coordinating bodies'. In this report we call them 'intermediary bodies'. We have rejected the commonly used words 'coordination' and 'coordinating' because the number of different senses in which they are used impedes a clear appraisal of the work of these bodies. Sometimes coordination is used to mean the machinery by which voluntary organisations of different types may be enabled to work together; sometimes the bringing together of organisations dealing with a particular subject; and sometimes a means by which the statutory side tries to bring under its umbrella those parts of the voluntary movement which can be of help to it. Intermediary bodies have important functions in providing support for voluntary organisations individually and collectively, and in reconciling the inherent tension between the autonomy of individual organisations and planning for the pursuit of common purposes. A more precise definition of these intermediary functions is provided below. At this stage we simply state that we are concerned with organisations that are intermediary between different voluntary organisations, performing the functions identified below. In saying this we exclude voluntary organisations that are predominantly involved in providing direct services to individuals, and organisations that form an integral part of central or local government. At the local level we have not identified any intermediary bodies with a statutory character, but at the national level there are several, which are discussed in the next chapter. A distinction that applies at both levels is between generalist and specialist bodies. Local generalist bodies exist in some, but not all, areas. Voluntary bodies of all types may belong to them. Specialist bodies are more limited in that they deal with a single human need, e.g. the elderly, youth, the mentally handicapped, though we recognise that they may cover a number of subjects in their respective fields. We start with the generalist intermediary bodies.

Many different titles are used for these bodies but in this report we have adopted some standard ones which we must now define. First we use the generic term 'local voluntary councils' (LVCs) to cover the most commonly met local intermediary bodies. LVCs include two

types whose titles we have standardised as 'Rural Community
Councils' (RCCs), which are found solely in the non-metropolitan
counties in England and Wales, and 'Councils for Voluntary Service'
(CVSs), found mainly in the urban areas. In speaking of RCCs and
CVSs, we follow the practice of the National Council of Social Service,
but we recognise that many different names are used in the country.
'Council of Social Service' is a name which is still much used, although
'Council for Voluntary Service' is becoming more common. We shall
also refer to another form of local intermediary body, the local resource
centre, which generally serves a small well-defined area such as part of a
large town. They are still few but are likely to grow in number. Some of
the settlements, many of which are members of the British Association
of Settlements, carry out a resource centre function. Community
Relations Councils assist ethnic organisations in the same way in many
of our towns. (For the sake of clarity we should perhaps explain that
the community councils which are being established under the Local
Government (Scotland) Act 1973, the various community or neighbourhood councils recently established voluntarily in a number of urban
areas in England and the community councils in Wales, which are the
equivalent of the parish councils in England, are not discussed
here.

In their evidence to us the Standing Conferences of RCCs and CVSs
said:

broadly CVSs and RCCs were founded to promote all or any
charitable purposes for the benefit of the community, in particular
the advancement of education, the protection of health and the
relief of poverty, distress and sickness; and to promote and organise
cooperation in the achievement of these purposes by bringing
together representatives of statutory and voluntary organisations.
Community development was also an objective, RCCs having a
special responsibility for the rural areas. Because their original
purposes covered such a broad field of activity, CVSs and RCCs
consider that their principal goals and objectives are still the same
today, but recognise that over the years the work in detail towards
these ends has in some cases changed or developed, and has
continually increased. The emphasis of CVS work has, however,
been shifting from community work with groups and organisations
in the personal service field to more involvement in environmental
matters, information services, and promotional work with self-help
and special activity groups. RCCs are not so conscious of their

methods having changed as of the widening scope of their services.

Rural Community Councils – England and Wales

Rural Community Councils exist in all the non-metropolitan counties
of England except Norfolk and the Isle of Wight, are all county-based
bodies usually consisting of member organisations and some affiliated
organisations such as village halls. They are funded in part by the
Development Commission (whose work we describe in Chapter 7). The
Commissioners do not normally grant-aid organisations below county
level. All RCCs are members of the Standing Conference of Rural
Community Councils, which itself is serviced by the Community Work
Division of the National Council of Social Service. Rural Community
Councils vary greatly in size and in the functions which they carry out
but they have certain common features arising from their activities for
rural development; for example the provision of a secretariat for the
County Parish Councils Association, giving advice on the provision,
improvement, management and use of village halls and on the means of
obtaining grants for them, and for playing fields, organising best kept
village competitions and so on. A recent development has been the
appointment by many RCCs of Countryside Officers with funds from
the Development Commission. Their work has been related mainly to
planning and to environmental problems including work on structure
and local plans, encouragement of local initiative in the formation of
voluntary amenity societies and in the study of problems such as rural
transport. We give some detailed information about RCCs in Appendix
5A. We have also seen two studies[1] of the work of RCCs made in fairly
recent times, for the Development Commission.

The Development Commission spent just over £567,000 in the
financial year 1975/76 on support for RCCs. The proportion of
Development Fund assistance to RCCs varies from county to county.
The Development Commission consider that ideally RCCs should
receive one third of their funds from the Development Fund, one third
from local government and the remainder from voluntary sources. They
say that in practice this is difficult to achieve and in most cases the
largest contribution is the Development Fund grant which probably
provides about half the total income of all RCCs, but only in exceptional cases will Development Fund assistance for an individual RCC's
general work exceed 60 per cent of its total income. This contribution
covers the cost of each RCC's chief salaried officer, of the salary of the
Countryside Officer where one is in post, and a sum for general work,
within a maximum figure dependent on the category of the RCC.

A total of twenty six RCCs receive grants to meet the whole cost of schemes in community initiative in the countryside. Grant-aid is also available for a few other special schemes and towards capital expenditure. In return each RCC has to submit annual returns of income and expenditure according to specifications laid down by the Development Commission whose members or officers may visit them. The Commission has a say in the appointment of chief salaried officers, though it may not dismiss them; it expects the RCCs to turn to the NCSS for advice and support, and it relies on the NCSS for advice about the work of RCCs. The Development Commission's grants to RCCs are made primarily for rural development and not directly for the encouragement of voluntary effort. These grants, and particularly the payment of the salary of the chief officer of the RCC, have however been of great indirect assistance to the voluntary sector.

The situation in Wales in approximately the same as in England but there is one important difference in that several RCCs are active in the field of Welsh language and culture. RCCs have been regrouped under various titles and their areas made coterminous with the new large rural counties. In the old County of Glamorgan, however, there is but one community council corresponding to an RCC, although the former county was divided and now forms three new counties. With the exception of the Counties of Gwent and Clwyd, Welsh RCCs are not involved to any substantial extent in urban work. The Development Commission ceased to operate in Wales on 1 April 1977. Responsibility for the funding of RCCs has been handed over to the Welsh Office.

Councils for Voluntary Service — England and Wales

RCCs and CVSs, which operate mainly in urban areas, are not mutually exclusive and their areas may overlap. There are about 165 CVSs in England. Some detailed information about them is in Appendix 5A. CVSs which cover metropolitan counties and districts and non-metropolitan districts are elegible for membership of the Standing Conference of CVSs which is serviced by the Community Work Division of the National Council of Social Service. Most eligible CVSs are members and the total membership figure of CVSs is about 100. The most conspicuous characteristic of CVSs is their diversity. In size, income and expenditure, variety of activities and calibre and orientation of their staff, they have far less in common with one another than have RCCs. They do not exist in all urban areas, and many large metropolitan communities are without a CVS, e.g. Wolverhampton, South Shields and Barnsley and ten of the thirty-two London boroughs. Some six

CVSs employ no paid staff at all, and seventeen employ only one. Honorary officers and volunteers therefore continue to be important sources of manpower for CVSs. About half employ a paid secretary and nearly a third have several staff. The eleven largest CVSs employ ten or more staff and so are quite substantial social agencies. There is also great variety in their incomes which range from a few hundred pounds of the small ones which employ no staff to well over £100,000 in a few cases, e.g. Liverpool, Birmingham, Camden and London. The majority receive some grant-aid from local authorities and many CVSs, both large and small, are largely dependent on this source of income. A few of the old-established CVSs have a significant income from charitable trusts and investments; some are able to obtain resources by direct fund-raising activities; and some obtain substantial funds from foundations, or other sources such as the Job Creation Programme.

The Standing Conference of CVSs sent to all English and Welsh CVSs in August 1976 and again in February 1977 a questionnaire which asked whether their current level of local authority grand-aid had risen or fallen, whether they had been obliged to make cuts in staff or services, or retrench in other ways, and what were their expectations of grant aid for 1977/78. The Standing Conference kindly made the results of this survey available to the Committee and some details are contained in Appendix 5A. It will be seen that the replies to the question about retrenchment in services and CVS staff during 1976/77 suggest that many of the increased sums in grant-aid were less than sufficient to maintain the real value of the grant, but it seemed that about two thirds of the CVSs had been able to maintain staff and services at their current level. Only one CVS, however, was in the process of expanding and 32 out of 116 responding mentioned retrenchment. The replies to the question on expectations for aid for 1977/78 appeared to indicate that even more CVSs will be obliged to retrench in 1977/78. If these pessimistic prophecies are borne out, only 7 CVSs will receive any increase in grant-aid in 1977/78 compared with 67 which recorded an increase in 1976/77 and, apart from 30 CVSs which did not know what level of aid they would receive, the remainder will experience cuts in their income in real terms.

The different interpretations of the CVS role can be shown by the following short descriptions of four CVSs.

(i)   Liverpool CVS has a long tradition of close support from the business community, from which much of its income comes, with another large amount from endowment interest payments.

Hardly any of its annual income of over £100,000 comes from the local authority. It places a strong emphasis on community development and social planning and deliberately avoids pro-. viding direct services itself. Many activities and agencies in Liverpool have been hived off from the CVS in the past or owe their origin to the CVS in a less direct way. This CVS has shown a special ability to span the business community, traditional voluntary organisations and the newer small groups.

(ii) Harlow CVS is of more recent origin. Nearly all its annual budget of over £50,000 comes from the local authority. It has working parties on pre-school provision, emergency accommo- dation and the disabled, and standing committees dealing with single-parent families, a voluntary warden scheme for the elderly, and family holidays. It provides a variety of direct services under the auspices of these committees but combines this with pioneering and social planning.

(iii) Tamworth Community Service Council was formed in 1972, pays its secretary only a small honorarium and has no full-time paid employees. It gets rent-free premises and a small grant from the District Council. Its main activities seem to be (a) administering the Carnegie Centre, a base for various volun- tary organisations in Tamworth, (b) promoting new voluntary organisations in the area (e.g. Samaritans) and supporting and coordinating voluntary effort.

(iv) The London Council of Social Service is unlike the three CVSs mentioned above in that it covers an area in which there are at least 20 other CVSs, its nearest counterparts being Greater Manchester and Merseyside CVS. Almost half its 1975/76 income of over £150,000 comes from local authorities. As well as seeking to promote cooperation among and provide services for voluntary organisations generally in London, it seeks to support CVSs in the individual boroughs and has recently become the base for one of the five community resource centres being established in different parts of the country. This centre will endeavour to provide support services for community groups and community workers throughout the London area. Perhaps the most important aspect of the LCSS's work is the attempt to influence social policy by looking at London problems as a whole, pressing for action on the part of government and local authorities and initiating pioneering projects. Thus recently the LCSS has made a substantial contribution to the debate on the social and economic problems of inner London.

In Wales there has traditionally been a different pattern for Councils
for Voluntary Service. We saw that in every rural county in Wales there
has been a Rural Community Council. In the more populated areas of
South Wales the Council of Social Service for Wales (CSSW) has been
responsible for initiating and coordinating work directly with voluntary
groups. There are Councils for Voluntary Service in Swansea, Colwyn
Bay and Dinas Powis, and it is the intention of CSSW to endeavour to
establish similar bodies in localities in the South and in the larger town-
ships of North Wales. The recent radical reorganisation of CSSW will, it
is hoped, help to achieve this object, despite the severe economic cut-
backs affecting the voluntary movement in the Principality.

Another way of considering the great variety which exists among
Councils for Voluntary Service is explained in a recent report by John
Lansley.[2] This dealt only with a limited area and covered a project set
up to establish a series of bodies for voluntary coordination and action
in Greater Manchester and Merseyside. None the less the conclusions are
of general interest. Lansley suggests that there are two possible ideolo
gies for a CVS, unitary and pluralistic:

> a CVS adopting a unitary frame of reference would take as its basic
> presupposition that all social service agencies are working to the
> same common ends, and that, given a degree of public spiritedness
> and rationality on the part of those involved, most problems are
> administrative in nature and can be solved by joint discussion of
> what needs to be done and how it may be achieved in the most
> effective way. This requires of the CVS that it acts as a coordinator
> and possibly also as a broker or umpire, to bring this joint and
> voluntary consensus about. It may provide various kinds of assis-
> tance to service giving organisations, such as disseminating informa-
> tion . . . it would also use its information networks to identify unmet
> needs by the same consensual principles.

Referring to the pluralistic model, Lansley says: 'the presupposition
that all sides are working together to common ends is challenged. So
equally fundamentally is the emphasis on voluntary organisations as
welfare providers. Instead it is assumed that different groups of providers and receivers within the area of social provision have different
and often competing interest and that social planning would at best
only be an arbitration between these interests . . . emphasis thus

frequently shifts from the providers of the services to their consumers.'
He adds that a CVS accepting such a view of social service provision
might give emphasis to the provision of such services as information and
technical expertise to voluntary action groups and will facilitate joint
action by voluntary groups: the CVS's relationship to the local authority will be one of critic. We have drawn attention to these comments
because of their interest and the pointer to a possible direction which
CVSs, especially in large towns, may take in future. But it is our
opinion that at the present time the great majority of CVSs would see
themselves as 'unitary' rather than 'pluralistic', in Lansley's terms.

Some Scottish Aspects

The nearest Scottish equivalents to the Rural Community Councils of
England and Wales are the local rural Councils of Social Service.
According to the Development Commissioners in their report for the
three years ending 31 March 1976[3]

> in Scotland there were many problems which led to difficulty in
> getting community development work under way. By 1965 there
> were only seven local rural Councils of Social Service and these were
> either on the islands or in small and widely separated areas on the
> mainland . . . however . . . by 1973 there were nineteen Councils in
> existence. Because the Councils are few and scattered the Scottish
> Council of Social Service itself employs field officers to promote
> community work in the rural areas and to help the local Councils
> [which] have been heavily dependent on assistance from the
> Development Fund.

The total number of local voluntary councils of all sorts (as we defined
them above) in Scotland is between forty and fifty. A variety of titles
are used, the most common probably being 'Council of Social Service'.
A total of twenty of these local voluntary Councils were being funded
by the Development Commission at the end of March 1977. Responsibility for them has now passed wholly to the Scottish Office where it is
exercised at present by the Social Work Services Group of the Scottish
Education Department which is maintaining the same policy in
1977/78. Generally speaking the pattern has remained almost the same
as mentioned above in that all the grant-aided Councils are in areas
fairly remote from the main centres of population, except for the
Clackmannanshire Council of Service, and in the Islands. Those Councils
which are grant-aided have certain common features, as do the English

and Welsh RCCs. The others vary from those in the large cities such as Aberdeen, Dundee, Edinburgh and Glasgow, to those in the smaller towns.

The variety of tasks undertaken by local voluntary councils in Scotland is very great. The Aberdeen Association of Social Service has in the past concentrated mainly on a wide range of direct services, running a large variety of residential care establishments, having its own team of professional qualified social workers for field work of various types and having its own community projects. It has been called an alternative social services department, but it is now putting more emphasis on a development role complementary to the reorganised statutory services. Other Councils operate less strongly in the field of direct provision and concentrate more on the roles of supporting other organisations and community development. The Glasgow Council for Voluntary Service was formed only in 1974 and has taken up the challenge offered by the extremely high levels of deprivation in the city. In so doing it has deliberately avoided the provision of direct services and is concentrating on acting to stimulate new initiatives in both statutory and voluntary sectors and to provide information and resources for voluntary organisations.

Local voluntary councils in Scotland have had to meet two great difficulties which differ from those south of the border. The changes in local government have brought into being the new large regions which have responsibility for education and social work services. This has meant not only that the councils, like all voluntary bodies, have had to form new relationships, quite different in kind from those which used to exist with the former smaller local authorities where 'everyone knows everyone', but also an organisational difficulty in that the voluntary sector has never been organised on a regional basis in the past. The other great change is the introduction of the community councils which are coming into being as we write. It is clear that local voluntary councils will have difficulties in determining their exact relationships with these new bodies, and it will take time to work them out. Much assistance and advice have been provided by the Scottish Council of Social Service over the first difficulty through the work of the Scottish Voluntary Organisations Regional Advisory Group set up while the Local Government (Scotland) Act was passing through Parliament; and over the second difficulty by the activities of field staff promoting public awareness, through the leaflets and information services supplied in conjunction with the Community Councils Forum. To complete this very brief survey we should refer also to a problem which applies very strongly in Scotland (and in some other parts of the United Kingdom) — that is, the combination of small population and great distances in the rural areas. This factor adds very greatly to the cost and complication of arranging meetings and of other aspects of voluntary work over much of Scotland.

Some Northern Ireland Aspects

There are about twenty 'umbrella bodies' of various sorts in Northern Ireland including councils of social service and community councils but excluding the two which cover the whole province; the Northern Ireland Council of Social Service (NICSS) to which we refer in Chapter 7 and the Standing Conference of Councils of Social Service and Community Councils. There are no RCCs and the Development Commission does not operate in Northern Ireland. The public funds of local voluntary councils, as we call them, come from the Area Health and Social Service Boards for those activities having a social services element and from the local district councils for such tasks as community centres and secretarial service. We do not however mean to imply that there is a common policy for all districts in their support of local intermediary bodies or of the voluntary sector. Local voluntary councils (the most common title being 'Councils of Social Service') also raise money from other sources and so may have a private income. There are no hard and fast distinctions in Northern Ireland between resource centres and local voluntary councils. Some are quite independent while some 'umbrella bodies' operate resource centres as part of their activities, e.g. East Belfast, Shankill and Strabane Community Councils.

As in other parts of the UK local voluntary councils in Northern Ireland are not standardised and vary greatly. The Belfast Voluntary Welfare Society (BVWS) has a long history of being not only a resource centre but also a service-providing body. It has its office in Bryson House, in the centre of Belfast, and this converted linen warehouse also houses the offices of a number of other voluntary organisations, some of them originally started by the BVWS. This has enabled many voluntary organisations to work under the same roof with consequent easy, informal communication and shared facilities. Some of the early tenants have now grown up and hived off into their own quarters, to be replaced by others. The North West Council of Social Service in Londonderry was created about ten years ago, partly as an information centre and partly to provide a night shelter. Its role is still divided between direct provision and assisting other organisations, and it undertakes new projects, such as looking into the problem of teenage alcoholism, as they arise. There has been in recent years in Northern Ireland an emergence of small community groups, especially in Belfast and Londonderry, and we note that their existence emphasises the importance of the function of providing information and resource centre facilities, whatever the name of the local intermediary body which provides them.

Local voluntary councils in Northern Ireland have had difficulties to face over local government reorganisation because the new districts differ greatly from the former local authorities. Outside the cities they also have the same problems of long distances which we mentioned earlier. They have in addition special problems arising from the present troubles. There is no Northern Ireland Parliament and the powers of district councils are limited. There are therefore no elected members of the NI Parliament and fewer councillors, with powers to remedy grievances, to whom the population may turn in times of difficulty. This increases the demand on the voluntary sector at the very time when the violence, mainly in the cities, is making many people suspicious of going for advice or help to any organisation which might appear, rightly or wrongly, to be part of 'the establishment' and which even makes movement itself very difficult. There is a real difficulty in matching the traditional work and areas of responsibility of the local voluntary councils with the needs of the new community organisations.

Functions of Local Intermediary Bodies

In our discussions we thought it right to try to identify the main functions which local intermediary bodies carry out. These functions are in the following list, which is not in order of priority; and it is not suggested that all councils carry out all of them.

(a) *Development* This can be described as a process of reviewing existing provision, identifying unmet needs and initiating action to meet them, seeing where duplication exists and trying to achieve a better match between needs and resources. In practice it may mean helping to bring new organisations into existence, seeking grants for new work, establishing working parties and initiating research and evaluation projects.

(b) *Services to other organisations* There are a variety of services which local intermediary bodies may provide for other voluntary organisations, such as access to typing and duplicating facilities, provision of information, help with the keeping of accounts, running training courses, giving advice about relationships with statutory authorities and so on.

(c) *Liaison* This is defined as the exchange of information and opinion between organisations. It may sometimes lead to agreements between organisations and policy changes by individual bodies, but the intermediary body promoting the liaison can exert no sanctions over the liaising bodies. If pursued as an end in itself liaison may often be unproductive, though as the by-product of the pursuit of other objectives it may be of great value.

(d) *Representation* Articulating views, protecting interests, pressing for changes through negotiations, and publicity, on behalf of the organisations represented. The effectiveness with which this function can be carried out is likely to be much affected by the extent of common ground between the organisations represented. Much of it is concerned with representing the voluntary to the statutory sector, and may in practice be difficult to distinguish from liaison.

(e) *Direct services to individuals* The large budgets of a few CVSs are for the most part accounted for by the provision of direct services. For example, Camden CSS run six Citizens' Advice Bureaux, two consumer aid centres, four adventure playgrounds. We do not count the provision of direct services as an intermediary function, but it should be recognised that many intermediary bodies do engage in direct service provision.

These functions will vary greatly from one part of the country to another and in accordance with the local needs. What is important is to distinguish the functions appropriate to any particular local voluntary council and to relate the organisation of that council to those functions and not vice versa. When there are limited resources decisions must be taken on priorities and this will have a bearing on which functions are to be carried out. In the list of functions there is a clear distinction between (e) above, direct services to individuals, and the remainder. We have been informed that it is difficult for an intermediary body to carry out service provision and to do the general information and representational functions, though we are conscious that there are many examples where both types of role appear to be successfully accomplished, for example, Aberdeen, Belfast and Harlow. In cases where there is a service-providing role the reason may sometimes be to obtain funds to cover expenditure on some of the other functions which have little popular appeal, though there may be other reasons too. In Liverpool

the Council of Voluntary Service avoids the direct provision role but
there is a long tradition of giving to the Council by local industry and
local philanthropists and there are endowments so that the Council is
assured of an independent income. In Belfast, there is much service
provision but there are special reasons for this, mainly the proximity
of the Northern Ireland Council of Social Service which fulfils the
development, information and representational functions: another
reason is the present troubled situation.

The representation function can be carried out in a number of ways.
Usually the intermediary body will make contact with the appropriate
local authorities and will make its member organisations' views known
to those authorities or vice versa. In addition local organisations which
are members of a LVC may put forward their views through that body
which may then raise the point in the appropriate Standing Conference
at national level and so it can reach NCSS and possibly the government.
Alternatively a local organisation may represent its view to its own
national headquarters which can bring it forward in the NCSS or the
appropriate government department. A combination of methods may
also be adopted. The representation role can be carried out also in the
reverse sense. For example many RCCs actually run the local branch of
a national organisation, e.g. of the National Playing Fields Association
or the Council for the Protection of Rural England, and so the views of
these bodies are directly represented at local level; and many national
bodies' local branches are in membership of RCCs and CVSs and can, if
they wish, express the ideas of their national organisation at that level.

Before we leave the question of functions we record the importance
we attach to the first one listed — development. There is much criticism
of the voluntary sector on the grounds of duplication and alleged waste
of resources. This criticism is stronger at a time of financial shortage.
But what one person regards as wasteful duplication another may call
providing a degree of choice, so that it is not easy to determine whether
the criticism is justified. There is also criticism of failure to discover
unmet needs, which may mean neglect of a certain task, or bad geographic distribution of resources, so that some places are over-provided
and others have little or nothing. Certainly it is inherent in the term
'voluntary sector' that it cannot be controlled and directed without
losing its essence; and we are not in favour of any compulsion or direction. There is, however, a place for some type of body with a watching
brief and an ability to look ahead to spot possible defects, to try to
anticipate them by persuading someone to take action in advance or, if
this is not possible to attempt to remedy the defects. The corollary is

to avoid wasteful duplication. It has been put to us that the development role should be the prime responsibility of the elected statutory bodies. In some activities, as in the hospital services, the resources needed are so costly that development planning must of necessity be mainly in the hands of the statutory side. But there is every reason for the voluntary sector to have views on how such development is carried out and to take initiatives itself when it can. In our opinion the partnership between the statutory and voluntary sectors is of great importance in the development role and the intermediary bodies should be ready to take the lead on the voluntary side.

Specialist Intermediary Bodies

The specialist intermediary bodies perform many of the functions we have listed in an earlier paragraph. Some argue that for this reason there is no need for the generalist intermediary bodies. They often add that coordination is usually overdone, wastes time and resources, and that voluntary organisations will get together on their own initiative to discuss points of common interest whenever there is a need to do so. In short they say that subjects which cover the whole range of the voluntary sector are few and can be handled on a temporary basis as they occur. We have sympathy with this view but we feel it underestimates the scope and frequency of occurrence of across-the-board subjects. We go into this matter in more detail in Chapter 7 when we consider the role of intermediary bodies at national level. In our opinion there is a need both for generalist bodies handling the across-the-board subjects and for specialist bodies which may be required either permanently, for example to handle old people's welfare, or on a temporary basis where a working party may be sufficient. But there is no model system which can be applied universally. From our locality studies we know of cases where a number of specialist intermediary bodies or voluntary organisations themselves in a particular locality have come together for the consideration of matters affecting the voluntary sector generally without there being a generalist intermediary body.

Local Resource Centres

We mentioned earlier another quite different sort of intermediary body, the resource centre. In a report published by the Calouste Gulbenkian Foundation,[4] a Community Work Group under the chairmanship of Lord Boyle suggested that Area Resource Centres should be set up

within existing organisations to serve the needs of community groups
within their area. It was stressed that the functions of such centres
would vary according to local needs and the services already available
but it was suggested that they might provide information services,
supporting services such as help in accounting, preparing documents
for publication, or skilled advice, the loan of equipment such as type-
writers and photocopiers, and facilities for meetings and exchange of
ideas. The similarity to CVS is obvious but there is no question of
providing services to individuals, playing a representative role, or
playing an active part in coordination.

During the past three years five such area resource centres have been
established on an experimental basis with funds from the VSU, the
EEC Poverty Programme, and the Calouste Gulbenkian Foundation.
Two of these, in Manchester and Newcastle, are managed by the Young
Volunteer Force Foundation, one in Strathclyde is to be managed by a
mixture of local authority and voluntary body representatives, one in
South Wales is managed by a consortium of local voluntary agencies,
and one in London is attached to the London Council of Social
Service. All the centres operate in different ways but they are
encouraged to exchange experiences with each other by the existence
of a central monitoring committee which will in due course produce a
report on the lessons to be learnt from the various approaches to
providing assistance for local groups.

Although these experimental centres are a direct result of the Boyle
Group's recommendations, there are many other intermediary bodies
which could be described as local resource centres. The settlements
have been fulfilling similar functions since the end of the last century
and more recent bodies such as the Islington Bus Company, which we
visited, and Interaction provide a variety of back-up services for local
groups. The Association of Neighbourhood Councils sees its member
Councils very much as intermediary bodies working closely with local
authorities while encouraging voluntary work and community
projects, but would also include a representative role among their
functions.

Most of these organisations have the desire to provide services
or help to small groups at a very local level such as a small part of a
large town or any compact area of comparatively small population. In
theory, such services would be open to all comers but in practice
limited resources would probably make some form of selection inevitable and groups holding extreme views might find themselves
excluded. It has been said to us that many small community type

organisations are unwilling for one reason or another to join a Council
of Voluntary Service or indeed to be associated with it, and perhaps this
applies with particular force to the ethnic groups and to some of the
Northern Ireland groups, but that they might readily accept help from
one or other of this range of organisations which we have classified as
local resource centres. We do not know whether or not this assertion is
accurate as a generalisation. We believe that the position varies in
different areas and according to the personalities concerned. But we
underline the importance of this type of intermediary body in certain
circumstances, not only because it is on the spot and readily available
to people who may be unable to afford the time and money to travel to
more distant centres, but also because it is less likely than any larger
federated body to be regarded as a threat to the independence of the
groups making use of it.

Some Local Authority Association Views

In our discussions with local authority associations the subject of local
voluntary councils was raised on a number of occasions. The Association
of County Councils referred to the unevenness to be found among
CVSs which, in their view, often depended upon the quality of the
permanent staff, and suggested there was perhaps a need to strengthen
the machinery. But they did not express any wish to reduce the tasks
now carried out by RCCs. In considering CVSs, they laid stress on
their value as resource centres and the danger of their overdoing the
role of taking the initiative, which would be regarded as interference by
their member organisations. The Association of District Councils felt
that the county level would be a little remote from voluntary organisations. They laid more stress upon the district as the basis for the local
intermediary bodies, but they added that it was not essential for these
bodies on the voluntary side to follow exactly the areas of local
government responsibility if these did not match with their own
feelings. The Association of Metropolitan Authorities also drew
attention to local variations in the effectiveness of CVS; although in
conurbations it was clearer than elsewhere that they should relate to
the district rather than to the county level. The National Association
of Local Councils mentioned the risk of there being too many
coordinating bodies. They doubted the desirability of organising the
intermediary function exclusively on the district and welcomed the
existence of RCCs and the work of the Development Commission as
having made some redress to the rural areas for the greater interest
which on the whole was shown towards the towns. They pointed to the

need for RCCs to be flexible, to be able to change the emphasis of their work if it was necessary. They stressed the RCCs' role as an agent for smaller voluntary organisations in negotiations with local authorities and generally in providing them with advice. They also had a role in identifying gaps in the services provided to the community. This association felt that the funding of RCCs by the Development Commission had not affected their independence, but, while recognising that fund-raising took up their time, they felt strongly that it was important for RCCs to have non-statutory sources of income.

Some Reflections and Conclusions

We have seen that the most commonly found local intermediary bodies today are the RCCs and the CVSs. The RCCs, though showing great variety, share some common characteristics arising from the fact that they are funded by the Development Commission and that they are all members of the Standing Conference of RCCs. CVSs on the other hand have no common source of funding and many of them are not members of their Standing Conference; there is a very great diversity between them and there is no uniform pattern of one CVS per district. The area of responsibility of a CVS is not necessarily coterminous with a local authority though there are moves in their Standing Conference to encourage a development in this sense. We can see certain obvious advantages from the point of view of representation in a CVS's area of responsibility being that of a local authority particularly in the metropolitan districts and in some urban non-metropolitan districts.

The point we wish to emphasise is the importance of identifying the functions which one wishes an intermediary body to play in any particular area. We have discussed these functions earlier in the chapter and have stated our view that development is by far the most important, though the other functions of providing services to other organisations, liaison and representation are also valuable. The coordination of local fund-raising activities can be a most useful service. As a general rule we believe that local intermediary bodies should not be concerned with direct service provision, though there are some exceptions of which we have given examples, because this is something which is nearly always best done by voluntary organisations themselves. Though the development role is something for which the local authority has a clear responsibility, there should be a partnership and an intermediary body can play a significant part in seeing that the partnership is not too unequal. Part of the exercise of this role by the intermediary body will be the encouragement of the formation of new bodies to meet unmet needs and bringing together existing bodies to try to eliminate wasteful duplication where this appears to exist.

It is only after one has determined the functions needed in a particular area that one can decide on the type of intermediary body and how it should be organised. From what we have heard, the present pattern of RCCs in the shire counties seems to be generally acceptable. We do not, however, for that reason suggest that there should be a similar standard pattern in the districts. In some cases the right solution may be to have a CVS for a district and we suggest that this will usually apply in the metropolitan districts and in those non-metropolitan districts which are more or less the same as the former county boroughs. This is not a universal pattern. There is a place for the specialist intermediary bodies and also there may be a need, particularly in the towns, for more local resource centres. Sometimes one may need a combination. Where one is thinking about CVSs, the question of their internal organisation is also of importance. If they are to carry out the development function effectively it is important that they should not simply be a federation of the larger existing voluntary organisations. They should, as many of them now do, include an element of individuals chosen for their general qualities and independence of mind and not simply as representatives of organisations. In the shire counties there is also a need to have practical working arrangements between the CVS and the RCC on areas of responsibility. Perhaps the most important point of all is the quality of the senior paid official and the method of his or her selection.

These considerations bring us to the question of finance. On the whole, direct service to individuals is the only one of the functions we have listed which is likely to command support from the public when it comes to raising funds. The other functions have little popular appeal. It is not reasonable to suppose that RCCs, CVSs and still less local resource centres, could exist solely by charging fees to the organisations they serve. There must therefore be some form of outside funding. In some cases local commerce and industry may provide some money, and we hope that there will always be some individual subscribers also, but on the whole, especially in the present time, most of the funding can only come from public sources, i.e. central or local government or a combination of both. We discuss in Chapter 10 the machinery by which public funding could be supplied.

Notes

1. 'Review of Social Work of the Development Commission Jan. to Jul. 1975', by Brian E. Lincoln; 'The Present State and Future Prospects of Rural Community Councils', by R. F. Bretherton (unpublished).
2. Lansley, John, *Voluntary Organisations Facing Change,* 1976.
3. 34th Report of the Developmental Commissioners.
4. *Current Issues in Community Work*, Calouste Gulbenkian Foundation, 1973.

7 NATIONAL INTERMEDIARY BODIES

National intermediary bodies differ greatly from one another and perform a variety of functions which may include regulation, a degree of control, general influence, supplying of resources and information, and occasionally funding. They play an important part in the life of many voluntary organisations and we feel they deserve a special chapter in our report. The same definitions apply as those given in the last chapter for local intermediary bodies and we again avoid using the terms 'coordination' and 'coordinating'.

There are very many national intermediary bodies which fall within our definition. We do not attempt in this chapter or elsewhere to list them all. We hope rather to show from a number of selected examples some of the different ways in which they may operate. There are also, as with voluntary organisations themselves, a number of different ways in which national intermediary bodies may be classified. In this part of the chapter we look first at the statutory bodies, of which some are much involved in grant giving, and then we turn to the voluntary side. Except for the National Council of Social Service and its counterparts in Scotland, Wales and Northern Ireland which we cover later in the chapter, we give only very brief notes about the selected national intermediary bodies as full details are available in published documents such as annual reports.

Some Examples of Statutory National Intermediary Bodies

The Housing Corporation was established in 1964, under the Housing Act 1964, and it consists of not more than nine members, appointed by the Minister of Housing and Local Government and the Secretary of State for Scotland acting jointly. Its responsibilities are to promote and assist the development of housing associations and through them to stimulate the building of new houses and flats for letting or for ownership. The machinery by which it does so is described more fully in Chapter 8. The Housing Corporation disposes of very large sums and in 1975/76 some £200 million was advanced to some 2,000 housing associations.

The Development Commission was established in 1909 under the Development and Road Improvement Funds Act 1909. It consists of a

Chairman and seven other Commissioners appointed by the Crown and its terms of reference are to consider and report to the Department of the Environment on applications referred to the Commissioners for advances from the Development Fund. The Commission gives advice, instruction and limited credit for small industries in rural areas, similar credit facilities for tourist enterprises in rural parts of the development areas, and it provides factory premises in rural areas where prevention of depopulation is a cardinal policy objective. As we saw in Chapter 6, the Development Commission gives grants to Rural Community Councils (RCCs) in England but has now handed over its responsibilities for similar bodies in Scotland and Wales. Grants from the Development Fund to RCCs are not made conditional upon the acceptance of any particular policy or course of action, as the Commission wishes RCCs to preserve their independence of thought and action, but they hope that RCCs will support their policies wherever possible. The salaries and conditions of service of RCC officers are determined centrally.

The Charity Commissioners have the general function of providing for the effective use of charitable resources by encouraging the development of better methods of administration, advising trustees on any matter affecting the charity and investigating and checking abuses. The Commissioners may order enquiries into charities and if misconduct is proved, have the power to appoint administrators and approve the use of the charity's funds. They also maintain a central register of charities. There are three Charity Commissioners who are civil servants appointed by the Home Secretary. Two of these are barristers. The Charity Commissioners are an independent body with quasi-judicial functions, and appeal from their decision lies only in the High Court. Their work was recently reviewed by the Goodman Committee on Charity Law and Voluntary Organisations.

The University Grants Committee has the task of presenting to the government, through the Department of Education and Science, its estimate of the financial needs of the universities. It then has the responsibility, when the government's decision is communicated to it, of distributing the total sum among the individual universities in accordance with its judgement of the needs of each. The grants for capital requirements are made on a project-by-project basis. For annual recurrent expenditure each university receives a block grant which it divides up through its own internal budgetary processes. Traditionally these block grants were made to each university on a five-year basis, but recent stringencies have reduced this period of predictability. A substantial majority of the members of the Committee are practising university professors, and it operates largely on the advice of subcommittees composed of experts in the relevant fields.

The Arts Council of Great Britain is an autonomous body whose functions are set out by Royal Charter. Its members are appointed by the Secretary of State for Education and Science in consultation with the Secretaries of State for Scotland and Wales. It receives an annual grant from central government and in turn makes grants to the Scottish and Welsh Arts Councils, which decide how the money should be spent in their respective areas. Most of the Arts Council's support goes to a multitude of organisations and individuals across the country ranging from orchestras and repertory theatres to individual artists. The great national companies, the National Theatre, the Royal Opera, the Royal Ballet, the Royal Shakespeare Company and the English National Opera Company are all subsidised by the Arts Council. Under the Housing the Arts Scheme the Arts Council makes capital contributions to buildings for the arts provided by local authorities. The Arts Council of Northern Ireland has similar functions in the Province and is funded by the Northern Ireland Department of Education.

The Countryside Commission was established in 1949 as the National Parks Commission by the National Parks and Access to the Countryside Act 1949; and was extended and enlarged as the Countryside Commission by the Countryside Act 1968. It covers England and Wales and has a Committee for Wales. The chairman and members are appointed by the Secretaries of State for the Environment and for Wales. The terms of reference include keeping under review all matters relating to the provision and improvement of facilities for the enjoyment of the countryside, designating national parks and areas of natural beauty, affording opportunities for outdoor recreation; recommending grants for the establishment of country parks; providing or assisting in the provision of publicity and information services on countryside matters; and advising Ministers and public bodies on matters relating to the countryside. The Commission has recently initiated a scheme to provide grants for voluntary organisations undertaking conservation work. There is a Countryside Commission for Scotland, with broadly similar functions, the members being appointed by the Secretary of State for Scotland.

The Nature Conservancy Council's functions are the establishment and management of nature reserves in Great Britain, the provision of advice for the Secretary of State or any other minister on the development and implementation of policies for, or affecting, nature conservation in Great Britain, the provision of advice and the dissemination of knowledge about nature conservation and the commissioning or support of relevant research. The functions include the continuing survey and assessment of nature conservation interests, the selection, establishment and management of national nature reserves, selection and notification to local planning authorities of sites of special scientific interest, research, and creating a wider public awareness of nature conservation values.

The Commission for Racial Equality has a duty to work towards the elimination of racial discrimination and to promote equality of opportunity. It has wide powers both to enforce the law and to play an advisory role in the pursuit of these objectives and to assist individual victims of discrimination to obtain redress. The Commission can give financial and other forms of assistance to organisations concerned with the promotion of good relations between different racial groups and may support research and education. Through these powers it will foster the work of the independent local community relations councils. The Commission is composed of fifteen members with a wide range of relevant knowledge and experience and including the racial minorities. The central government grant is subject to the consent of the Home Secretary and the Treasury.

There are a number of matters to be considered when deciding whether or not to establish statutory national intermediary bodies. Voluntary organisations may be helped by dealing with a statutory intermediary body, whose members will, from the fact of their appointment, be likely to understand a voluntary organisation's problems and will know the personalities concerned. Central government for its part may see a case for setting up a national intermediary body if it appears that exclusive or predominant local authority provision seems undesirable; if government does not itself want to provide services directly, as, for example, when the service requires a special flexibility and discretion; and if it is desired to find a way of involving public figures and representatives of various interested parties in the development and implementation of policy. It may also be a convenient source of information and opinion from a large and complex array of voluntary organisations. From a wider point of view the intermediary body may to some extent protect the independence of the voluntary organisations which receive public money; it may be more effective because it will be smaller and perhaps more approachable than a government department; and it may provide greater continuity of administration and consistency of policy. On the other hand voluntary organisations may look upon the intermediary body as an unnecessary link or even an obstacle between themselves and the statutory side and they may consider, as they do sometimes with independent intermediary bodies, that their very existence is a waste of scarce resources both material and human. Their view will probably be affected by the size and accessibility of the intermediary body and the personalities of its senior permanent staff. Central government may also see the intermediary body's existence as a waste of resources which could be avoided if they themselves provided direct grants, and they may feel that it is not fully accountable because it is not directly subject to the process of questions in Parliament and other similar checks.

There is no universal pattern which will meet all cases. Normally we would expect national intermediary bodies to be used. But there may be cases where a government department wishes to aid a particular task in furtherance of the department's policy. In these cases it is probably not necessary or desirable to use an intermediary body.

This leads us directly to the question of whether there is any need for an overall grant-giving intermediary body for voluntary organisations. It is sometimes suggested that there should be such a body taking the same form as the University Grants Committee, which we described earlier. Although this idea is often mooted in general terms we have found little support for it in our evidence nor any serious arguments in its favour in our own discussions. It may help to summarise the arguments against the idea. If such an intermediary body were dealing with organisations in the area of activity of a single government department, it would always have to consult that department before it could act. More time would therefore be spent and there would be a need for additional manpower. If the intermediary body dealt only with those voluntary organisations and subjects which crossed the fields of responsibility of different departments, its influence would only be marginal, though it would certainly have the power to take decisions on matters in which a department might perhaps be reluctant to assume responsibility. It could, however, hardly establish sensible priorities over an almost limitless field. We feel there is no case for such a solution to be adopted. But this does not necessarily apply to the possibility of setting up a national intermediary body responsible for grant-giving in a limited field of activity, and we discuss this matter more fully in Chapter 10.

Independent National Intermediary Bodies

On the voluntary side there are many organisations which carry out intermediary functions of one kind or another at national level. We make a broad distinction between generalist and specialist bodies. The generalist bodies cover the voluntary sector as a whole and consist of the National Council of Social Service and its counterparts in Scotland, Wales and Northern Ireland. These are discussed later in this chapter. There is also the Volunteer Centre. It covers both statutory and voluntary social services, with the remit to encourage voluntary service generally. We recognise that it carries out developmental and support functions for the voluntary sector generally but, since its essential responsibility is volunteers rather than voluntary organisations, we do not discuss it further here. Specialist national intermediary bodies do not form a homogenous group although there is a broad similarity in the functions they carry out and in their relationships with their constituent members. We have studied a number of them as examples covering a wide range of activities:

Age Concern
Central Council for the Disabled[1]
National Association of Women of Great Britain
National Association of Youth Clubs
National Children's Bureau
National Council for Voluntary Youth Services
National Council for One Parent Families
National Council of Voluntary Child Care Agencies
National Federation of Community Associations
National Federation of Housing Associations
National Playing Fields Association
National Society for Mentally Handicapped Children
National Youth Bureau
Royal National Institute for the Blind
Royal National Institute for the Deaf

The structures of these independent national intermediary bodies are often elaborate but there are points of similarity between them. None of them have local branches, although most have affiliated local autonomous organisations which may implement the policies accepted by the central body, but are not compelled by reason of their membership to

do so. Some of the national intermediary bodies have a regional structure but there is considerable variation in the way that these regional
agencies are used. The RNID have seven regional associations which are
autonomous but act in consultation with RNID over work being undertaken by local organisations within their areas. The National Society for
Mentally Handicapped Children has twelve regional offices professionally administered by the national society with paid staff; it is through
these that local societies elect members to the central governing body.
The National Children's Bureau has twelve local groups where the
Bureau membership in a particular locality can meet to discuss current
issues or projects; they are non-executive and have no formal constitutions although the Bureau lays down guidelines and provides some sup-
portive resources.

The overall structure of national intermediary bodies is well illustrated by Age Concern. The governing body, selected triennially by members, decides on general policy. It elects an executive committee with
authority to act within the general policy framework without reference
to the governing body. It may also delegate some powers to its finance
committee and may establish advisory or working groups. Another
example is the RNIB. The governing body of the RNIB is its executive
council. This is composed of members nominated from five different
categories of constituent organisations. The policy-making body of the
National Council for One Parent Families is its committee of management. This is elected by council members at an annual general meeting
and one third of the committee retires each year. The committee of
management appoints subcommittees on special subjects, for example
housing or legal and social policy. A director with other administrative
staff works within the scope of general policies approved by the committee of management.

The composition of an independent national intermediary body
may include voluntary organisations active within its specific terms
of reference; voluntary organisations working outside these terms of
reference; professional associations and possibly hospitals or research
institutes; statutory authorities; individual members. The relative power
of these different categories varies according to the number of their
representatives at the centre and according to the terms of their membership. Most of these national intermediary bodies give greatest controlling interest to their voluntary organisation members active within
their specific terms of reference. The voluntary organisation membership is in several cases fairly broad ranging. Membership of Age Concern,
for example, includes the National Association of Alms Houses,

National Association for Mental Health, Family Welfare Association. The
organisation membership of intermediary bodies which cover a restricted area is usually limited to those whose work is confined to the relevant field, but there are notable exceptions. The Central Council for the
Disabled,[2] for example, has societies such as the National Children's
Home, Girl Guides Association and Scout Association among its associated members as well as societies for disabled people.

Local authorities are given the opportunity for close communication
with the independent national intermediary bodies. There may be direct
representation of local authority associations with full membership
rights, as with the Executive Council of RNIB, or local authorities may
be nominated by their associations, or there may be direct representation of local authorities. Another arrangement is for local authority
associations to have observer status, as on the Executive Committee of
the Central Council for the Disabled. They may also take part in a consultative capacity through professional associations as in the case of the
Association of Directors of Social Services membership of the National
Children's Bureau.

Central government is represented by an observer of consultative
status in all the national intermediary bodies we examined. The RNIB
has observers from the Departments of Health and Social Security,
Education and Science and Employment. Age Concern has observers
from the same Departments as the RNIB and also one from the Department of the Environment. The National Council for One Parent Families
has an observer from the DHSS and one from the Supplementary Benefits
Commission. These formal arrangements are usually strengthened by
informal links between the national intermediary body and central
government officers. Of the bodies studied only the National Council
of Voluntary Child Care Associations has no formal statutory relations
with either central or local government although it is often asked to
provide consultative documents by the DHSS for example.

Besides local authority associations, some professional associations,
universities, colleges of education and hospital authorities may be members of certain national intermediary bodies such as the National
Children's Bureau, Age Concern or the RNIB. Certain national intermediary bodies also have a small number of individual members who
are usually people who have been specially concerned with the field of
interest of that organisation or who have been given honorary membership of the organisation.

Client participation in centralised policy-making is clearly present in the Royal National Institutes for the Blind and for the Deaf. It is not so evident in the composition of the National Council for One Parent Families, though clients are indirectly represented by virtue of Ginger-bread's affiliation, and we were told in the event of a merger of the two organisations client participation would become more significant.

Most independent national intermediary bodies act as a collective voice for their constituent organisations in negotiations with statutory bodies over policies affecting their objectives and in influencing and informing public opinion. As nearly all include statutory bodies in their membership in one form or another, they can decide with them on needs to be fulfilled. Although national intermediary bodies nearly always represent the collective voice of their constituents, individual voluntary organisations can also initiate and arrange joint action. For example the Child Poverty Action Group (CPAG) has collaborated with other interested organisations, such as the Association for One Parent Families and Shelter, in approaching government. These organisations set up a 'lobby group' for the purpose. CPAG, however, may also take direct unilateral action to affect government policy, as with the alleviation of family poverty. In this it differs from an organisation such as the National Children's Bureau which, by reason of its constitution and structure, can only inform government of its opinion in the sense of the collective view of its constituents.

Some independent national intermediary bodies do some direct service provision. For example, in mounting a building project or setting up a training centre, they may experiment and so demonstrate a method of supplying or conducting services to clients. Some of them give consultative and advisory services directly to clients and thereby gain direct experience of the field in which they are working and of the problems encountered. Direct contact with the recipients of services can lead to greater sensitivity to changing needs. Sometimes the national intermediary body will provide direct services to clients because it is less wasteful to do this centrally than through small organisations with few resources. On the whole, however, direct service provision tends to be a means to an end, not an end in itself.

The national intermediary bodies depend upon their constituents' subscriptions for much of their income. The National Council of Women of Great Britain relies entirely upon its subscription income and Age Concern England receives as much as 76 per cent of its funding from this source. Most of the other national intermediary bodies receive about 50 per cent. Many receive grants from other national intermediary

bodies both statutory and independent. The National Playing Fields
Association gets a 10 per cent grant from the Sports Council and the
National Federation of Housing Associations receives 23 per cent of its
income from the Housing Corporation and from other outside bodies.
Central government grants received by national intermediary bodies are
often quite substantial in absolute terms and some amount to sizeable
proportions of their total incomes. Age Concern receives 20 per cent of
its funding from central government departments and the National Youth
Bureau as much as 85 per cent. The Civic Trust, although getting
almost all its income from voluntary sources and from companies,
receives government grants for specific projects. Certain national intermediary bodies receive money in the form of fees and charges where
they provide direct services. This is true, for example, of the RNIB and
of the National Society for Mentally Handicapped Children.

Independent national intermediary bodies carry out a wide variety of
functions of which we give some short examples. The National Children's Bureau provides a means of encouraging 'multidisciplinary cooperation' between voluntary organisations, statutory authorities and
professional bodies concerned with different aspects of provision for
children. It provides an information service and library, circulates litera-
ture and holds conferences. It has a children's centre which mounts
demonstration projects linked with seminars, and it undertakes research into provision for children and children's welfare which helps to
identify gaps and overlaps in statutory and voluntary services and encourages action to eliminate them. The National Council for Voluntary
Youth Services provides a centre for the pooling of information and
sharing of resources, it enables joint consideration of youth work training and provides courses and training programmes for those working
with young people. It plays an educative and informative role both
generally to the public and specifically to its own constituent members.
It also serves as the medium through which the DES provides grants to
national voluntary youth organisations. One of RNIB's main roles is to
develop pioneer services for the blind. It undertakes research into the
development of technical aids and into the changing needs of blind
people and the nature of services available to them. It has for example
identified a shift in the age level of blind people in that, though fewer
children become blind, people are living longer and more are becoming
blind late in life. Therefore more resources should be applied to services
for the elderly blind. RNIB has many other activities and its experience
and advice are often called upon by relevant government departments.

It may be of interest to mention the Civic Trust, though it does not fit into the classification we mentioned at the start of this section. Its subscribing amenity groups have no say in its policy or representation on a central governing body, but there is a two-way exchange between the Trust and local groups. While the local groups may benefit from the Trust's expertise and influence, the Trust in turn relies on local groups for the information they supply concerning local opinion and local issues and gains this expertise by its involvement in local disputes.

The few examples we have chosen give a general impression of the work of independent national intermediary bodies. They are designed more to encourage others to implement policies than to undertake this task directly. They gather information from constituent members and from outside and through research projects, surveys and other investigations and therefore can or should be able to detect gaps or defects in provision and to consider improvements. They may persuade and encourage others to take up and implement policies by distributing research findings and information about particular issues which might be worthwhile following up. They may provide consultative services and advice and practical help in such matters as providing training courses.

Functions of National Intermediary Bodies

We have shown above the enormous range of activities covered by both statutory and independent national intermediary bodies. Most of them fall into the classification of functions given in Chapter 6. But there are two that do not: regulation and funding. Regulation derives from powers conferred by statute and is clearly exemplified in the conditions that have to be fulfilled for registration as a charity and as a housing association with the Charity Commission and the Housing Corporation respectively. Of itself we do not count the provision of funds as an intermediary function: otherwise we would need to bring into consideration every trust and foundation in the country. But we were interested in funding vested in an intermediary body like the Development Commission with related planning and developmental functions. We discuss in later chapters the case for the provision of funds through an intermediary body rather than directly from central or local government. Here we should add that with one interesting exception we came across no instance of funding through an intermediary body at the local level. The exception was Liverpool Play Action Council which had the responsibility for allotting, between many different play schemes, funds provided for play by the local authority.

It may be useful to show briefly how these functions are sometimes exercised in practice. The Charity Commissioners and the Housing

Corporation are regulatory; The Development Commission, the University Grants Committee, Arts Council and the Housing Corporation have considerable funding powers. All these bodies have some of the other functions such as development, giving services to organisations and representation. On the non-statutory side, the national intermediary bodies do not have a regulatory role. NCVYS has a part to play in funding and many of the others could easily have a similar part in that they would be giving advice on funding which almost merges into the function of representation. As we saw when we were discussing local intermediary bodies, the prime responsibility for carrying out the development function must rest with the statutory side, especially in those cases where expensive resources are in question, but the voluntary sector must also be involved mainly through the independent national intermediary bodies. We must therefore consider how the system works in practice.

The Generalist Independent National Intermediary Bodies

The National Council of Social Service

The National Council of Social Service was set up by the voluntary sector in 1919 'to be a focal point and a resource centre for national and local voluntary organisations concerned with social service'. They sent us two papers of written evidence and we had two discussions with their representatives during the enquiry. In the Council's own view 'they believe that social welfare is concerned with raising the standard of living and the quality of life for man'. They therefore interpret the word 'social' in their title broadly and not simply in the narrow sense of what are now called the personal social services. It is an interesting fact that many people would prefer to change the title to the National Council for Voluntary Service. The NCSS plays a very large part in the voluntary sector as a whole but has made it clear to us that it does not claim to speak for all voluntary organisations, nor for all registered charities. It would repudiate any idea that there is such a thing as the 'voluntary sector' in a finite sense with the NCSS as 'headquarters'. NCSS also explained that the Northern Ireland, Scottish and Welsh Councils of Social Service are autonomous, self-governing bodies responsible for coordinating voluntary agencies in their respective countries and for their own finances, but NCSS has by agreement with them a special role in formulating these policies which have significance for the whole of the United Kingdom. We refer to all four bodies collectively as 'the national councils of social service'.

In their evidence to us NCSS representatives referred to the good relations which they had always had with various government departments but they also spoke of their disappointment at the occasional failure of the government to consult them in advance on important subjects which are bound to affect the voluntary sector as a whole. They quoted as examples the introduction of Value Added Tax and the Community Land Act and the National Insurance Surcharge (though we note on this last point that their representations appear to have contributed to an important concession which has since been made). They referred also to the more particular relationship with the Voluntary Services Unit which we discussed in Chapter 4. In their words the creation of VSU

> does not mean that an independent, central body is not required to perform a cooperative and representational function within the voluntary sector. Such a centralised role is necessary because any suggestion that a Government body should be responsible for collecting and processing the opinions of voluntary organisations and should then interpret them to other Government departments would not be acceptable to the voluntary movement itself . . . it would be equally unacceptable if Government were to attempt to speak for the voluntary sector internationally. By common agreement the NCSS attempts to represent the views of UK voluntary organisations internationally to bodies such as the UN agencies, Commonwealth Secretariat and the EEC. Indeed the existence of NCSS, set up by the voluntary movement, is an expression of the need felt by the voluntary organisations for an independent focus. At all times the voluntary sector should practise and be seen to practise constructive cooperation within its own ranks and this is especially true at the present time of financial difficulty . . .

In discussing with representatives of the NCSS how they saw themselves carrying out their representation function, we asked how far they could express the views of 'the voluntary sector' or a part of it as opposed to merely obtaining a consensus of views. They told us that NCSS certainly has its own views on the main subject of the day; and, though it usually bases them on those of the member organisations and the voluntary sector generally, they are by no means a consensus. For example, in the recent past advertising on television and gambling have both been subjects on which NCSS has formed and given a clear view, though in each case there was considerable difference of opinion among individual voluntary organisations. Its views in these matters are formed not simply by reporting those of organisations but also from general experience, particularly perhaps that of the senior officers, from their contacts and from the widely attended one day conferences held from time to time on specific 'across-the-board' subjects. It is not, however, always wrong in their opinion to give a consensus of views and there may be occasions when there is great merit in setting out as clearly as possible in the early stages of consultation the arguments for and against a particular policy.

The representational function of NCSS raises the question of its relationships with the specialist national intermediary bodies such as Age Concern, National Playing Fields Association, RNIB and many others, some of which we have described at the beginning of the chapter. All these autonomous intermediary bodies go to the particular government department concerned over matters of interest to them and they can and do carry out their own representative function very effectively. But the pattern is not tidy, and some of those we have called the specialist intermediary bodies often have interests across a wide range of departments (e.g. Age Concern). This does not in our view in any way detract from the importance of the representational function of NCSS or from the need to have somewhere an organisation which is constantly on the alert for these across-the-board subjects and ready to take them up. The bodies we have mentioned themselves usually turn to NCSS when it is a question of dealing with government over general subjects such as charity law, taxation of charities, land legislation, charity stamps and EEC issues affecting voluntary organisations. Recent examples are the report of the Goodman Committee on charity law and a UK non-governmental document on the future of social policy in the EEC. Not all issues are of interest to all organisations so that occasionally groups of organisations are called together by NCSS. Examples are the Youth Charter, social effects of disasters, rural transport and the recent report on the minibus working party, which was based on 755 replies from separate organisations.

The development function of NCSS brings in the question of newly identified needs, which can come to light from varied sources both inside and outside the voluntary movement, and of unnecessary duplication. Social welfare in the broad sense (i.e. going beyond the limited field of personal social services) stands much to gain by having ideas and innovatory work produced by both statutory and voluntary sectors — NCSS has given us many examples of having set up organisations to deal

with newly discovered needs, such bodies then in the course of time
becoming independent (see Appendix 5B). Duplication of effort by
voluntary organisations may, as we said in the last chapter, provide a
useful element of choice or it may be a waste of resources. It may be a
requirement for statutory funding to ensure that it is not the latter. The
independent national intermediary bodies, especially the national
councils of social service, are well placed to give impartial and independent advice in this matter.

In carrying out its support centre role NCSS provides a general
information service through regular news bulletins, a quarterly journal,
special briefing papers and other matters including a publications service. It provides some training courses in management. The NCSS representatives, however, stressed to us the absence of coordinated intelligence
about the voluntary sector generally, and the lack of advice on the
question of management (though the free service provided by the British
Institute of Management, which they support, helps to fill this gap) and
there are also the services provided by the Action Resource Centre.
NCSS added that they did not wish to enter into the research field but
felt it better to commission research through the universities and other
bodies which have the facilities and knowledge to embark on these projects. We come back to this question in Chapter 8.

Although the NCSS does not provide any direct services to individuals, it does provide direct services for a number of national bodies representing local organisations. These services are provided by the two main
divisions of the NCSS. One of these is the Community Work Division,
which is responsible for secretarial and other assistance to the Standing
Conferences of RCCs and CVSs which were mentioned in Chapter 6, to
the National Federation of Community Associations and to the Village
Halls Committee. The other is the National Organisation Division which
provides the secretariat and supporting services for a wide variety of
bodies such as the National Council for Voluntary Youth Services, the
Women's Forum, the Standing Conferences for Amateur Music and
Local History, and the National Drama Conference.

NCSS at present receives from the Voluntary Services Unit a grant at
the rate of 50 per cent of approved expenditure which covers all the
Council's work with the exception of the following areas which are
grant-aided at higher rates: staff dealing with CVS at 80 per cent from
the VSU; rural work at 80 per cent from the Development Commission;
Citizens' Advice Bureaux development at 100 per cent from the Department of Prices and Consumer Protection; the Secretariat of the British
Volunteer Programme at approximately 75 per cent from the Ministry

of Overseas Development. The balance of income has to be obtained
from voluntary sources such as donations, subscriptions, affiliation fees
and from the sale of publications. Excluding the National Association
of Citizens' Advice Bureaux, which is to become independent of NCSS
as soon as this can be arranged, a very large part of the Council's work
falls within the category receiving 50 per cent grant. In 1975/76 the
expenditure attracting this grant amounted to £614,000. The raising of
the necessary £307,000 of voluntary money is a prodigious task and
imposes a very strict control upon expansion. It is certainly doubtful
whether the Council will be able to continue its present scale of operations without increased statutory funding.

The Scottish Council of Social Service

We received written evidence from the Scottish Council of Social
Service at an early stage in our deliberations and had an opportunity
later of meeting their representatives for a session of oral evidence. The
Council told us that their present purpose, which had not changed much
from the original goals at the time of the foundation in 1943, was:

> to promote all or any of the purposes for the benefit of the com-
> munity which now or hereinafter may be deemed by law to be chari-
> table, and in particular the advancement of education, the further-
> ance of health and the relief of poverty, distress and sickness: to
> promote and organise cooperation in the achievement of the above
> purposes and to that end to bring together in council nationally and
> locally representatives of voluntary agencies and statutory authori-
> ties engaged in the furtherance of the above purposes or any of them.

There is perhaps a difference between these purposes and the aims of
NCSS in that NCSS refers to its work in the context of the voluntary
sector whereas the Scottish Council specifically mentions its responsibility for bringing together voluntary agencies and statutory authorities.
In discussing its functions the Scottish Council sees as one of its
objectives the need to stimulate and encourage the development
and effectiveness of voluntary action in Scotland with a view to encouraging social change and it works 'to affirm and emphasize the importance and distinctive nature of voluntary activity'. It also stresses that
the main weight of activity is through indirect services characterised as
inter-organisational work and community work and, as does NCSS, it
encourages newly developed organisations to become independent

voluntary organisations. In looking to the future the Scottish Council particularly stressed to us three points:

(i) That there is a persistent human need to give oneself in service to others though this has been in danger of submersion in the floodtide of the statutory and professional service provision. The word altruism needs rehabilitation and new ways for the expression of this human need to give of oneself in service will have to be found.

(ii) That voluntary activity should become increasingly concerned not only with the quantity of services provided by the state but also with the affecting of statutory policies in a positive way. Consequently voluntary organisations will need to think more and more in terms of public social policies and how the voluntary agencies can contribute to those policies by expressing views and demonstrating by their own activities possible alternative methods.

(iii) That voluntary organisations themselves must learn the necessity of proving their own case, to realise that their freedom and independence should be accompanied by a responsible attitude towards accountability and that they must constantly review their own position about what they are doing.

In exercising the function of representation the Scottish Council of Social Service does not seek to represent the views of the voluntary sector as a whole but follows a policy of enabling the views of those interested in specific issues (e.g. the disabled, the homeless, urban aid) to be expressed. This is done, for example, by promoting the formation of *ad hoc* working parties rather than by the creation of standing conferences. The very considerable changes in the local government pattern in Scotland have shown how SCSS fulfils the roles of information giving and development, for example in the setting up of the voluntary organisations regional advisory group referred to in Chapter 6. They had two main problems, that of single service bodies relating to a new level of authority and that of arrangements for different organisations to co-operate with one another at regional level. The Scottish Council has also done a great deal of work in explaining to its member organisations about the new community councils, has given progress reports on their establishment and has helped to advise local councils of social service on how to relate to these new bodies.

The future of the government's proposals for devolution is still uncertain as we write. If there is to be an elected Scottish Assembly with functions similar to those proposed in the Scotland and Wales Bill 1976-7, which included devolution of responsibility for education, the arts, recreation, health, social welfare (other than social security), the environment and the countryside, housing, local government and charities, the voluntary sector will have a new situation to deal with. SCSS will then have a stronger part to play in the formulation of policies which have a significance for the whole of the United Kingdom and to which we have already referred in our consideration of NCSS. In one sense devolution has been anticipated in that a number of organisations which were on an all United Kingdom basis with headquarters in London have now split themselves so that there is either a separate independent organisation of the same character in Scotland or at least an almost independent branch. We refer to this point again in Chapter 11 on future trends. We note here that there is a major role for the Scottish Council in promoting the new relationships which will inevitably develop between the voluntary and statutory sectors.

The Scottish Council of Social Service is financed about 81 per cent by the government, about 3 per cent from subscriptions and charges for services and the remaining 16 per cent comes from voluntary sources of one sort or another. Funding is always a difficulty for an intermediary body which does not provide direct services and even though statutory funding provides such a high proportion of the total expenditure, the problem still remains.

The Council of Social Service for Wales

The Council of Social Service for Wales (CSSW), whose representatives we met for a general discussion, was established in its present form in 1946 and exists to bring together voluntary organisations in free association. They explained that CSSW serves to pioneer, develop and strengthen work throughout Wales in social welfare, health, education and community development, in consultation with central and local government and in cooperation with other agencies. Its general aim therefore is much the same as that of the National Council of Social Service. Like the NCSS it would like in future to provide a general resource agency and to deal with questions of research, intelligence and information and training for voluntary organisations across-the-board in Wales and to represent the views and opinions of voluntary organisations. After a review of the CSSW's work initiated by the Welsh Office there have been many changes implemented since 1 April 1977. The principal departments of CSSW initiated and funded by it since their inception have become independent, with their own constitutions, committees and staff members of CSSW seconded to them now employed by the new bodies. These are: Age Concern Wales, Wales Council for the Disabled and the Council for Wales of Voluntary Youth Services. By mutual agreement these organisations will remain physically within the new premises of CSSW at Caerphilly, and will pay for rentals and common services on an agreed basis.

The independence of these organisations has led to a marked reduction in the staff of CSSW, which will now work to a completely new and more flexible policy. It will continue as a general resource agency dealing with research, intelligence, information and training but will concentrate upon aspects of coordination of voluntary groups, especially those that have been severely hit in areas of high unemployment, redundancy and social deprivation. CSSW is already engaged in schemes dealing with certain sections of young unemployed. It has also received the approval of a wide cross-section of voluntary agencies to act as a clearing house for the forwarding of applications to the EEC for grants from Regional and Social Funds. Upon the fulfilment of its function of setting in motion committees for specific purposes, CSSW is now turning its attention to fresh problems, concentrating on the more economically deprived part of the Principality and on work outside the range of the statutory agencies.

CSSW's representatives told us of the great difficulties caused by the very extensive reorganisation of local government in Wales in that many of the new authorities did not continue grants which had been made for many years by their predecessors. They mentioned a particular difficulty in Wales that there were few financial resources available to voluntary organisations apart from central and local government: such industry as was Welsh-based did not have the same tradition of giving to the voluntary movement as was the case in parts of England, and there were few Welsh Trusts. Further, bodies such as theirs which sought to be primarily information and resource centres had little popular appeal particularly as they did not feel it right to compete against local voluntary councils for aid from local government. They were therefore in a position in which they must be very much dependent on statutory aid; and they drew attention to staff redundancies caused by financial reasons. They told us that: 'the money anticipated from local authorities which had formed the basis of roughly 25 to 30% of the Council's income over a period of 40 years, was dramatically reduced during the year following the reorganisation of local government in

Wales', and added: 'the severe economic climate that existed throughout
the year made it impossible to obtain money from voluntary sources to
bridge this serious financial gap.'

The future of the movement towards devolution in Wales is
uncertain as we write, but if a Welsh Assembly is set up, it seems likely
to be followed by an increasing need for independent Welsh organisations as opposed to Welsh branches of London-based United Kingdom
organisations. In this respect voluntary organisations in Wales are not so
far forward as in Scotland. There may also be an increase in the number
of Welsh speaking organisations such as Urdd and Merched Y Wawr. If
these developments do take place then there will be an increasing role
for some central body representing the across-the-board interests of
voluntary organisations in Wales to give a lead in giving advice and
information.

The Northern Ireland Council of Social Service

We received evidence from the Northern Ireland Council of Social
Service (NICSS) and subsequently met representatives for a discussion
in Belfast. In addition we recognise the considerable assistance we
obtained from NICSS who collected evidence for us from about fifty
Northern Ireland organisations, a few of whom we subsequently saw.
The general purpose of NICSS, which was formed in 1938, is the
development of social services in Northern Ireland and it seeks progress
in a number of fields of which the first (in their own words) is 'to make
contact with existing provincial and local social services with a view to
effective coordination and development'. There is also reference to pro-
secuting research and encouraging the formation of social service and
community organisations. The evidence to us stressed that since 1938,
though goals and objectives remain the same, there is now a greater
emphasis on community development. The Council points however to
two difficulties: the fact that the Roman Catholic minority has tended
in the past not to involve itself in the institutions of the Province, including the work of NICSS, though this attitude is changing, and that
some of the new locality based groups of both communities have some
suspicion of the NICSS as being, as they see it, a middle-class body. In
speaking to us NICSS representatives explained that they had had to
work very hard to try to become regarded as an impartial body which
brought in all forms of organisation and that this was a continuing
difficulty. It was necessary to have personal contact and this required
great patience and was in the main the job of some of their younger
members of staff. Another method of approach was the organisation of

meetings and conferences concerned with particular problems, a fairly recent one being that of the teenage alcoholism.

NICSS both in their written evidence to us and in discussion stressed the importance of their role as a central resource agency, particularly since the former Northern Ireland Community Relations Commission had been disbanded. They said that through the medium of their publication called *Scope* and through the visits of their staff members and their informatory leaflets they try to fulfil the great need for information on the part of many, particularly the smaller, organisations. They explained that local government reorganisation had posed a problem: that ideally one would expect to find a Council of Social Service for each of the twenty-six districts (and this might perhaps be thought necessary as district councils have been given, as we have seen earlier, a measure of responsibility towards community development) but that this is not the position so far. Indeed the question of relationships between the district councils and the local councils of social or voluntary service is not yet clear as we write, due in part to the recent considerable changes in the district councils' duties and powers. NICSS in the year ended 31 March 1976 obtained rather over three fifths of its income from the Northern Ireland Government but this still left a large sum to be found from other sources and this is always a difficulty for an organisation whose prime role is administration and the provision of services.

Some Reflections and Conclusions

We have discussed in some detail the organisation and methods of operation of the National Council of Social Service and the other national councils of social service because we feel that their central position and 'establishment' image can lead to misunderstanding and ignorance of their role. We do not feel it necessary to go into the same sort of detail about the specialist independent national intermediary bodies. This is not only because they cover such an enormous field and differ so very greatly from each other (a fact which is shown even from the few examples quoted earlier in the chapter though the range is much wider than the study of these examples alone might suggest) but because more importantly their existence is generally accepted from the very nature of their functions and because of tradition. The voluntary sector is expected to concern itself with people suffering from physical handicap so that the existence of those bodies which seek to coordinate organisations working for the handicapped, e.g. RNIB and RNID, is usually accepted without question. The voluntary organisations which provide the service wish the intermediary body to exist; and it is a convenience to the statutory side to have some body of this nature to which it can turn for advice and help. There may be criticisms of the ways in which some of these specialist intermediary bodies work; and it was sometimes suggested to us that more should be done to devolve power to the sufferers of a particular handicap rather than their being in the position of beneficiaries. There are also those who raise objections to any form of intermediary body at all on the grounds that any effort taken away from service provision is wasted. On the whole however intermediary bodies which deal with a limited field command general acceptance and do not have quite such great difficulties over funding as some of the others.

We are naturally conscious in this part of our work as elsewhere of the difficulty of trying to make classifications. Many of what we have called the specialist intermediary bodies can be put into that classification without further qualification but there are some, such as the Central Council for the Disabled and Age Concern to quote two examples, whose terms of reference are rather broad and who therefore take on something of the character of what we have called the generalist intermediary bodies. They may therefore have greater difficulty in justifying their existence and consequently in raising money, and they may be more dependent upon public funds than their more specialist fellows. There is little to be gained by our attempting to set out long and detailed arguments on the relative merits of generalist, specialist and semi-specialist intermediary bodies. It would be a waste of time to justify the need for the specialist bodies, as that is not seriously questioned. What seems to us to be important is to say something about whether there is a need for the generalist bodies as well and we deal with this below.

We have thought a great deal about the evidence given to us by the national councils of social service and we have compared what they said with the functions which we identified earlier in this chapter for national intermediary bodies. The role of representation is essential in our view. As legislation becomes more difficult and complicated, so it becomes more necessary to have a body able to speak about it on behalf of the voluntary sector, though we recognise that there will not normally be a common view on all major points. If there were no such bodies as the national councils of social service we believe the government would wish to encourage the creation of organisations on these lines. But the complaint that the government does not always consult the national councils in advance on all important subjects which may affect the voluntary sector does raise difficulties. Voluntary organisations cover an enormous range of subjects which touch on almost every aspect of our national life. The general responsibility of a democratically elected government is to the electorate as a whole and there must be times when a government has to take action without consultation, though there can be very close consultation in the implementation of their policies. Specific issues, for example fuel debts and minibuses, are a different matter and there is a very strong case for the voluntary sector to take the initiative and the national councils of social service are the best placed of all organisations to do so. Part of the reason for their existence is their success in this type of cause and the more they succeed the more likely they are to be consulted. In short the right to be consulted has to be earned.

We believe that quite apart from the representative role of all national councils of social service in their own areas, a strong case also exists for the work of NCSS in its representative capacity on behalf of the whole of the voluntary sector in the international sphere. By agreement it represents the other national councils of social service as well. No doubt it consults with them and disseminates information to them and this process will be developed in the light of devolution. There is also a clear need for all the national councils to provide, as they now do, an information and support service for voluntary organisations generally. Although, as we saw in Chapter 4, VSU has a role in giving advice to voluntary organisations on their best points of contact in government departments and of encouraging cooperation between organisations wherever possible, we do not believe that this undermines the need for independent bodies performing similar functions nor do we think that there is any real danger of duplication of roles. VSU is not large enough to act as a general coordinator for the voluntary sector, nor has it any desire to do so. We see the roles of VSU and the national councils of social service as complementary, not competitive.

We need hardly stress further the importance of the development role which is a feature of the work of the Scottish Council of Social Service in particular. The NCSS's Annual Report for 1975/76 contained a summary of a management review carried out within the NCSS in the summer of 1975. One of the recommendations of the review was that the National Organisations Division should move towards a greater emphasis on the initiation of new work. We believe that NCSS may well wish to place a greater weight upon this function in the future, both in studying the question of whether to set up new organisations to meet new needs, or bodies to attack common problems which cross the boundaries of existing organisations, and perhaps in pressing even more strongly the avoidance of wasteful duplication. In saying this we recognise that this is a difficult area because the voluntary sector is free and changes can only come from persuasion. None the less the point is particularly important at a time of financial stringency and no doubt it is something to which the government will in future give increasing attention when deciding on levels of grant-aiding.

We have stressed the important role which we think the intermediary bodies of all sorts can perform and we have also explained that we are not in favour of any rigid pattern being imposed all over the country, but that the type of organisation needed should depend upon the functions which must first be identified. The local intermediary bodies of various sorts will all need access to a central organisation for the provision of information, facilities for meeting and so forth. It seems to us that the national councils of social service in each country are the obvious bodies to provide such services.

We also suggest that there should be some central funding for intermediary bodies in urban areas on the lines of that provided for RCCs in England by the Development Commission. We examine this matter in detail in Chapter 10. For our present purposes it does not matter whether there is to be a single funding agency covering all local intermediary bodies or separate ones for town and country. This agency (or these agencies) in order to operate efficiently will need to work in close connection with the national councils which have the experience and knowledge. This point is important for practical reasons, and also because it is in our view necessary in the interests of the well-being of the voluntary sector for advice to any funding agency to come from the voluntary side.

We were struck by the extent to which the NCSS provided the secretariat and administrative services to its constituent bodies.[3] We recognise that the provision of such services may well be an important step in helping new organisations to find their feet but we question the need for support of this kind to be continued for more than a very short initial period. The NCSS representatives themselves informed us in one of our talks that the criteria for granting independence to constituent bodies are whether independence would be to the ultimate good of the voluntary movement, of NCSS itself and of the organisation concerned, and whether the organisation has the resources and leadership to act independently. There are practical problems here, but we feel there may be some confusion of thought between independence and physical separation. As the recent experience of the Council of Social Service for

Wales has shown, independence does not necessarily involve physical separation and there is no reason why organisations should not employ their own administrative staff and determine their own policies while possibly continuing to occupy offices on NCSS premises and sharing some of the NCSS common services on an agreed financial basis.

The arguments against separation for most of the bodies currently receiving direct services from the NCSS, such as the Women's Forum, the Standing Conferences of Amateur Music and Local History, and the National Drama Conference, would probably be mainly practical, e.g. that their size or the infrequency of their meetings fail to justify a separate establishment which would inevitably require extra resources. In the case of the Standing Conferences of RCCs and CVSs, however, NCSS representatives have argued that their retention within the Community Work Division is necessary to enable the NCSS to keep in touch with 'grass-roots' feeling, particularly bodies which are geared to the needs of the whole community rather than to a specialised interest. They told us that they would miss the mutual support and fellowship of these organisations with their wide coverage of town and country and that to give them independence would be to exchange the unifying influence of NCSS support and combined national coverage for weak but separate voices. We understand but do not support this view. We consider that if a number of local intermediary bodies wish to combine together in a Standing Conference or any other central organisation they have every right to do so. This central organisation would need a small staff and might deserve some government funding. But it does not seem to us to follow that the central organisation must be part of the NCSS in order to keep the latter in touch with the 'grass-roots'. NCSS in our view should maintain its contact with the general community as it now does through the wide knowledge of its officers, which in turn comes from frequent and regular meetings with representatives of voluntary organisations throughout the country and at centrally convened conferences.

We also have a more specific reason for suggesting that there might be advantage in separating the Standing Conferences of RCCs and CVSs from the NCSS. We have suggested that the NCSS has an important role to play in servicing local intermediary bodies. We hope that this role will become stronger and will cover a greater variety of bodies, especially if different kinds of intermediaries are funded by central government. But if the NCSS, presumably through the Community Work Division, is to provide a central service for all local intermediary bodies, it seems to us that there could be some conflict if it simultaneously has a special relationship with particular groups of intermediary bodies such as the Standing Conferences of RCCs and CVSs. This can be illustrated by reference to CVSs. As Appendix 5 shows some are members of the Standing Conference of CVSs and some are not. The Standing Conference has recently been seeking to establish tighter conditions for affiliation to it and under the present relationship it would be natural for it to expect the Community Work Division to give priority to member organisations. This would be incompatible with the more general role we envisage for the NCSS. We therefore think that there is a case, which we hope that the interested parties will examine carefully, for the two Standing Conferences to be separated from the NCSS.

We have paid particular attention to the question of separation of the Standing Conferences of RCCs and CVSs because it raises issues different from those raised by separation of the other constituent bodies of the NCSS. But the crux of the matter is that the NCSS seems to us to have too wide a field to cover. If it could free itself of responsibility for direct servicing of constituent bodies, its staff would be more able to concentrate on the roles which we have suggested as most important, and they would be relieved from any possible embarrassment, which could arise from having to serve two masters. The separated bodies would have to make their own cases for funding from both statutory and voluntary sources. The NCSS, more clearly defined as it became less of a direct servicing agency, might well find its own ability to raise funds, particularly from statutory sources, increased.

We believe that the functions of liaison, representation and development are of great importance for all four national councils but that they should not be involved in the maintenance of other bodies except in the initial pioneer stages. We would stress that the difficulty lies not in accepting the principle of what is said but in having the determination to put it into practice.

Both in Scotland and in Wales the great changes in local government reorganisation have given added force to the need to have independent intermediary bodies concerned with the interests of the voluntary sector as a whole. The situation is not the same in the two countries, as evidence submitted to us shows, but there is a plain need in both for some organisation which is prepared both to exercise the representation and development functions in relation to the statutory side and to give a great deal of help to voluntary organisations in preparing themselves for changes. The probable advent of devolution and the creation of new Assemblies with their elected members would also introduce new problems of adjustment for the voluntary and the statutory sectors; and the national councils would, we hope, take the lead in bringing them together. It would be a different aspect of the role of development. With the advent of devolution, it would also be necessary for all the national councils of social service to look again at the present arrangements by which, at an international level, the International Committee of the NCSS may speak for the interests of the voluntary sector in the United Kingdom. Issues could well arise on which the four national councils of social service might each wish to express their own views. In Northern Ireland there is a need for assistance to voluntary organisations, particularly as the elected Provincial government is at present not in existence, so that in effect organisations have to adjust in the opposite direction from their counterparts in Scotland and Wales. There is also a great need to provide services of the information type which can be of assistance to the many resource centres being developed for the small community groups.

To sum up, we are convinced that there is a strong case for the generalist independent national intermediary bodies in each of the four main parts of the United Kingdom and that their role in the future is likely to be more important than ever. If they are to concentrate on the types of functions we have suggested it follows that a substantial amount of their income must come from government funds. In our view it is not a high price for the services they engender from the voluntary sector.

Notes

1. Now amalgamated with the British Council for the Rehabilitation of the Disabled and known as the Royal Association for Disability and Rehabilitation.
2. See note 1.
3. See list in Appendix 5B.

8 INDEPENDENCE, RESPONSIBILITY AND EFFECTIVENESS

The general subject of 'independence, responsibility and effectiveness' was often raised in our oral evidence sessions and in discussion among ourselves. There are many issues involved: the effect of grant-aiding upon the independence of voluntary organisations; financial probity and account keeping; whether or not there is any responsibility on the part of a voluntary organisation to the public and its supporters for the type of service it provides; and whether effectiveness should be and can be measured or assessed in any way. A minor difficulty is that in discussing this subject people attribute different meanings to the words they use. To avoid confusion we shall use the word 'accountability' strictly in the financial sense, as in auditing accounts; and we speak of 'responsibility' when we are referring to the wider matter of any duty which an organisation may or may not owe to its supporters, clients and the general public.

We start by setting out some propositions each of which would probably be acceptable to most people if taken individually:

(i) It is the essence of a voluntary organisation that it should be independent of control by the statutory side or other agencies.

(ii) There is a general duty on any person or organisation responsible for the spending of other people's money to account openly for the way in which it is being spent.

(iii) There is at least a moral responsibility to see that services provided for others are of reasonable standards.

When one considers these propositions together, however, it is clear that if one tried to apply them simultaneously there could be some tension in practice. It is one of the purposes of this chapter to discuss whether or not the existence of this tension is a problem to be resolved or something which is creative. We look first at the question of accountability in our sense of the term, then at some aspects of independence, and finally at the wider question of responsibility and effectiveness.

Accountability

The work of a voluntary organisation can be sustained by the service of

146

committed individuals, by money or aid in kind from one or more
sources, or by a combination of such personal and financial resources.
Sources of income can be classified as follows:

(a)   The general public by subscriptions, gifts and legacies.
(b)   Central and local government, whether by grant or by pay-
       ments for services rendered to those authorities. We do not
       here distinguish between money paid directly from central or
       local government and that paid through some kind of interme-
       diary body. We do not in this context regard as income assist-
       ance in kind, whether from rate relief, free premises or any
       other means.
(c)   The tax reliefs received from the Inland Revenue.
(d)   Corporate bodies, whether endowed foundations or trusts or
       companies incorporated for industrial and commercial
       purposes.
(e)   The exertions of the organisation itself through revenue from
       publications, fees or other sales which either may directly con-
       tribute to the purposes of the organisation or may be an
       independent money raising venture.

These different sources of income are not in practice all accounted
for in the same way:

(i)   Central government funds come under the strict principles and
       rules for the provision and expenditure of public money refer-
       red to in Chapter 4. There must be parliamentary approval of
       departments' estimates year by year and there are also well-
       known checks on the expenditure of public money. Roughly
       the same principles apply at local government level in that all
       expenditure is subject to public audit. An organisation which is
       in receipt of statutory money is therefore under a strict obliga-
       tion to account for it annually, usually in a prescribed form;
       and there may be other forms of control which we discuss later
       in this chapter.
(ii)   Trustees of foundations and directors of companies are in
       general less strict in their financial controls in the sense of
       approving items of expenditure in advance but they normally
       require to see accounts.
(iii) Income received by way of tax rebate from the Inland Revenue
       is in a sense public money but is not subject to the same finan-

cial control as are funds provided directly from central or local government. The Revenue must be satisfied that the tax was paid by the original donors and that the rebate is correctly claimed, but they are not normally concerned with how the tax rebate is then spent provided it is for charitable purposes.

(iv)   Income from sales of goods or services is relatively free from any form of financial control other than in the annual accounts as is the case of income from gifts and subscriptions and from investments. Legacy income can be a little different as there may be particular conditions imposed by the testator and these must be obeyed.

Although there are various ways in which the different sources of income are accounted for, they do not make much difference to the 'accountability' position of a voluntary organisation in the narrow sense in which we have taken it. Central and local government, trusts and companies if they are donors must see accounts. Though there would appear to be less strict requirements on the other sources of income, most voluntary organisations in any case, either because of their own constitution, their registration with the Charity Commissioners, or to meet the requirements of the Companies Acts will publish audited accounts. Chapter 8 of the Goodman Report discusses the administration and surveillance of charities and considers the various controls which apply or should apply to fund raising and also the wider question of accountability of charities. The conclusions reached by the Goodman Committee on recording and auditing procedures and on the presentation of relevant information to the public seem to us to apply to voluntary organisations generally. There may be different degrees of control which are exercised in accordance with the source of income but some form of financial accountability is attached to all of them. Some of the smaller organisations may need advice and help on how to keep and present accounts and this is the sort of service which a local intermediary body can provide as we have shown in Chapter 6. But on the whole 'accountability' does not in our view normally lead to serious problems.

Independence

Difficulties, however, start when the fund provider seeks to go beyond merely seeing that the money has been honestly spent. In a general sense anyone accepting money from anyone else is under an obligation to them and 'he who pays the piper calles the tune'. But can he also determine what the piper is to wear, the tempo of his playing, how hard he works his assistant, and so on? The statutory side is probably regarded as most likely to try to exercise control through funding, and the question came up a number of times in our discussions with organisations. We encountered very different attitudes in this matter. At one end of the scale there are organisations which take the view that any form of central or local government subsidy is unacceptable because of its effect on independence, for example the Royal National Lifeboat Institution and some of the newer organisations with a critical role. At the other end there are organisations which can only work with a very high percentage of central or local government funding, e.g. WRVS and Family Service Units. In these cases the framework in which the organisation, national or local, is to operate is agreed in advance and within it there is usually a considerable degree of independence. Organisations which are paid fees or act as agents to provide services for the statutory side are between the two extremes and they usually operate within a previously agreed framework, but are subject to inspection (e.g. residential homes).

Obviously the proportion of the statutory contribution to the organisation's total income is a most important factor. As the government evidence in Chapter 4 shows, if the grant represents only a small percentage of the income of the organisation, the only conditions of grant may well be that some form of annual report and audited accounts should be submitted to the government department and any grant unspent at the end of the year should be returned. But if the grant represents over 50 per cent of an organisation's income, as far as the government is concerned it is regarded as a controlled fringe body and becomes subject to government approval for levels of pay proposed and conditions under which the staff are employed. Local authorities naturally vary a great deal but the same degree of wider control is often encountered when they are providing a large proportion of a voluntary organisation's income, and this for excellent motives. They are democratically elected bodies and they urge that they cannot support with the ratepayers' money an organisation which does not treat its staff properly; they cannot subsidise 'sweated labour'.

The degree to which control is exercised by other sorts of donors varies but it is generally lighter. Trustees of foundations do not, however, exhaust their statutory and personal responsibilities for the funds they administer when they receive a receipt for a contribution to a body whose work falls within their terms of reference. Indeed, they may not delegate their powers, but remain responsible for ensuring that the funds they have passed on are used directly for the intended purposes and that the gift is an effective means of achieving the objects of the trust. But these responsibilities, though important, relate more to seeing that the legal requirements of the funding trusts are observed and do not normally extend to a concern about such matters as salaries and conditions of employees. Directors of public companies have a direct responsibility to their shareholders for the spending of their companies' moneys and a general responsibility to their work people. They have to see that aid to voluntary organisations is given in accordance with agreed company policy, but in general their freedom in choosing the causes to support and the amounts to be given is greater than in the case of trusts. With the other sorts of donor no question of control usually arises, though it could perhaps be argued that some stricter control might be exercised on behalf of the Inland Revenue for money received in the form of tax reliefs since it is in a sense public money.

Seen from the point of view of central or local government, the controls which may cover conditions of service, including salary scales, hours of work, holiday periods and many other details, may be regarded as benevolent supervision and an exercise of constitutional authority by a democratically elected body. It may still, however, seem like undesirable interference to the recipient. Trusts in forming their policies can, as we have seen, act indirectly as a form of control. It is these considerations no doubt which lead so many voluntary organisations to yearn for some private endowment or other wholly independent source of revenue. Indeed we have been told several times in the course of our discussions with organisations how important it is not to be too much in the hands of any one outside agency, particularly on the statutory side, for one's income. In its essence the argument is the same as that advanced by the owners and workers of a small factory seeking to avoid becoming too heavily committed to any one wholesaler in selling their products. We can understand these fears and indeed we would suppose that the government itself and most local authorities would fully understand and respect them, because they come from the same source from which the voluntary sector derives its inspiration. Certainly there may be unimaginative local authorities which do not understand the purposes or motives of all the voluntary organisations which they support and do not realise that to try to exercise too much control may endanger their freedom and so harm their effectiveness. There may be some who do not actively try to foster good relationships which will at any rate ease the problem. But the responsibility does not lie solely with local authorities. The voluntary sector itself does not always understand that it must go further than mere accountability, and accept that the funder too has rights and duties to his own constituents. The voluntary sector must be able to demonstrate its general responsibility and effectiveness.

There is however a more subtle way in which the payer may have a strong influence on the piper. Many persons in the voluntary sector acquire great skill in the matter of seeking grants and learn to know how government departments, local authorities, trusts and foundations organise their business and the sort of work and projects which they are likely to support. It is a fairly small step from that knowledge to the adaptation of one's work to meet the possibilities of obtaining money. This is not necessarily harmful either to the organisation or to the public, and it could be regarded as a desirable method of general control which does not have the effect of detailed interference. But there is another side to it. It was well expressed to us in a memorandum we received from the Howard League for Penal Reform. They said:

> a charity which runs homes or hostels, for example, may feel pressed into seeking publicity which is distasteful to the residents in them. Secondly, charities often advocate reforms of various kinds. Some of these are helped by publicity; others, especially where sensitive factors such as staff attitudes have to be taken into account, might be better dealt with by quiet diplomacy or informal and unpublicised exchanges of view, rather than by press statements and public conferences. But an organisation which is struggling for survival is strongly tempted to choose methods which will show the world how active it is, in the hope of attracting more members.

It is matter of degree, and on the whole we feel that an organisation which has an excellent cause to put forward is not likely to be diverted from its course because of the difficulty of obtaining funds. We feel therefore that any tension which may arise between the potential donor's policy and the organisation's proposed activity is likely to be constructive rather than a serious problem.

It may be convenient to mention here that a problem of control and independence could arise in the future over the unionisation of voluntary organisations. It is not far advanced at the moment but some trends can be identified. The headquarters staff of national bodies like the National Council of Social Service and the National Consumer Council have been joining mainly the Association of Scientific, Technical and Managerial Staff (ASTMS), though some staffs have been joining the Transport and General Workers' Union (TGWU). Among community workers and the staff of small specialist agencies, many employees have joined the TGWU through the medium of its Association of Clerical, Technical and Supervisory Staffs (ACTSS): in other places the National Union of Public Employees (NUPE) is the main union. In the health field, NUPE is the most active union. In our discussions with MIND they said that a number of staff had joined ACTSS, and that they were in favour of it, thinking it would be helpful to staff. They also pointed out that there could be difficulties in practice if unions tried to be associated in policy-making and to go beyond questions of wages and conditions of service; though policy decisions could have an effect on both. It may be that in the past some voluntary organisations have not been good employers. We need hardly stress the importance of their consulting with their staff on salaries and conditions of service, and also involving them as much as possible in policy-making. If unionisation serves to prevent voluntary organisations' staff being paid less than the 'going rate' and encourages grant giving bodies to fund at adequate levels, the effects will be positive and helpful. Unionisation in the voluntary organisations has not, in our view, yet gone far enough for anyone to draw any firm conclusions. But in general terms we can see that there could be tension between a voluntary organisation and a union in very much the same way as can now exist between an organisation and a funding local authority or central department.

Responsibility and Effectiveness

Effectiveness is another word used in a number of different senses. One may consider whether a voluntary organisation is doing the right job, whether it has kept up to date, or whether it is providing a service which may no longer be so greatly needed as when the organisation was founded. Accepting that the client's right to choose is important, are steps being taken to avoid wasteful duplication? Is the service efficiently provided from the point of view of the organisation and is it cost-effective, particularly as compared with the statutory side? Are attempts made to monitor the work and to see whether the receivers of the service and the subscribers to the organisation are reasonably satisfied with what is being done? All these questions came up frequently in the written evidence and in our discussions with organisations and others. We can only give a general summary here.

We found many examples of organisations which took great trouble to keep themselves up to date and to meet public demand. Both Barnardo's and the Church of England Children's Society have after detailed enquiries decided to change the emphasis of their work from residential care to day care and other preventive work for children in need, in tune with modern demands. Age Concern told us of the changed emphasis of their work from the coordination side more to that of asserting and claiming rights. The Royal National Lifeboat Institution pointed to the setting up of the inshore lifeboats to meet the very considerable expansion of boat sailing as a sport. The Board for Social Responsibility of the Church of England wrote to us about the move away from the specialised service for the unmarried mother to a service concerned more with general pioneering and gap filling in the field of the personal social services. There are many other examples, but these are sufficient to show that many voluntary organisations realise the need to re-examine their methods from time to time and are prepared to modify themselves accordingly. We do not need to underline the importance of this practice.

Avoidance of unnecessary duplication is a much more difficult problem. If freedom is of the essence in the voluntary sector it could be argued that any organisation can be established to do what it likes and by any method it chooses, irrespective of what other people are doing. This freedom can often be a positive advantage in that it may provide choice for those to whom the service, of whatever type, is being offered. But there is also a continuing need to avoid wasting human and material resources. This question is the same on a smaller scale as that which is discussed in the whole of this chapter, that is how far can one reconcile the independence of the voluntary sector with its responsibility to the community. This again is a subject which often came up in our evidence and it is clear that it is very much in the minds of many organisations. The National Council for One Parent Families, for example, spoke of the seriousness of wasteful duplication in the present economic crisis and mentioned steps they were taking to work more closely with Gingerbread. The Scottish Standing Conference of Voluntary Youth Organisations stressed that one of the main lines of operation is to encourage the conservation of resources and to avoid overlapping in the work of voluntary youth organisations. Some organisations, however, fear that avoiding duplication means merger and several, the Cyrenians being one example, have stressed the theme that 'small is beautiful'. The Chase Charity in their evidence to us pointed out that it was seldom that the aims and methods of one voluntary organisation exactly duplicated those of another and continued

> but there are many instances of complementary aims which could be slotted into one administrative set up where several now exist. This involves waste of money and time whether paid for or voluntary.

It means competition for funds, statutory or charitable, and, often, two or more inadequate administrations and inadequate budgets. Too often there is no attempt to coordinate effort; indeed, not infrequently, there is hostility between rival organisations which espouse the same cause.

Anyone who reads the newspapers will see examples of this type of thing in advertisements which appeal for funds for organisations of almost exactly the same title and between which it is almost impossible for the ordinary subscriber to distinguish. In the nature of things there can be no short answer to this problem. But there is a clear need for the voluntary sector itself to keep a close eye on the possibility of wasteful duplication and it is very much a matter in which the intermediary bodies, both national and local, should take the initiative and give a lead.

Effectiveness in the sense of how well the job is done is very hard to measure. As the Society of Local Authority Chief Executives said to us

> there are great limitations in evaluating the cost effectiveness of human service, and sophisticated techniques of measuring cost effectiveness can be so complicated that the system becomes more important than the objective. There is a challenge in society to show efficiency and not to waste money. But even within local government itself, where there is direct contact and direct opportunity of cost effectiveness control, very little is being done or is likely to be done in a short span of time. It is obviously much more difficult in the voluntary areas. The obvious things such as examining balance sheets are done, but how does one evaluate the contribution of care of the aged, the battered wife, the one parent family, etc. Certainly one could try to be systematic in assessing voluntary organisations and many authorities do this by producing a check list of the questions that ought to be asked before giving or renewing a grant.

We think that this states the difficulty very clearly. Yet one should not go to the other extreme and assume that nothing at all can be done. We know that there is increasing realisation of the importance of monitoring both projects and the work of voluntary organisations. We give some examples of how this can be done later in this chapter.

One method of assessing effectiveness is to compare costs. David Ennals, Secretary of State for Health and Social Security, recently stated: 'This whole field is one in which local authorities should make the fullest possible use of voluntary bodies; pound for pound they are a better buy' (*Municipal Review*, August 1976). Where voluntary organisations are making substantial use of volunteers this is certainly true. Thus a Meals on Wheels service operated by the WRVS will cost less than one operated by local authority employees; and a great many services provided by voluntary organisations do have this advantage.

It is more difficult to tell whether voluntary organisations are more cost-effective than local authorities where both are relying predominantly on paid staff. In order to examine whether there were any differences, we initiated some studies of situations where voluntary organisations and local authorities were providing comparable services. One of these dealt with housing. Serge Lourie was commissioned to appraise the evidence on the relative costs of housing associations and local authorities. In general the differences that emerged were small. In the case of new building both local authorities and registered housing associations have to conform to Parker Morris standards, and this makes costs very similar. In rehabilitation work there is evidence that housing associations tended to be quicker, partly because they operate on a smaller scale. Management and maintenance costs were similar, with the exception of the London area where local authority, but not housing association, costs are exceptionally high. In addition the research staff of the committee made comparisons of the running costs of hostels for single homeless people in London and of children's homes. Of the sample chosen, six local authority hostels were about one fifth more expensive than the two religious-orientated ones studied. A small part of the difference was due to higher administrative overheads, but most of it could be attributed to the higher wages and salaries paid by the local authority hostels. It should be added that the local authority staff were faced with more social problems and more difficult physical conditions.

The children's homes presented a more complex picture in terms of costs. We examined three local authorities' homes and those of three large voluntary organisations. The main finding was the wide variation between the homes run by the same agency. However, when the averages were calculated, one of the voluntary agencies did emerge with distinctly lower costs than the other five. This was attributable mainly to lower expenditure on staff. Research into how far differences in costs are related to the nature of the care and the facilities provided has yet to be completed. To generalise, in the light of the evidence we have about services relying on paid staff, it seems clear that voluntary organisations are certainly not less cost-effective than statutory ones, and on one or two points they may have some advantage over statutory services. Perhaps the most basic question is whether voluntary organisations may have any intrinsic characteristics which enable them to be more cost-effective. Apart from their ability to mobilise more volunary help, it might be suggested, for example, that they operate on a smaller scale with greater flexibility and have smaller overheads, that the staff are more committed and thus work harder or accept lower salaries, and so on. We did find a little evidence of such tendencies, but only a little. We also found a tendency, exemplified particularly by the housing associations, for the voluntary sector, once well established in a given field, to adopt the same standards and formulae as the statutory authorities, with a consequent evening-up of costs.

Another way of measuring the effectiveness of a service is to see how far the recipients are satisfied with it. We have the impression that the question of client satisfaction is not always considered sufficiently seriously by either the statutory or the voluntary sectors and that there may be too much attention given to satisfying the requirements of gifts and grant makers and too little to the views of the beneficiaries. We recognise that this is a most difficult area and with some groups, notably small children and the mentally handicapped, one can hardly proceed by the ordinary methods of surveys though one can obtain help in many cases from parents and relatives. Again we have been struck when speaking to the representatives of national organisations which have local branches by the degree of importance that they attach to the independence of these branches. Usually less emphasis is placed upon the need to see, by some means or other, that local branches provide for their clients the sort of service which the latter are led to expect from an organisation operating under a well-known national name. Some organisations do carry out their own internal system of inspection and withhold the right to operate under their name from any local branch which does not meet their standards. Others rely more on persuasion, using development officers, or staff having a similar title, with the ultimate sanction of removing recognition from a local branch which will not conform. There are those, however, who take the view that nothing whatever can be done in this sensitive matter. We give below some examples that have come our way of how internal discipline, external surveillance and the informed criticism of beneficiaries can together enhance both the quality and the economy of the service.

An allied question is client participation since, if clients are involved, then satisfaction or dissatisfaction with what they receive is more easily discovered. The National Federation of the Blind of the United Kingdom in speaking to us emphasised the importance of consumer participation and, in their own field, of increasing the proportion of blind people on the RNIB's Council, though they recognised the improvement on the position of some years ago. The point can be clearly demonstrated by making the contrast between organisations for the handicapped and organisations of the handicapped. Mutual aid organisations demonstrate the principle of client participation and we were greatly struck by the work and growth of the pre-school playgroups throughout the United Kingdom. The Pre-school Playgroups Association referred to the young mother suddenly finding 'that she now has a role to play herself. As a result her confidence increases firstly in handling her own child and secondly in relation to other adults.' They continued: 'those who learn to cooperate with other adults within these groups develop interests and recognise responsibilities. A unique feature of playgroups is that in deprived areas where it is almost impossible to get people to attend political meetings, church congregations, etc. there are many mothers experiencing the responsibility of participating in playgroup organisation'.

The Pre-school Playgroups Association of Northern Ireland referred to the fact that 'mothers developed to a marked degree and this often helped fathers to develop too. But though mutual aid organisations may have the advantage of providing client participation, they have their problems, caused usually by their small size and spontaneity. To quote again the Pre-school Playgroups Association of Northern Ireland: 'Local officers [i.e. of associations] need a great deal of help and advice even in quite simple matters of administration' and later 'the keenness of the playgroup movement . . . needs to be supported if it is to be maintained'. We consider that one of the important functions of the local intermediary bodies is to provide this sort of support to mutual aid groups.

Examples

We begin with the Family Fund which is new, but large enough in scale from the outset to illustrate the application of several of the forms of surveillance we have advocated. The government at the time of the thalidomide disaster wished to recognise a responsibility to the parents of the very severely handicapped children — numbering perhaps 85,000 families — for whom no provision was possible remotely comparable to that made for the less than 700 children affected by thalidomide. Thus a substantial bridging operation was needed, immediately available, whilst longer term policy for this group was considered. To date, a total of £10½ million has been handed to the Joseph Rowntree Memorial

Trust to be administered at its discretion within the most general guidelines agreed with the government. It was inherent in the nature of the
Trust that the money became part of the Trust's resources so that the
decision of the Trustees as to its allocation was absolute. How in such
circumstances could the evident duty of public responsibility be
properly discharged? First, safeguards against misappropriation were
needed for the Trust's entire resources; the protection of the government contribution was no more, and no less, necessary than the protection of the Trust's ordinary revenue. It was provided by professional
audit. Second, responsibility to Parliament for the use of public money
was discharged by the Comptroller and Auditor General whose officials
spent several days at the Trust office observing its procedures and the
kind of decision to which they led. Third, the Trustees themselves felt
that their discharge of this unusual task should be independently
monitored both as an exercise in public administration and, more
immediately important, as an experimental method of meeting ascertained family distress. The help of a university was called upon to
mount a research and monitoring operation the results of which were
continuously available to the appropriate government department and
would in due course be published. Fourth, an attempt was made to
secure the views of the families whose needs were to be met; the
developing procedures of the Fund and the help given were discussed
with a consultative committee bringing together members of all the
main organisations representing handicapped children, which through
their branches are in touch with a large proportion of the families likely
to be eligible for help. The important role of the medical profession in
such an exercise was recognised by an invitation — gladly accepted — to
four consultant paediatricians from different parts of the country to
serve as a medical advisory panel under the chairmanship of a professor
of child health. Here therefore was a service requested by government
which could not have been mounted in the time available in any other
way save at prodigious expense. The Trust has sought to discharge its
public responsibility, internally by professional audit, by independent
assessment through a university and by the oversight of a panel of
consultants; external surveillance has been the statutory responsibility
of the Comptroller and Auditor General; the interests of the beneficiaries have been continually before the Trust through the responsible
bodies which the different groups of handicapped people have themselves established. None of this could remove the ultimate responsibility
of the Trustees in law for the use of what had become their funds; but
neither were the various measures in conflict with it. Our view is that

the one reinforced the other.

We take as our second example the voluntary housing movement. In recent years some £200 million annually has been put at the disposal of some 2,000 housing associations for the building of new houses and the acquisition and rehabilitation of those that have decayed. Expenditure incurred on administration and on the management of the dwellings has also been met from public funds. How, and how effectively, has this massive use of public money by a wide variety of voluntary organisations been safeguarded? And have the necessities of surveillance reduced the individuality and capacity to experiment of the assocations – historically the nation's pioneers in housing development? The structure of a housing association must conform to the law. To ensure that in each case it does so is a duty discharged by the Charity Commissioners, the Registrar of Friendly Societies, or the Department of Trade and Industry. Which of them acts in relation to any particular association need not concern us here; their constitution and their powers are and always have been prescribed and enforced. To qualify to deploy public funds for housing, the association must further register with the Housing Corporation – an important example of what we have called elsewhere an intermediary body. The Corporation requires exhaustive information about the structure and resources of each association, the private interests of members of its governing body, the status and qualifications of its staff and details of its professional advisers. The initiative in launching housing projects and in implementing them rests with the association alone; but the Corporation must be satisfied that the project is within the resources of the association given the support of public funds for housing purposes. The quality and financial efficiency of the association's particular methods of management are subject to continuing monitoring by the Corporation but this is designed to stimulate disciplined self-monitoring within each association. Drastic powers of intervention and even of dispossession are available to the Corporation at need. The persons for whose benefit the whole operation is intended are the occupants of the houses. The practice of the best associations in involving those they house in the management of the property is made widely known in order to increase the variety and effectiveness of this aspect of housing management. Within this statutory framework more than 40,000 dwellings a year – nearly 20 per cent of the national output – have been provided. They include the rehabilitation of some of the worst property in our stress areas, experimental schemes for the handicapped and other special groups, and a large number of schemes incorporating different amenities to secure independent lives to those who are elderly. The 'voluntary' component, in the sense of unpaid service, is given by the members of the governing bodies of the associations and not, except in small and local associations, by those who manage the dwellings. The benefit to the community lies in the multiplication of 'centres of initiative' for enlightened housing development throughout the country; in the range of provision and experiment; in the different patterns of management; and in the increase in housing choice offered to those seeking a home. Here responsibility is differently exercised. The massive scale of public expenditure and the numerous and disparate bodies by which it is deployed mean that a framework of law has been established to preserve for the purposes for which they were supplied the buildings thus provided by public funds. Within that framework the scope for initiative and experiment is remarkable. But the quality of the performance of each association is monitored and compared with that of its peers and in that assessment the Corporation invites the views of the appropriate local housing authority to supplement those of its own officers.

The two examples given are of a large trust and of a corporation which has extensive controls over the associations which it funds. Organisations of this size can without much difficulty command the resources of money and expertise necessary to monitor their activities, appraise the course they are pursuing and adapt to changing circumstances. The cost of monitoring in fact was not high in our examples. But smaller organisations may find this more difficult. They may not be able to afford this sort of activity and they may not know where to turn for appropriate professional expertise. In the case of groups which possess few resources beyond the voluntary work of their members, failure to adapt and to develop may be of little moment: the organisation will wither away as it becomes less relevant to its members. One might perhaps say that if irrelevant organisations do die, this fact is a sign of health in the voluntary sector as a whole. There are, however, some organisations, typically those of medium size, which possess significant resources in the form of premises, investments, a reputation or well-known sponsors, in which declining vitality can raise issues of waste and ineffectiveness. The Settlements illustrate the situation well. Most observers would agree that some fifteen years ago a good many of them lacked a clear sense of purpose and had not been notably successful in reinterpreting the objectives that led to their foundation. The renewed vitality of the Settlement movement arises in part from a general revival of interest in deprived areas and community-based approaches to social problems. But it also owes something to the British

Association of Settlements (BAS). There are two aspects of the recent work of BAS that particularly deserve to be noted. First it has initiated campaigns into which individual settlements have been drawn. Besides attracting public attention to the needs of adult illiterates, the 'Right to Read Campaign' has helped to develop a sense of common purpose among settlements. Second, BAS has sought to promote the exchange of ideas among settlements, and to provide advice, consultancy and information services to member organisations. In our view the work of BAS illustrates well the scope for development work among a group of loosely affiliated agencies, and how it can be tackled in spite of limited resources. Development work is, as we have pointed out earlier, a most important function of the independent intermediary bodies.

Some General Reflections and Conclusions

We started this chapter by referring to the complicated nature of the subject and said that we would try to see whether in practice it caused tensions which amounted to serious problems or which were on the whole creative. As we have already indicated we do not believe that accountability is a real difficulty for the great majority of voluntary organisations. It may perhaps arise in the case of those organisations which raise money from the general public for work which they alone deem it right to undertake. In this connection we welcome the increased attention that the Charity Commissioners have given in recent years to the affairs of charities which raise very large sums from the public for purposes which are necessarily imprecisely described. Perhaps some advertisements should be more carefully checked to see that the cause for which the money is requested is clearly stated and that the appealing picture fairly represents those to whom the money raised by the appeal will go. But we think the problem can easily be overstated. It is to the credit of our society that an appeal, for example, to send aid to the victims of some disaster whether at home or abroad, has sometimes produced a response which is embarrassing in its generosity. In the light of experience, careful consideration is now given to such appeals even when decisions have to be made very quickly; the main relief organisations, the media and independent persons of experience consider whether, and if so how, such an appeal should be launched. We have been aware too that the public can show considerable discrimination in failing to respond to appeals which show little promise of using the results of public generosity effectively and promptly.

There is no short answer which will resolve the question of reconciling the independence of voluntary organisations with a measure of control by whoever funds them, whether the statutory side, trusts or any

other sources we have mentioned. Provided that the question can be
approached from a background of mutual knowledge and understanding, there should not in most cases be serious difficulties. But problems
may arise where the objectives of a project are interpreted differently
by those funding it and those carrying it out. This may happen if they
were not clearly defined to begin with, or if changing circumstances
lead to divergent reinterpretations. Such conflicts are not easily resolved,
but they may be obviated by clarification of objectives at the outset and
steps to ensure that funders are kept fully informed of the implications
of changing circumstances.

The pursuit of efficiency or effectiveness is a cause to which everyone subscribes in theory, but there are no simple formulae by which it
can be pursued. Our general impression is that taken as a whole voluntary organisations are no less effective or efficient than statutory
organisations. The financial position of most of them is less secure than
that of statutory agencies and there are a lot of pressures to prevent
them from vegetating. But as we have noted earlier, the performance of
the voluntary sector is uneven: its very diversity could hardly make it
otherwise, and it would be wrong to convey an air of complacency.
Hence we devote the rest of the chapter to a discussion of ways in
which the health of voluntary organisations individually and collectively
can be sustained.

Research and Statistics

We have commented already on the difficulties that we have encountered
as a result of the paucity of research on voluntary organisations. Our
own small research team has gone some way towards meeting the need
for more systematic knowledge in this field, but the scope of its work
has necessarily been circumscribed by the immediate needs of the
Committee and its existence is temporary. We believe that better
statistics and further research are essential if there is to be more
informed and more effective development of the voluntary sector. In
Appendix 6 we indicate ways in which the collection and analysis of
data by official bodies could be improved so as to yield a clearer
picture of the activities of the voluntary sector and how these change
over time. Beyond this, if there is to be the new examination of the
roles of the voluntary, informal and statutory sectors called for in
Chapter 4, a substantial research and development effort will be
required. Probably the most direct way to give powerful and sustained
impetus to research would be to establish a centre specialising in the
study of the voluntary sector. In a period of severe financial restraint it

may be difficult to find the necessary funds. Whether or not a unit is established it may be helpful to Trusts and government departments to identify the areas of enquiry in which we believe research and development are most urgently needed.

(a) *The emergence and performance of voluntary organisations* What factors affect the emergence of voluntary organisations in different fields and the degree of support they achieve? Why are some activities and causes so much more popular than others? Where important needs remain unmet can ways be found of stimulating voluntary action? How can the effectiveness of voluntary organisations be assessed? What are the different systems adopted for decision-making and how effective are they? Where performance measures can be identified, what factors appear to determine variations within organisations over time, and between different organisations? In particular, how does the performance of statutory, voluntary and commercial organisations offering similar services compare?

(b) *The relationship of statutory and voluntary sectors* What factors determine the varying patterns of interaction between these sectors which we have noted in this report? How far can the 'best practice' form the basis for changes where relationships are currently less effective?

(c) *The relationship of voluntary and informal sectors* What factors affect the willingness and capacity of individuals voluntarily to provide support for others through family and other informal networks? To what extent and in what ways can voluntary organisations reinforce them in doing so?

(d) *Action research* based on experimental projects in chosen areas should be an integral part of any programme concerned with reshaping the relative roles of the three sectors.

Education and Training

Many professionals and administrators in the statutory field such as doctors, social workers, local and central government officers, work in areas where frequent contacts with voluntary organisations are involved and where cooperation with them can play an important part in their daily round. Although we have not carried out a systematic analysis of the training of such people, it is our impression that the voluntary sector receives at best cursory treatment in most of the courses concerned. For example, very few social administration and social work courses in our universities have separate specialisms dealing with the voluntary sector. In part, of course, the dearth of teaching in this area can be attributed to the lack of published research and the absence of regular statistical reports of the kind that are available in abundance on the statutory sector. We have already emphasised the need for such research and information. However, we suspect that the relative weakness of teaching on the voluntary sector may also reflect the general scepticism about its potential and that if the sector was considered significant enough, it would be found there was already sufficient material on which to base introductory courses. We urge the educational institutions concerned with training in these areas to take more account, in future course planning, of the need to prepare their students for collaboration with voluntary organisations, and to give the subject a prominent place in their curricula. A more specific need for training results from the emergence of local intermediary bodies, and this will become more important if our recommendation for extending the funding of these bodies is accepted. In the last few years increasing attention has been devoted to training for community work and various opportunities now exist for attending in-service and full-time courses. But it is still not very securely established, and we suspect that more emphasis is given to work at neighbourhood level than at the inter-agency level. It is the latter that is more relevant to work in intermediary bodies. We believe there is a strong case for building up the in-service courses that have been developed by the NCSS and for encouraging a small number of universities and polytechnics to give more sustained support for training in this field.

Support services

In discussing intermediary bodies we pointed to their role in providing a variety of support services for voluntary organisations. Earlier in this chapter we suggested that small- and medium-sized voluntary organisations may have some difficulty in gaining access to the appropriate professional expertise for appraising their existing work and for examining ways in which it might be developed; and we pointed to the work of BAS in fostering change in the settlement movement. In the last few years there have been discussions about establishing a consultancy service for voluntary organisations. In our view the characteristic ethos and problems of voluntary organisations are in some respects different from those found in the statutory and commercial sectors, and further development of professional and managerial expertise in the voluntary sector would be desirable. In this context we see the work of the Action Resource Centre as a step in the right direction, as is the professional support being made available through the British Institute of Management and the application of cost-comparison techniques to voluntary organisations by the Centre for Interfirm Comparisons. Further encouragement for this sort of work should be among the priorities of the strengthened national and local intermediary bodies that we are advocating.

9 FINANCE

Factual information about the income of voluntary organisations has been presented briefly in Chapter 3 and more fully in Appendix 6. To summarise, the income of voluntary organisations active in the field of the social and environmental services amounted in 1975 to about £1,000 million. Nearly half seems to have come from donations of one kind or another from individuals, companies and trusts and the remainder from charges for services, rent and investment and government grants. In thinking about the future it is important to ask whether voluntary organisations are keeping up with inflation and with the expenditure of the statutory sector, and whether their sources of income are changing in ways which may affect the role they can play. In making judgements on these topics the effects of rising prices have to be taken into account. The most widely used indicator of price changes is the official index of retail prices. This rose by 84.5 per cent between 1970 and 1975. But it is not an ideal measure for assessing the effect of rising prices on voluntary organisations, since some of their costs, e.g. postage, printing and travel, have risen faster than inflation generally. For many purposes a better index is that used for PESC (Public Expenditure Survey Committee) in calculating expenditure on the personal social services at constant prices. This shows a rise in prices of 124 per cent, between 1970 and 1975.

The evidence we have on the actual performance of voluntary organisations in raising money from 1970 to 1975 is summarised in Table 9.1. The figures have been adjusted so as to discount inflation, the first column using the index of retail prices, the second the PESC personal social services index. Although many organisations rely entirely or mainly on unpaid voluntary effort, which may well be increasing, there are many others which rely to a greater or lesser extent on raising money. For the latter the figures in Table 9.1 do not present a very encouraging picture. Some organisations have continued to raise money very successfully, for example Help the Aged, the Royal Society for the Protection of Birds, and the National Trust, but the failure of private giving to keep pace with inflation is striking, though readily understandable.

The financial position of many voluntary organisations has always tended to be somewhat precarious and many organisations giving

Table 9.1. Trends in the Income of Voluntary Organisations 1970-75

	Adjusted by Retail Price Index	Adjusted by PESC PSS index
Voluntary organisation income from all sources:		
The largest fifty fund-raising charities (see Appendix 6D for details)	plus 11%	minus 8%
Income from voluntary giving:		
As recorded by Family Expenditure Survey:	minus 32%	minus 44%
Under covenant from companies and individuals:	minus 5%	minus 22%
The largest fifty fund-raising charities	plus 3%	minus 15%

evidence to us mentioned financial problems. But the Committee has not received evidence suggesting that the number of voluntary organisations in financial difficulties has risen dramatically. We carried out a small survey of organisations that had applied unsuccessfully for grants to the DHHS and the VSU. It was our impression that the organisations with what appeared a strong case had been able to obtain funds from a trust if not from a public authority. But in general it seems that more serious crises have only been avoided by increased government funding. Our information is too patchy to establish firm trends back to 1970. However, grants by central government departments have risen from £19 million in 1974/75 to £35 million in 1976/77. This is considerably faster than inflation. In addition, in the eighteen months following its inception in October 1975, the Job Creation Programme made grants to the value of over £30 million to voluntary organisations. The latter do not represent deliberate policy decisions to support voluntary organisations, but the fact is that voluntary organisations have been quick to profit from temporary measures to counteract unemployment.

Our knowledge about funding from local government is even more patchy. Up to 1975/76 there seems to have been a quite rapid rise, but since then voluntary organisations seem to have been relatively hard hit by the cuts in public expenditure. We have obtained some recent information about the situation of CVSs. Most of these depend heavily on local authority grants. It would appear from evidence collected by the NCSS that in 1976/77 a third of local CVSs had had to curtail their activities. In 1977/78 the situation promises to be worse; hardly any expect to receive a grant that takes account of inflation and some grants will be cut even in money terms (see Appendix 5).

We know of no other well-defined group of organisations like the

CVSs that is being so severely hit by present economic circumstances. Our evidence on the largest fifty fund-raising charities (see Appendix 6D) precedes the period of strict constraint on public expenditure. In any case these larger organisations seem to have been doing relatively well and are much less dependent on grants from local authorities than are many smaller voluntary organisations. On examining the largest fifty fund-raising charities by need area, the seven medical research organisations seemed to be doing well and the only category that as a whole seemed not be be keeping its head above water was the four international relief organisations, but this was probably because there were no major world disasters in 1975. Most of the six organisations for children were compensating for a drop in voluntary giving by making higher charges for their services.

We cannot provide an authoritative explanation for the relative decline in private giving, but inflation, the rise in direct taxation, the squeeze on many salary earners and rapidly increasing public expenditure on the social services are all factors which might be expected to have a deterrent effect. Our data relate to a period preceding the fall in real incomes that is taking place as we write. We expect that this will further discourage private giving. We also expect that when the economic situation improves there will be a recovery in private giving. But house to house street collections depend upon the availability of collectors and too many flag days in the same area can lead to a resistance to giving. In thinking about the future we recognise that the voluntary sector will probably not be able to place as much reliance as previously on private giving. As we are looking for a strengthening of the voluntary sector lack of money could prove a serious brake.

There are a number of ways in which the shortage of funds might be overcome:

    (a) New devices for raising money, for example schemes for payroll deductions.

    (b) Tax concessions which would be of value in themselves and might encourage people to give more.

    (c) Increasing reliance on statutory funding.

New devices

As regards the first of these, keen and competent fund-raisers have been at work for a long time and we do not believe the situation could be revolutionised by the invention of new methods. Although some organisations are more vigorous and successful than others in raising money, we doubt very much whether there is a large pool of untapped resources. What might alter the situation is a system of payroll deductions, from which the individual employee would have to opt out if he did not wish deductions to be made from his pay. Any scheme along these lines faces the problem of how the money is to be distributed. If donors are allowed to decide individually which charity is to receive their money, administration of the scheme becomes complex and costly. If a committee decides, one could argue that not a great deal distinguishes such a scheme from taxation. Private giving will remain an important safeguard of the independence of the voluntary sector, and continuing efforts to improve methods of fund-raising are needed, particularly ones directed at sections of the population for whom charitable giving has not been customary. Nevertheless two points should be made. First, in our own study of the largest fifty fund-raising charities, information on fund-raising expenditure was available for twenty-five organisations. The expenditure of these organisations on fund-raising rose slightly between 1970 and 1975 as a proportion of their income from voluntary giving; but their income from voluntary sources did not keep pace with incomes generally. Second, our NOP survey showed that fund-raising was the type of activity most frequently reported by volunteers. Many volunteers would be unwilling to embark on any other type of activity and fund-raising activity may benefit the image of an organisation as well as its bank balance. There is still a case for saying that the diversion of some of the time and effort devoted to fund-raising to direct service giving would be beneficial.

Tax Concessions

A variety of tax concessions were considered by the Goodman Committee. They all have the merit of providing assistance to charities with very few strings attached, and, in so far as they are seen as equivalent to public expenditure, the converse disadvantage of being unselective in their effects. In addition, concessions to donors encourage giving so that, it can be argued, a concession costing the revenue a given amount may do more to benefit the voluntary sector than the expenditure of an equal sum in direct grants. It is not our intention to go over the ground covered by Goodman. We prefer to direct our attention towards the broader issue of whether tax concessions could do much to meet the future financial needs of the voluntary sector.

The Goodman proposal likely to produce the greatest financial benefit for voluntary organisations is that covenanted donations

should be allowable against the higher rates of income tax.
In 1975/76 some £30 million was paid to charities by the Inland
Revenue in respect of relief on covenants. A substantial part of this
sum is attributable to companies rather than individuals. Thus even if
the implementation of this proposal brought about the doubling of
monies received by charities in respect of covenants made by individuals
it would not make a substantial impact on the financial situation of
voluntary organisations. Together with all the other Goodman
proposals it is unlikely that it would improve the financial position of
voluntary organisations by more than one or two per cent. The
Goodman Committee took the view that there would be little
advantage to charities even in a more radical concession, along the lines
of the United States system whereby all charitable gifts by individuals
are tax deductible. Hence, though further tax concessions would
certainly be helpful, even in conjunction with more effective fund-
raising, we do not see them as the solution to the financial problems of
the voluntary sector. There will therefore have to be greater reliance on
statutory funding. This is a conclusion with important implications.

Statutory Funding

The rise in central government grants from £19 million to £35 million
over three years has already been mentioned. Full details are presented
in Appendix 6B. Data about local authority grant giving is much more
patchy. What we do know is also presented in the appendix. It shows
that the level of support for the voluntary sector varies immensely
from one local authority to another. Grants by the London Borough of
Islington amounted to £7.22 per person resident in the Borough in
1976/77. To this can be added grants made by the ILEA, the GLC and
the London Boroughs Association amounting in all to a further £1.64
per person. Nearer, if somewhat below what appears to be the normal
level, are the grants made in Humberside. In 1976/77 the county gave
grants of £0.24 per capita and the districts averaged out over the whole
county £0.06 per capita. The Islington to Humberside ratio is approximately 30:1. In addition local authorities make facilities and resources
available to voluntary organisations without charge; at any rate in
Islington this form of support is quite substantial.

   In thinking about funding from central government sources it may
be helpful to distinguish different rationales according to which funds
may be provided:

(a) *Voluntarism as an end in itself* The encouragement of voluntary work or of voluntary organisations may be regarded as an end in itself, though in practice this objective is not usually on its own regarded as a sufficient basis for the allocation of resources.

(b) *Voluntary organisations as deliberate instruments of policy* Much of the money that voluntary organisations obtain from government is given because the voluntary organisation is recognised as the appropriate instrument for the pursuit of a particular policy, e.g. Home Office support for NACRO, Housing Corporation grants to housing associations, Development Commission support for Rural Community Councils. In these situations the existence of the voluntary organisation is seen as desirable from the point of view of departmental objectives, so that overhead costs may be covered by grants and funding is not confined to precisely specified pieces of work.

(c) *Voluntary organisations as incidental instruments of policy* In this situation the voluntary organisation obtains funds because it happens to be able to do work desired by the statutory authority. Thus in the case of the Job Creation Programme, both voluntary and statutory agencies can apply for funds to employ people: whether a voluntary organisation is successful depends on the merit of its application. Voluntary organisations which charge fees for services provided (e.g. children's homes) and those which operate on the basis of agency payments (e.g. various social work agencies) might also be placed in this category.

Another consideration is the extent to which and the terms under which central funding is directed towards local activities. As indicated in the government evidence (Appendix 4), in fields where the local authorities have responsibilities central funding is usually confined to support for the headquarters of the voluntary organisation concerned. Local projects generally have to be funded locally, although in the case of the Urban Programme the DOE (previously the Home Office) covers 75 per cent of the costs of projects selected by it from lists put forward by local authorities. But there are examples of situations where local and central government fund the same kind of project separately. For example, some local law centres have been funded by the Lord Chancellor's Office, others by local authorities. More commonly where central funding for local activities occurs, it is channelled through an intermediary body, e.g. the Commission for Racial Equality, Housing Corporation. In the case of the Commission for Racial Equality, funding for local community relations councils and Development Commission funding for RCCs, a central contribution is dependent upon a local authority contribution.

We argued in Chapter 6 for central funding for local intermediary bodies, and in the next chapter explain how it might be provided. The consequent growth of a lively set of intermediary bodies ought to strengthen the capacity of the voluntary sector to attract financial support from one quarter or another, but none of the suggestions that have been made so far amount to more than a partial answer to the financial problems that have been identified. In Chapter 7 we rejected the idea of an all-embracing voluntary organisation grants committee. For the most part statutory funding for voluntary organisations will have to be on the basis that, directly or indirectly, the voluntary organisation acts in furtherance of a specific policy. While voluntary organisations should not be funded in such a way as to discourage voluntary effort, it is a simple fact that a quite small reallocation of resources by the mass of local authorities towards the level of grant aid of the more generous ones would significantly improve the position of voluntary organisations. An equivalent point deserves to be made in respect of the health authorities, except that we know of none that could at present be described as generous.

As regards central funding in general, we reiterate the view that for the most part it ought to be based on specific policy objectives. In Chapter 4 we urged central government departments to develop a clearer view of the ways in which voluntary organisations could contribute to departmental objectives and we hope that this will lead to a continuation of recent increases in central funding for voluntary organisations. In Chapters 6 and 10 we argue for central support for local intermediary bodies. There are two further situations where central government might do more. First, there are local bodies that tend to fall between the responsibilities of different statutory agencies, all of which lie clearly within the territory of one central government department. An obvious example is organisations for alcoholics and drug addicts, the activities of which may be relevant to the Area Health Authority, the local office of the Supplementary Benefits Commission and the local Social Services Department. Voluntary bodies in this position can provide an integrated service that may be very difficult to mount within the statutory sector, but they do encounter special difficulties in seeking grant aid. Where equivalent boundary problems occur as between different central government departments, funding by the VSU is proving invaluable in ensuring that voluntary organisations do not fall between two stools. We hope the

DHSS will become more willing to act like the VSU in funding projects that lie across different parts of its territory. The fact that voluntary organisations were mentioned as possible recipients of funds in the second DHSS Circular on Joint Care Planning (Joint Care Planning: Health and Local Authorities: HC(77)17, LAC(77)10; May 1977) is an encouraging sign.

The second situation where present practice should be extended concerns the readiness of central government departments to fund innovatory development work. At present most government departments have resources to fund outside research projects. An extension of such funding to support and sustain research and development projects mounted by voluntary organisations is what we have in mind. Some but not all such projects would succeed. Hence in supporting innovatory work government departments would have to be confident that funds for the continuation of some of them beyond the initial phase would be available from one source or another.

We recognise that in arguing for more explicit policies towards the voluntary sector on the part of central and local government and for more statutory funding there is a risk of placing the voluntary sector under closer statutory control and undermining the pluralism we advocate. It is to safeguard against this that we advocate central funding for local intermediary bodies. We have also argued that, as is already often the case, independent criticism and autonomy in pursuit of agreed general objectives should be accepted by central and local government as a necessary part of their relations with voluntary bodies. In any case the income of the voluntary sector from statutory sources, taking into account all grants, charges and agency payments, will remain only a minority of their total income, even if substantially increased. A lot of it will continue to come from charitable sources. We decided not to give attention to trusts, but they do play an important part in sustaining the pluralism of the voluntary sector, particularly those larger ones which, like our two sponsoring trusts, evolve their policies in the light of a broad and informed view of developments in the social and environmental services. We urge trustees to remember this.

10 CENTRAL FUNDING FOR LOCAL SOCIAL DEVELOPMENT

In earlier chapters we argued that some of the funding required by local intermediary bodies should come from central government. In the previous chapter we underlined the case by saying that voluntary organisations generally are likely to require increased statutory funding, and that local CVSs are being hit particularly severely by current economic constraints. But how should such funding be provided?

In order to answer this question the object of the exercise needs to be restated and clarified. In Chapter 6 we distinguished the different intermediary functions that could be performed in relation to the voluntary sector — development, support services, liaison and representation. Elsewhere we have pointed out that the voluntary sector is uneven in coverage and performance as between different localities and need areas, and that if the voluntary sector is to have an important role, steps need to be taken to counteract this. The effective performance of these intermediary functions should serve to strengthen the voluntary sector generally. But more particularly the intermediary body should be the agent for reinforcing the voluntary sector where it is weak.

An important part of the intermediary functions concerns relationships between voluntary organisations and local authorities. We have seen how the policies of local authorities towards the voluntary sector vary and how very widely the levels of financial support from local authorities differ. An essential element in the work of an intermediary body should be to encourage on the part of the local authority the formulation of policies that enable the voluntary sector to maximise its contribution to the well-being of the community. We have argued for a less unequal partnership between the voluntary and statutory sectors, and we see local intermediary bodies as having an essential part to play in defining the terms of this partnership.

In Chapter 6 we gave considerable attention to local voluntary councils. These are the most widespread form of local intermediary bodies either in their RCC or CVS manifestation, and have a considerable record of achievement. The simplest solution, administratively, would be to adopt this as the universal pattern, so that every county would have its RCC and every town of any size its CVS; and these would be the only recipients of central funding for intermediary

functions. We do not advocate this. First, the essential element in the
constitution of local voluntary councils is that they are federal bodies.
Voluntary organisations are often specific in their commitments.
Member organisations often do not have a great deal in common and
they may be more aware of their differences than of any community of
purpose. Indeed, they are not infrequently to some extent competing
with each other for volunteers, donations and grants. Bodies of this
kind therefore have in-built obstacles to agreeing on any definite and
positive initiatives. Second, local voluntary councils are generalist
intermediary bodies usually covering the area of a local authority.
Some of the intermediary functions we have discussed may in some
cases be more effectively carried out by bodies with functions more
specialised in terms of need area, e.g. local councils for the disabled, or
localised in terms of geography. Settlements, the new area resource
centres and neighbourhood councils (in Scotland, community councils)
are all bodies which could be the most effective instruments for
carrying out some of the functions we have discussed. For these reasons
we do not support the idea of an identical institutional framework for all
areas. What requires funding is functions rather than bodies. Of course
bodies are required to carry out functions, but the choice of bodies
should be made according to local circumstances. We expect that
existing voluntary councils and new ones formed on the same pattern
would be the main recipients of central funding, but they should not be
the only ones.

The emphasis on functions rather than bodies will make it especially
important to recruit able and enterprising people to carry them out. We
have not looked closely into the staffing problems of voluntary
organisations, but we are encouraged by the fact that recruitment to
the social services was at a high level in the early 1970s, and that many
young people have been attracted into posts with a community work
element in them. There should not therefore be a dearth of suitable
people, provided the right framework for them to work in is established.

One word of warning is needed. Some local authorities may feel that
they are the appropriate body to carry out many, perhaps all, of the
intermediary functions, and appoint their own officers for this purpose.
While there will often be much to be welcomed in such an approach,
however benevolent the local authority there will always remain a case
for an independent voice and an independent source of initiatives. The
balance between what the local authority does and what is done
within the voluntary sector will vary over time and between places, but
a monopoly is contrary to the concept of a partnership.

From what source should central funding come? There are a number
of different possibilities — the VSU, the Development Commission, the
Urban Programme, from the DOE direct or from a newly devised body.
The VSU has recently taken steps to encourage the formation of CVSs
in those metropolitan districts where they have not yet been established.
This is a welcome indication of government support. We also welcome
the recent establishment of the five community resource centres (which
we mentioned in Chapter 6) in London, Glasgow, Manchester,
Newcastle and South Wales with funds from the VSU, the EEC Social
Fund and the Gulbenkian Foundation. The growth of such national
and local agencies as the Action Resource Centre and the Islington Bus
Company is also encouraging. However, if similar arrangements became,
as we hope, more widespread and were to depend largely on VSU
funding, the special character of the VSU would alter. It would lose its
flexibility and smallness of scale; as it attracted more public scrutiny,
its activities would be subjected to greater constraint; and more
exacting conditions might be imposed on recipients of funds. All this
would impair its capacity to play its present valuable role.

The Urban Programme has recently been transferred to the DOE, so
all the alternatives to the VSU mentioned above would involve making
the DOE the parent department in England. In view of its general
responsibilities for local government, its interest in neighbourhood
councils and its present responsibility through the Development
Commission for social and economic development in rural areas, it
would be the appropriate government department. An important
question then arises as to whether funding should come directly from
the Department or indirectly through an intermediary body. If directly,
the Urban Programme or some new departmental arrangement could be
the vehicle: if indirectly it would have to be the Development Commission or a new organisation created for the purpose.

An important part of the case for central funding for local social
development is to give local intermediary bodies greater security and
safeguard their independence by avoiding complete dependence on the
local authority. It can be argued that central funding is what is important in this context, and that whether this funding comes directly or
indirectly from a government department is much less significant. But
is this true? Direct funding would mean closer accountability to
Minister and Parliament for the grants awarded. This, it could be
claimed, would be more democratic; but it could also have the effect of
encouraging a close adherence to rules and precedents and thus inhibit
the flexibility we have advocated. As compared to a government

department, an intermediary body might be better for maintaining continuity of personnel and building up stronger expertise and knowledge of the field. The Development Commission is in some respects the obvious intermediary body for the work we have in mind. First, it already has long experience of supporting social development in rural areas; and its experience of economic development might be of value in inner city areas. Second, the boundary between rural and urban social development is unclear, and indeed is drawn in different places in different counties: this issue would give rise to recurrent problems if urban and rural work received central funding from separate sources. Third, it would not be necessary to bring a new public body into existence. On the other side, such an expansion of the Development Commission's responsibilities, which are at present entirely rural, would represent a very substantial change for the Commission and could well be seen as threatening its rural commitments. If its role was to be extended it would be essential to safeguard the rural work now being carried out. Separate subcommittees and a separate allocation of funds for urban and rural work might be an appropriate device. At the same time it would be necessary to ensure that the Commission adapted itself sufficiently to make a good job of its new responsibilities. Additional staff and members with experience of social development in urban areas would certainly be needed. All this might be seen as a large, unwelcome graft.

One further funding mechanism should be mentioned: the idea that the NCSS should itself distribute the money. This is not one espoused by the NCSS itself and in our view it would not make sense. As we have argued earlier, the main functions of the NCSS are to represent the voluntary sector and to provide services for it. We do not think it could satisfactorily both represent the voluntary sector to government and, as the government's agent, act as the paymaster of part of the voluntary sector.

Most of the responsibilities of the Development Commission in Scotland and Wales have recently been devolved to the Scottish and Welsh Development Agencies respectively. The remainder rest with the Scottish and Welsh Offices. In these two countries, responsibility for social development and support for intermediary bodies could be given either to the Development Agencies or to the respective Offices. In Northern Ireland there is no equivalent development agency, so for the time being responsibility for the work we are discussing would have to rest with the Northern Ireland Office.

We have already stated the case against concentrating funds on a single type of local organisation and in favour of funding functions rather than bodies. If this is to be done there will certainly be difficulties in deciding what kind of work and what sort of agencies should or should not be funded. Clear definitions would have to be worked out at an early stage. It is not for this Committee to provide an operational manual, but it is necessary to be sure that what we are advocating is not completely impractical. The following points can be made :

(a) We think the activities to be funded should include community development work aimed at helping individuals to form or join organisations and the work of organisations like the Volunteer Bureaux which concentrate on placing volunteers. It should not include the provision of direct services for individuals.

(b) In so far as an intermediary body was providing services for other organisations, there would have to be evidence that a service was valued by the other organisations. Such evidence could well take the form of contributions to the cost of the service.

(c) In so far as an intermediary body was representing other organisations, evidence that it was an authentic representative would be necessary. This could relate to the number of subscribing member organisations and their level of involvement in decision-making.

(d) It would make sense if central funding was concentrated on generalist bodies, i.e. those that cross several need areas. Specialist bodies such as Age Concern and local councils for youth or for the disabled are likely to fall clearly within the responsibilities of local authority departments, which might thus be expected to fund them.

The attitude of the local authorities will have a major influence on the success of what we are advocating. We see the non-metropolitan counties, the metropolitan districts and the London boroughs as the English authorities with which our local intermediary bodies would be mainly, but not exclusively, concerned. If central funding was provided in direct opposition to the wishes of the local authority, we see little chance of the local intermediary body making much headway. Consequently central funding should depend on local authority agreement. One of the objectives of such funding would be to secure greater recognition on the part of local authorities of the potential of the voluntary sector generally and local intermediary bodies in particular.

Hence the continuation of central funding after a pump-priming period should depend on the willingness of local authorities to provide some financial support. We suggest that at least half the funding should come from one local source or another. Equivalent evidence of support from local voluntary organisations should also be a condition for the continuation of central funding.

The practical steps by which appropriate organisations are selected for central funding will be for the funding body to work out for itself. But the following suggestions indicate how it might approach the task. The funding body will have to deal with areas where intermediary bodies are well established and the voluntary sector generally is strong, as well as with areas where the opposite is the case. We hope it will give first priority to areas it suspects are in the latter category. Whatever the funding body's priorities, it will have to review the situation in each county, metropolitan district and London borough in consultation with local authorities and voluntary organisations in order to establish what existing organisations are carrying out intermediary functions, how effectively they are doing this and whether new organisations may be needed. In the light of this review and of understandings with the local authorities about the support they were prepared to give, the central funding body would be in a position to decide the amount of funds to allocate to each local authority area, and which local organisation or organisations should receive them.

The one specific proposal that we are directing towards government is that the DOE should assume responsibility for encouraging social development in urban as well as rural areas. We have discussed the different channels through which the DOE might provide financial support. It seems that no one of these is unambiguously the best. Hence we feel the DOE should be asked to work out the best machinery taking into account the points we have made earlier in this chapter. The cost of what we have in mind would be small by any standards of central government expenditure. There are 32 London boroughs, 36 metropolitan districts and 16 non-metropolitan districts with a population of over 150,000. If on average £12,000 was allocated to the intermediary bodies in each of these and if on average £6,000 was allocated, for example, to another 100 towns not included in the previous category, and if resources were allowed for special projects and for administration, the cost would still not exceed £2.5 million per annum. The consequent strengthening of the voluntary sector's contribution would be worth that sum many times over.

11 TRENDS

Our Approach

So far this report has been concerned essentially with the past and present activities of voluntary organisations. Yet our terms of reference require us to look forward into the next twenty-five years. This is not an easy task, and there are a number of ways in which it could have been carried out. At the outset it is important for us to explain the approach we adopted.

One possibility would have been to undertake a major exercise in futurology. This would have meant attempting to identify all the more important needs and socio-economic trends likely to exist in the years to come and suggesting which of them the voluntary sector ought to be meeting. However we felt that any forecasts we might make would be so unreliable as to form a quite inadequate basis for making suggestions about what voluntary organisations ought to be doing. Thus we did not spend a lot of time pondering the imponderable and rejected the blueprint approach to the future.

An approach making fewer demands on powers of prophecy is one which does not attempt a complete blueprint, but simply takes existing known trends and projects them into the future. This has limitations; it ignores the possibility that trends may be reversed. Nevertheless there are a number of assumptions which can safely be made about the future on this basis. To take an obvious case, the proportion of the population aged over eighty is going to rise over the next ten years, with clear implications for the social services. However, even if there are some needs which can be forecast in this way, there are bound to be many which cannot be foreseen, particularly those that arise from changing norms and values. For example, who could have foretold the recent recognition of the needs of battered wives? As far as we can tell, this has come about not because of an increase in battering but because women are less willing to tolerate it. Even if we had devoted a lot of effort to the extrapolation of existing trends, we could at best have come up with no more than an extremely patchy scenario for the next twenty-five years. Hence we rejected the attempt to predict needs even on this less ambitious basis.

Nevertheless we clearly could not attempt to discuss the future without taking cognisance of the directions in which our society is now moving and making certain assumptions about future developments. We decided it would be most productive to concentrate our attention on trends in the scope and functions of the four main sectors providing social and environmental care, and to use this as a basis for discussing their relative roles in the future.

Before looking in turn at developments within the informal, the statutory, the commercial and the voluntary sectors, certain general assumptions need to be stated. In the first place we decided to take for granted the continuation, in very broadly its present form, of the existing political and economic system − of what one might loosely characterise as a mixed economy presided over by a parliamentary democracy. But we could not be so confident about the continuation of economic growth. Until recently most people would have assumed steady economic growth and have anticipated that the social and environmental services would continue to attract an increasing proportion of the nation's resources. Now it seems that growth may prove to be slower and more fitful. Forward planning will have to be based on less optimistic assumptions and the need for voluntary activity will be greater rather than less. There may well be less money for the development and extension of services, and improvements will be more dependent on voluntary effort or on the strengthening of informal caring arrangements. Over the next twenty-five years economic circumstances are bound to fluctuate, but in our view, it cannot be assumed that these fluctuations will necessarily take place around a strong upward trend.

Trends in the Informal Sector

Whatever the economic situation the future of the informal system is particularly difficult to assess, since this sector has hitherto received very little attention. Thus we cannot say confidently what social changes are likely to strengthen it or weaken it. Moreover it consists of four different elements: the nuclear family of parents and children, the whole body of relatives that comprise the extended family, neighbours and friends. What we can say about the future of all these can only be speculative, but there may be some merit in drawing attention to a number of relevant considerations. The nuclear family is now much less often broken prematurely by death than in former centuries, but a rapid increase is taking place in the number broken by separation and divorce, if often only temporarily pending remarriage. In addition to marriage breakdown there is a steady trend towards the smaller household, partly but not only because people are living alone. The proportion of households with cars continues to rise despite the increasing cost of motoring. This has the effect of making those without cars relatively more isolated, but except in those extended families where no one has a car, we suspect that the motor car does cross the barriers created by geographical separation and thus serves to facilitate the caring functions of the extended family. A similar point could be made regarding the effect of the telephone.

The 'local community' is something that is often alleged to be breaking down. Certainly recollections of the past usually present a picture of richer and stronger community life. But these tend to be nostalgic recollections by elderly people of their childhood, and while it is certainly true that some communities are very obviously being broken down by slum clearance and rehousing or by loss of employment due to industrial change, others are slowly and less dramatically being built up. Whether the relative rates of destruction and accretion have changed markedly or will be different in the future it is difficult to say. If only on account of television watching, the nuclear family does seem to be nowadays more home-centred. For many people the motor car means they spend more time outside their own locality. Thus there are reasons for thinking that the community of the local neighbourhood may occupy a lesser place in people's lives and so perhaps form a less effective source of care. Certainly there is evidence of more organised efforts being made to compensate for inadequate informal arrangements.

Perhaps the most significant point emerging from this discussion is that the pattern of relationships between family, friends and neighbours is a changing one, and will continue to be so. Some changes will weaken in certain respects the capacity of the informal system to provide care; a few may strengthen it. We place a high value on this system of care, both because of its intrinsic value and because its replacement by a more institutionalised form of caring would be intolerably costly. If its role is to be strengthened in the face of changing circumstances, it will need deliberate encouragement.

Trends in the Statutory Sector

During the present century the statutory sector has increased steadily in size; this is not just a matter of the once and for all creation of the welfare state, but of a rise in the number of employees and in the share of the national income absorbed by it. An important feature of the recent history of local government and the health service is reorganisation. Both have been rationalised in the interests of supposedly more effective administration. There are now 460 local authorities in England and Wales, where in 1961 there were over 1,400. Much of the reaction to the reorganisation of both local government and the health service has been unfavourable. Even allowing for the need to allow time for the new systems to settle down and for the fact that some of the criticism can be seen as part of a national mood of doubt and discontent, we feel that the public dissatisfaction is not without some foundation. Partly it is a response to tendencies to which all large-scale bureaucratic organisations are prone — long hierarchies generating high administrative costs and slow responses, problems of communication and sensitivity, the over-protection of vested interests within the organisation and so on. Within the voluntary sector many of the newer bodies are organisations of or for the consumers of statutory services, and the multiplying amenity societies and community groups are generally preoccupied with planning decisions: thus current developments often result from the extension of the responsibility of public authorities and the feeling that they have become too distant and cumbersome. Within the statutory sector there is widespread recognition of the need to find ways to bring about a measure of decentralisation. Hence the trend towards larger-scale operations in the statutory sector is one which we hope will in the future be weakened, if not reversed.

Trends in the Commercial Sector

One possible response to these trends in the statutory sector is advocacy of the expansion of the commercial sector. Statistics about it are scarce, but while pay beds within the health service have been under attack, the amount of private health insurance, mainly paid for by employers, has been increasing. Proposals for voucher schemes in education and health are being actively canvassed and there is a possibility that the commercial sector will advance rapidly as a result of political decisions. As explained in Chapter 2 we would have serious reservations about such a development. We would prefer to see the extension of choice in social welfare brought about through the medium of voluntary organisations.

Trends in the Voluntary Sector

The voluntary sector lacks the wealth of statistics that measure the activities of the statutory sector. Nevertheless we know that is it growing. The annual reports of the Charity Commissioners show that in recent years well over one thousand new charities have been registered annually, while hardly more than a handful become defunct. Our own enquiries show that a great many voluntary organisations are of very recent origin, and came into existence primarily to make an extended and centralised statutory sector more responsive to the needs of particular groups.

To get a fuller picture of trends we made a study of directories of voluntary organisations. The Councils of Voluntary Service in Bradford, Leeds, Liverpool, Oldham and Plymouth were able to supply us with a current directory and with ones for 1950 or earlier. We are most grateful for their help. Although uncertainties about their coverage mean that directories are not an ideal source of data, we did feel able to draw the following conclusions:

(a) Since 1950 the number of voluntary organisations has grown rapidly; births have easily exceeded deaths. It seems that while some organisations may have died during the Second World War and others may have been supplanted by the rapid development of the welfare state after the war, there has, since that time, been a revival of the voluntary sector and certainly since the 1960s a remarkable proliferation of organisations. Our main locality studies showed that a quarter of the organisations had come into existence in the previous six or seven years.

(b) Growth has been especially rapid among organisations that are the local branches of national organisations catering, often on a mutual aid basis, for those with a specialised set of needs and interests. This applies particularly to organisations for people suffering from specific handicaps and diseases. Many of the newer organisations are concerned to influence the policies and practices of the public authorities as well as engaging in the provision of activities and services themselves.

(c) Some directories do not give full coverage to local community-based organisations like playgroups and tenants' associations. However, it is clear that many organisations of this kind have been coming into existence recently, often as a result of deliberate community development.

(d) The growth of ethnic organisations of various kinds in towns with immigrant minorities and of organisations concerned with the environment is also noteworthy. The former indicates a reassertion of the role of voluntary organisations as a source of separate social provision for minorities.

(e) Apart from those organisations concerned with health and poverty which were supplanted by the welfare state, not many organisations have died. Among those that have, local organisations without a national affiliation and ones concerned with moral welfare and having explicit religious allegiances seem to be relatively more numerous.

Summing up the changes over the past quarter of a century, it seems that today there are more voluntary organisations and that growth has been in the direction of organisations that are: (i) more specialised in their objectives and membership; (ii) based on mutual benefit rather than benevolent paternalism; (iii) concerned to influence the policies and practices of public authorities; and (iv) secular and materialist in outlook rather than inspired by the desire to rescue or evangelise.

Although the growing number of organisations is strong evidence of increasing voluntary activity, it is less clear whether the number of people involved and the incomes of the various organisations have also been rising. We cannot provide authoritative answers on these matters but a number of points deserve comment. Organisations concerned with the recruitment of volunteers are one of the groups of organisations that have increased recently, particularly those concerned specifically with young volunteers such as Task Force, Outset and Community Service Volunteers. There are also numerous volunteer bureaux and provisions for community service in schools. Our National Opinion Poll Survey showed that those aged sixteen to twenty-four took part in voluntary work as frequently as older age groups. In comparison with the past many more young people are not in full-time employment, either because they are in full-time education, or because (recently) they are unemployed. We suspect that their level of participation in voluntary work has increased substantially and could perhaps increase still further. We suspect also that there is a relatively large untapped potential for voluntary work among the recently retired. Certainly this will become true if people are afforded greater opportunities to draw their pensions earlier than the present normal age of retirement. Two specific developments should also be mentioned. An increasing variety of employers now provide time for members of their staff to work for voluntary organisations, some with a view to widening the experience of trainees, others to provide 'sabbaticals' for older employees; and attempts are being made to recruit volunteers through the mass media, especially television programmes. Both trends are welcome and could make a significant contribution to the manpower of voluntary organisations.

Since the Second World War the percentage of married women going out to work has gone up sharply: thus of those aged forty-five to fifty-four, 24 per cent were working in 1951 and 57 per cent in 1971. It might well be argued that this trend would severely curtail participation in voluntary activity. Our NOP data indicated that there was not much difference in the level of participation in voluntary work of men and women. Also, as between women going out to work and those not doing so, the proportion involved in voluntary work was not very different. However there was a small number of women who reported ten or more hours of voluntary work in the preceding week, and these were all women who were not in employment. Thus the continuation of the trend towards married women working may not have a large numerical effect, but it could reduce the contribution made by a small but important element. Financial trends are discussed more fully in Chapter 9 and in Appendix 6. However it is important to note here that since 1970 voluntary giving has fallen behind the average rise in incomes. Instead a greater proportion of the income of voluntary organisations has been coming from statutory sources.

Before going on to identify those trends which we would like to see encouraged, there are a number of more specific developments which should be mentioned. As we write this report the progress of the legislation in favour of devolution for Scotland and Wales has come to a halt. Nevertheless we do not expect the demand for devolution to disappear. It forms part of the general resistance to the concentration of power we noticed in Chapter 2. Whatever measures eventually emerge the immediate practical effect for voluntary organisations is likely to occur through their impact on intermediary bodies. The functions of the Development Commission as they affect Scotland and Wales have already been devolved to the Scottish and Welsh Development Agencies respectively. Equivalent changes in relation to other bodies we consider elsewhere. An opposite trend is represented by the European Economic Community. So far it has not made a great deal of impact on voluntary organisations in this country, but its Social Action Programme through which a number of anti-poverty projects have been funded, is indicative of possible future developments. The NCSS has been enterprising in establishing its own European desk, and it will be important in the future to ensure that voluntary organisations remain abreast of and ready to act together in response to developments in the Community.

Signposts

The earlier part of this chapter has drawn attention to certain existing trends. We now examine a small number of trends we believe it is particularly important to encourage. The aim is to direct attention towards a few key signposts.

(a) We stressed above the desirability of supporting and strengthening the informal system. Chapter 3 distinguished three roles which voluntary and statutory services could play in relation to it: reinforcement, relief and replacement. The strengthening of the informal system will require emphasis on the reinforcement role and, to a lesser extent, on the relief role. The reinforcement role is exemplified by organisations for handicapped children which help parents to cope with the problems of rearing a handicapped child; the many schemes for neighbourhood visiting and street wardens which seek to strengthen caring arrangements for the elderly in the community; the work of organisations for one-parent families. The statutory sector also provides reinforcement and relief services, but many of the voluntary organisations in this field are mutual aid ones. These of their nature cannot be fully replaced by statutory agencies. The voluntary sector therefore has an important part to play in the encouragement of the reinforcement role and its activity in this direction deserves further support.

(b) Earlier in the chapter the hope was expressed that the trends towards increasing the scale of statutory services would be halted, if not reversed. Perhaps this was a covert way of saying 'small is beautiful'. It did not imply reservations about the desirability of social and environmental services or of extensions to them. Rather it was suggesting the need for a change of direction in the way they are provided. Such a change of direction suggests two more specific propositions about the future of voluntary organisations:

(i) There will be an important role for voluntary organisations that act as alternatives to statutory services. Alternatives are not viable in all services: hospitals are too capital-intensive to be replicated simply so as to offer a choice, and social security has to be provided on a uniform basis. But in a number of situations, notably in the residential, domiciliary and day-care fields, voluntary provision does already to some extent and could to a greater extent in the future, offer clients or those acting on their behalf, a choice. This could be interpreted as a broad endorsement of almost any kind of voluntary provision. It is not intended as such, but rather as a justification of voluntary provision where it extends the range of services available; where the voluntary sector possesses advantages by way of specialist knowledge and skills and flexibility; and as an encouragement to voluntary organisations to make well judged entries into those fields where, without a wasteful use of capital resources, a leavening of choice and variety could be introduced.

(ii) A reappraisal of attitudes to the extension of statutory provision is needed, both because of the problems of bureaucracy and scale already discussed and also because we cannot in future be so confident about the availability of resources. Instead of imposing new duties on public authorities whenever additional needs are recognised, a less automatic assumption of statutory responsibility can be envisaged. In some situations it may be more desirable to encourage the voluntary and informal sectors to remain or become major instruments of social service. These situations would most likely be those where voluntary bodies were able to involve the local community and the intended beneficiaries themselves in the provision of care. By encouraging the kind of community-based organisations whose growth has already been noted, we could be giving a fresh interpretation to Lincoln's famous words, encouraging service of the people, by the people, for the people.

(c) Chapter 3 drew attention to the uneven coverage of the voluntary sector. At the same time this report advocates an increasing role for it. Where the voluntary sector is a marginal part of social provision the existence of uneven coverage is not of much significance. But if it is to play a larger part it will become more important to find ways of stimulating the kind of organisations that transcend social barriers, to encourage voluntary activity among groups whose level of involvement is now low and to guide voluntary effort towards needs which it at present neglects. This should not detract from the overriding responsibility of the public authorities to ensure the equitable distribution of resources and to maintain standards of care and coverage; but it also points to the desirability of intermediary bodies actively involved in social and community development.

12 FINAL REFLECTIONS

We have said that at the beginning of our enquiry we were setting out
on uncharted seas. If we had known how vast was the ocean on which
we were embarking, or how rich and varied the living organisms it
contained, we might have been daunted and discouraged. In another
metaphor, we said that our description of the voluntary sector must be
a 'still' in the constantly moving film of a living growth and development. If we had known the gigantic size of the screen needed to show
it, we might have shrunk from this cinematographic task.

We have called attention many times, perhaps to the point of tedium,
to the incredible diversities between the bodies which are collectively
known as 'the voluntary organisations'. They are as different from each
other as the ant is from the elephant or the whale from the hermit crab.
But they all have in common with each other the characteristics that
they are born, they live and grow, and they are liable to die.

They are born because an inspired individual, or a group of like-
minded individuals, sees a need or a shortcoming in our society and is
determined to do something about it. The range of such perceived
needs is as wide as the range of society itself, from books for the blind
to the protection of birds or from rescuing shipwrecked mariners to
helping battered wives. It seems that no area of need can be too large
or too small to attract attention and consequent action.

The motives of those who intervene in this way may well be mixed —
human motives usually are. Some may see themselves in a position of
power or social importance; others may find that such activity fills a
gap in their own emotional lives; others may hope that success there
will build up a general self-confidence in other spheres; others may
hope, on the lines of Good King Wenceslas, that they will 'in Heaven
find blessing'; others, lonely, may simply enjoy the company of fellow-
workers; others may band together for mutual help and support.
However all this may be, or may have been in the past, we reject the
cynical assumption that anybody who is active in this way is simply
building up an ego or giving sops to conscience; and we deplore the use
of the word 'do-gooder' as a term of hostility or contempt. On the
contrary, we assert that there is such a thing as altruism. Ever since the
time of the Good Samaritan (and, doubtless, before that) there have
been people who simply want to help other people 'not with the hope

of gaining aught, nor seeking a reward'. Most of them would not understand introspection or self-examination about motive. They just want
to do what they can to help somebody else. They may act through what
we have called 'the informal sector', giving spontaneous help to relatives
or neighbours who need it; they may work as volunteers inside the
statutory sector; or they may be attracted to a voluntary organisation.
The point is that there are millions of such people in our society; and
one of the most encouraging features of that society is the growing
evidence of this quality in its younger members.

We have adduced evidence of the size of the contribution made by
the voluntary organisations — that is, by their members — in numbers,
man-hours and money. And there can be no doubt that without this
contribution the lives of an immense number of our fellow citizens
would be the poorer. To say this is no criticism of the statutory
sector. We have argued throughout for a pluralistic pattern in this
whole field. Our primary concern is the present state and, especially,
the future role of the voluntary organisations.

For the most part we have been impressed by the health and vitality
of the voluntary sector. We have not found perfection, and if we had
done so we should have suspected our own judgement. We have called
attention to one of its major weaknesses, the unevenness of its
distribution and performance. At its best, standards are very high; but
there are areas where shortcomings cannot be denied. And there are
areas of need which are relatively neglected by comparison with those
which make a strong and direct emotional appeal. Consequently,
despite the number and variety of organisations there are some needs
which are not met. This is a weakness which arises from the very
nature of the voluntary sector, from the freedom of individuals to
intervene where they choose or to abstain, and from the inherent
appeal of some causes rather than others.

Another feature which is often regarded as a weakness is duplication or overlapping between one organisation and another. There are
two sides to this. On the one hand, there are many who feel — and
some of us agree with them — that there must be some waste, of effort
if nothing more, when there appear next to each other in the Press
financial appeals which are almost identical save for the addresses of
two different bodies operating in the same field, apparently in open
competition with each other for funds. On the other hand it is argued
— and some of us accept this argument — that the British are on the
whole particular and 'specific' in their support of voluntary activity.
That is to say, they are less likely to support, for example, old people's

homes in general than homes for widows of Baptist ministers in particular. Consequently, we have been told, any attempt to amalgamate a number of similar specific bodies into one more comprehensive one, while it might seem more efficient and 'rationalised', would result in a drop in the total volume of public support. We have no means of knowing whether that would be so or not. But we would urge the voluntary organisations not to present their critics with evidence damaging to the whole image of voluntariness.

Perhaps a stronger argument for the continued existence of similar or overlapping bodies is that it extends the range of choice available to the consumer. We have stressed this point of alternative provision in connection with the relationships between the voluntary sector and the statutory sector. Much the same general principle applies to the relationships between one voluntary organisation and another. Obviously not every consumer can have provision tailor-made to suit his own requirements. But there may well be valid reasons, perhaps religious or ethnic, why one organisation is more appropriate to his needs than another, even if the outside world finds them almost indistinguishable.

On a different level there is a criticism to which we have called attention in Chapter 8. It concerns the responsibility, in the widest sense, which the voluntary organisations owe to the public which supports them. We urge them to be eternally vigilant in this matter if they are not only to deserve, but be seen to deserve, their freedom. There is more to be done than is done at present, in self-criticism, keeping up to date, monitoring performance, studying how far users and consumers are satisfied with what they receive. We are not asking that they should be perpetually pulling themselves up by the roots to see how they are getting on. But we do suggest that once every five years or so each and every voluntary organisation should engage in a deliberate self-examination about its aims, purposes, successes, failures, and, especially, possibilities for redirection of its activities. Our own enquiry has provided an occasion for such a self-appraisal by the organisations which submitted evidence to us; and we think it would be salutary if they voluntarily repeated the exercise at regular intervals.

One area in which such an operation might be particularly productive is that of management and its techniques. We are certainly not suggesting that all voluntary organisations are inefficient or that they are not cost-effective. But there still clings to them, in the minds of many, an aura of amateurishness, and for their own sakes it would be well that this should be dissolved of their own volition. They owe it to themselves to earn and deserve a reputation for the maximum amount of straight-forward efficiency which is compatible with the spontaneity and freedom which are their primary characteristics. This will not be easy, especially for the smaller and less wealthy among them. But there has recently been made available to them, through the Action Resource Centre, the British Institute of Management, and individual firms, a very generous range of practical help and advice. It would be both impolitic and unappreciative not to make the fullest use of the professional skills which are being offered. In this way, too, they will be greatly helped in resolving their perennial dilemma between freedom and responsibility.

But in day-to-day operational reality the organisations will, if they are wise, work very closely, both at national and at local level, with what we have described as the independent intermediary bodies. From them can come services more expert than any one body can hope to command, so that the stronger bodies may be reinforced and the weaker ones supported. And from them can flow stimulation towards the meeting of newly-discovered needs and proposals for a degree of collaboration inside the voluntary sector and between it as a whole and the statutory provisions. We have deliberately rejected the notion of a uniform pattern for these bodies, because we are well aware that local circumstances vary and that at national level the best may be the enemy of the practicable. What is essential, in our view, is that the particular need should in each area determine the structure, rather than bringing into existence a uniform overall pattern to which local or national needs were made to conform.

In this whole area we warmly welcome the establishment of the Government's Voluntary Services Unit and its activities. We know that its officers are, so to speak, walking several tight-ropes at once. They must not dictate to the voluntary sector: yet each of their decisions will be taken as an indication of official policy. They must not lay down hard-and-fast criteria for their support of the voluntary sector: yet they cannot support an indiscriminate free-for-all. We recognise the empirical commonsense with which they have interpreted their role in the implementation of governmental policy towards the voluntary organisations and we hope that they will be given, as we have suggested in Chapter 4, a more powerful governmental base.

We would not wish it to be thought that we believe the survival of voluntary organisations to depend solely on the injection of public funds, either at national or at local level. At the present moment many organisations are, as they have told us, uneasy about their financial future. This is not surprising, in view of the national financial situation. At the same time, we find no evidence that the voluntary sector is in danger of financial collapse. We have been reassured by the capacity of the voluntary sector to mobilise voluntary effort and by its readiness to tap new sources of help. But people and ideas are not enough. If there is to be substantial growth and development and if the contribution of the voluntary sector is to be extended and diversified, then it will need more financial resources. Especially, the present disparity between local authorities in their backing for voluntary effort leads us to believe that there is a case for a more liberal deployment of central government finance into this sector, to encourage and stimulate initiatives and provision.

We have not attempted to draw up a detailed programme for the development of the voluntary organisations over the next twenty-five years. That would be particularly hazardous at the present time and would in any case be incompatible with the spontaneity of growth inside the voluntary sector. We have painted a picture, admittedly incomplete, of what we have seen. We have tried to analyse it and show how the voluntary sector relates to the informal and the statutory forms of provision. We have suggested that, nationally and locally, these relationships need to be developed and have drawn attention to signposts pointing towards routes for advance.

We end not with the conventional summary of specific recommendations but with a two-fold challenge. We repeat and underline the appeal we have made to the voluntary organisations to maintain, improve and extend the vital contribution which they are making to the pluralistic system of social provision. By the same token we address an appeal to the government, as the central strategic makers of social policy. It is for them to take, urgently, the initiative in working out, with the variety of agencies which are now operating in this field, a collaborative social plan which will make the optimum and maximum use of resources. We are not, of course, proposing a super-monolith. That would be contrary to our whole philosophy. But we do believe that in this vast field there is need for a synoptic view, so that each system may make its full and appropriate contribution. If this initiative is not taken soon, there will over the next twenty-five years be not only an incomplete realisation of the potential contribution of the voluntary organisations but also an inadequate provision of help to our fellow citizens who need it.

APPENDIX 1

List of organisations and individuals who gave evidence, written, oral or both, or who were visited by committee or staff members

The Abbeyfield Society
Aberdeen Association of Social Service
Action Resource Centre
After Six Housing Advisory Trust Limited
Age Concern (England)
Age Concern (Scotland)
Age Concern (Wales)
Albany Trust
Alcoholics Anonymous
Arthritis and Rheumatism Council
Association of Agriculture
Association of British Adoption Agencies
Association of County Councils
Association of District Councils
Association of Inner Wheel Clubs in Great Britain and Ireland
Association for Jewish Youth
Association of Leagues of Hospital Friends
Association of London Housing Estates
Association of Metropolitan Authorities
ASRO (Association of Social Research Organisations)
ASBAH (Association for Spina Bifida and Hydrocephalus)

Bangladesh Women's Association in Great Britain
Bangla Educational Culture Centre
The Baptist Union of Scotland
Barker, Mr D. J.
Barnardo's
Belfast Voluntary Welfare Society
Birth Control Campaign
Board of Deputies of British Jews
Board of Education (Church of England)
Boys' Brigade
Bradmore 'Sons of Rest'
British Association of Hard of Hearing

194

British Association of Settlements
British Council for Rehabilitation of the Disabled
British Epilepsy Association
British Federation of Music Festivals
British Federation of University Women
British Polio Fellowship
British Red Cross Society
British Trust for Conservation Volunteers
Brook Advisory Centres
Burgoyne, Mrs M. G.
Bury and District RSPCA
Bury Metro Society for Mentally Handicapped Children
Bury Voluntary Language Tutorial Scheme

The Camping Club of Great Britain and Ireland Ltd
Cancer Research Campaign
The Carnegie Trust for the Universities of Scotland
Caribbean Family Group
Catholic Housing Association
Catholic Marriage Advisory Council
Central British Fund for Jewish Relief and Rehabilitation
Centre for Environmental Studies
Centre for Studies in Social Policy
CHAR (Campaign for the Homeless and Rootless)
Charity Law Reform Committee
The Chase Charity
Cheshire Foundation Homes for the Sick
The Chest and Heart Association
Child Poverty Action Group
Childrens' Country Holiday Fund
The Chindits Old Comrades Association
Christian Aid
The Church Army
The Church Lads Brigade
Church of England Board for Social Responsibility
Church of England Childrens' Society
Church of Scotland Committee of Social Responsibility
Church of Scotland Womens' Guild
The Coeliac Society
Commons, Open Spaces and Footpaths Preservation Society
Commonwealth Society for the Deaf

Communicare
Community Service Volunteers
Community Shop Association and North Belfast Community Resource
     Centre
Conservation Society   .
Consortium
Contact
Convention of Scottish Local Authorities
Council for British Archaeology
Council for the Protection of Rural England
Council of Social Service for Wales
Council for Wales of Voluntary Youth Services
Countrywide Holidays Association
Credit Union (Wimbledon) Ltd
CRUSE (Widows and Children)
CURE
The Cyrenians Limited

Dartmoor Preservation Association
Disabled Living Foundation
Disablement Income Group

Emmerson Park Ward Residents Association
Enterprise Youth

Family Crisis Centre (Southwark Womens' Aid)
The Family Planning Association
Family Service Units
The Family Welfare Association
The Fawcett Society
Fermanagh Association for the Handicapped
Forces Help Society and Lord Roberts Workshops
Friends of the Children Society
Friends of the Earth
Friends of the Elderly and Gentlefolks' Help
Friends Service Council (Quakers)

Gatliff Trust
Gibson, Mr Ashton
Giles House (Helping Hand Association)
Gingerbread

The Girls' Brigade
Girl Guides Association
Glasgow Council for Voluntary Service
Granville House
Guide Dogs for the Blind Association

Hackney Community Link-up
Harlow Council for Voluntary Service
Harvey, Mr Michael
Help the Aged
Housing Corporation
Howard League for Penal Reform

Ilkley Playgroup for Handicapped Children
Independent Adoption Society
Inland Waterways Association
Institute of Cancer Research
Institute of Race Relations
Interaction Trust
Invalid Children's Aid Association
Islington Bus Company
Isserlis, Mr A. R. (Centre for Studies in Social Policy)

Jewish Blind Society
Jewish Welfare Board
Joint Committee, Order of St John of Jerusalem and British Red Cross
    Society

Kelly, Mr Cuthbert
Keys Association
King Edward's Hospital Fund for London
Kingsbridge Fair Week Committee
Kingston Polytechnic

LAG (Legal Action Group Information Service)
League of Jewish Women
Leeds Council for Voluntary Service
Leeds Diocesan Rescue Protection and Child Welfare Society
Leukaemia Research Fund
Liverpool Council of Social Service
Llandaff, Bishop of

London Borough of Croydon Social Services Department
London Borough of Islington
London Boroughs' Association
The London Boroughs' Training Committee
London Council of Social Service

Manor Road Church and Youth and Community Centre
Manchester Jewish Social Services
Mardyke Tenants Association
Merched Y Wawr
Methodist Homes for the Aged
MIND (National Association for Mental Health)
Multiple Sclerosis Society
Muscular Dystrophy Group of GB

National Adoption Society
National Adult School Union
National Children's Bureau
NACRO (National Association for Care and Resettlement of Offenders)
National Association of Local Councils
NAMCW (National Association for Maternal and Child Welfare)
National Association for Multi-Racial Education
National Association of Boys' Clubs
National Association of Citizens' Advice Bureaux
National Association of Leagues of Hospital Friends
National Association of Voluntary Help Organisers
National Association of Women's Clubs
National Association of Youth Clubs
National Childbirth Trust
National Children's Home
National Corporation for the Care of Old People
National Council for Civil Liberties
National Council for One Parent Families
National Council for the Single Woman and her Dependants
National Council of Social Service
National Council of Social Service: Community Work Division
National Council of Social Service/London Council of Social Service/
    Association of Scientific, Technical and Managerial Staff Group
National Council for Voluntary Youth Services
National Council of Women of Great Britain
National Council of Young Men's Christian Associations

National Deaf Children's Society
National Educational Research and Development Trust
National Elfrida Rathbone Society
National Endeavour Group
National Federation of the Blind (UK)
National Federation of Business and Professional Women's Clubs of
    Great Britain and Northern Ireland
National Federation of Credit Unions
National Federation of Housing Associations
National Federation of Women's Institutes
National Federation of Young Farmers Clubs
National Free Church Women's Council
National Marriage Guidance Council
National Playing Fields Association
National Society for Clean Air
National Society for Epileptics
National Society for the Prevention of Cruelty to Children
The National Trust
The National Trust for Scotland
National Union of Townswomen's Guilds
National Voluntary Civil Aid Services
National Youth Bureau
Nature Conservancy Council
Neighbourhood English Classes
Northern Ireland Association for the Care and Resettlement of
    Offenders
Northern Ireland Association for Mental Health
Northern Ireland Council of Social Service
Northern Ireland Pre-School Play Groups
North Reddish Friendly Club
North Romford Community Association
North Wales Society for the Blind
North West Council of Social Service

Order of St John
Outset
Oxfam

Parkinson's Disease Society
Patchwork
Peacock, Miss Primrose

Peter Bedford Project
Physically Handicapped and Able-Bodied Residential Courses and Clubs
The Pipers' Guild
Pre-Retirement Association
Pre-School Playgroups Association

Queen Elizabeth's Foundation for the Disabled

Railway Invigoration Society
Ramblers Association
Ramsbottom Fraternal of Christian Ministers
The Richmond Fellowship
Rotary International
Royal Alfred Seamen's Society
Royal Association in Aid of Deaf and Dumb
Royal British Legion
Royal Humane Society
Royal National Institute for the Blind
Royal National Institute for the Deaf
Royal National Lifeboat Institution
Royal Scottish Society for Prevention of Cruelty to Children
Royal Society for Prevention of Cruelty to Animals
Royal Society for Protection of Birds
Royal Yachting Association
Rowe, Andrew (Director Community Affairs Conservative Central
    Office)
The Runnymede Trust
Rural Music Schools Association

St Andrews Ambulance Association
St Dunstans
St Giles Centre, Camberwell
St Giles Crypt Day Centre
The Saltire Society
The Salvation Army
The Samaritans
Save the Children
Scottish Amateur Music Association
Scottish Association for Mental Health
Scottish Association for Study of Dyslexia Ltd
Scottish Association of Boys' Clubs

Scottish Association of Voluntary Child Care Organisations
Scottish Council for Single Parents
Scottish Council for Spastics
Scottish Council of Social Service
Scottish Marriage Guidance Council
Scottish Mothers' Union
Scottish National Council of Young Men's Christian Associations
Scottish Paraplegic (Spinal injuries) Association
Scottish Pre-School Play Groups Association
Scottish Society for the Mentally Handicapped
Scottish Spina Bifida Association
Scottish Standing Conference of Sport
Scottish Standing Conference of Voluntary Youth Organisations
Scottish Wildlife Trust
Scottish Women's Rural Institutes
The Scout Association
Sefton Council for Voluntary Service
SHAC (Shelter Housing Aid Centre)
The Shaftesbury Society
Shankill Community Council
Shaw, Mrs Clair
Society of Local Authority Chief Executives
Society for the Promotion of Nature Reserves
Society of St Vincent de Paul
Society of Voluntary Associates
Soldiers' Sailors' and Airmen's Families Association
Southern and Western Regional Association for the Blind
South Stoke Newington Community Association
The Spastics Society
Standing Conference of Voluntary Social Work Organisations in
    Staffordshire
Stepney Jewish (B'nai Brith) Clubs and Settlements
Stevenage Council for Voluntary Service
Stockport and District Federation of Townswomen's Guilds
Stockport Maternity Child Welfare Voluntary Committee
Sunderland Council of Churches

Tamworth Community Service Council
Task Force
Thornhill Project
TOC H

Town and Country Planning Association

Ulster Institute for the Deaf
Union of Lancashire and Cheshire Institutes
Urdd Gobaith Cymru
Upminster and Cranham Ratepayers and Residents Association

Victoria Boys' and Girls' Clubs
The Volunteer Centre

Wakefield Metropolitan District Council
Wales Council for the Blind
Wales Council for the Disabled
The Wates Foundation
Welsh Association for the Deaf
Welsh Association of Youth Clubs
West Indian Welfare Association
White Lion Street Free School
Women's Aid
Women's National Commission
Women's Royal Voluntary Service

Youth Hostels Association (England and Wales)
Youth Service of the Community
Young Volunteer Resources Unit
Young Women's Christian Association (Great Britain)

The questionnaire sent to those giving written evidence

GUIDELINES FOR GIVING EVIDENCE

Introductory

The Committee is to review the role and functions of voluntary
organisations in the United Kingdom in the last quarter of the twentieth
century. We need facts about present organisations but we need them
for the purposes of the future and not for their own sake. We have
therefore divided our request for evidence into three parts: the first
being background material, mainly factual; the second being the current

situation; and the third asking for your views on the future. It would be helpful if you were to follow the guidelines broadly when dealing with the points which are raised in them, but you are not restricted to these questions and we shall welcome your views on any other relevant matters which you wish to put forward.

Section 1 – Background

(a) For what purpose or purposes was your organisation founded?

(b) (i) Are its principal goals or objectives still the same today?

    (ii) If so, have the methods used to achieve these goals changed?

    (iii) If not, in what ways have the goals or objectives changed?

(c) How is your organisation structured to achieve its goals?

    (i) What is the legal form of your organisation (e.g. trust, members association, company limited by guarantee, etc.)?

    (ii) What geographical area is covered by your organisation? If there are separate corresponding organisations in the various parts of the United Kingdom, what is your relationship with them?

    (iii) If your organisation has local branches, what forms do the relationships to the centre take?

    (iv) What is the governing of policy-making body, and how is it appointed?

    (v) What is the administrative structure?

    (vi) Does your organisation have members? If so, how many? How are they recruited? What is their role? What services are provided for them?

    (vii) To what extent does your organisation depend on unpaid staff?

    (viii) Does your organisation have a paid staff? If it does, how many? How are they recruited? What proportion of the staff have formal qualifications related to their work for the organisation?

    (ix) What part is played by paid staff in the management and policy determination of the organisation?

    (x) What proportion of the paid staff belong to (a) staff associations, (b) professional associations, (c) trade unions?

(d) (i) How is your organisation financed? (Please show the proportions of income received in the last financial year under the different categories (e.g. government grant, local authority grant, subscriptions, legacies, charges for services, etc.).)

(ii)   To what extent do you receive aid in kind (e.g. free accommodation or free facilities)?
(e) What forms do your relationships with statutory bodies take?
    (i)   central government
    (ii)   local government
    (iii) other statutory bodies
(f) What forms do the relationships with other voluntary bodies take?
(g) What methods are used to evaluate the work of the organisation? What criteria are used for the evaluation? What conclusions have been reached about the effectiveness of the work of your organisation over the last two or three years?
(h) How does your organisation make its work known to the public?

Section 2 – The Current Situation

1 *Functions*

(a) What are the main current functions of your organisation? Do they include, for example, a pioneering role, filling the gaps left by the statutory services; such matters as coordination, education, information, research, cultural or social/recreational activities?
(b) Are there any subsidiary functions to which you wish to draw attention?
2 What is the justification for a voluntary organisation providing these functions at the present time rather than their provision by a statutory or commercial body?
3 (a) What other organisations are to your knowledge working in the same or a similar field to your own?
    (b) How do their functions differ from yours?
    (c) Has any merger been considered?
    (d) Do you belong to a coordinating organisation or do you cooperate with these other bodies on certain activities?
4 *Problems*
What in the view of your managing or policy-making body are the main problems encountered by your organisation? (It may be possible to explain them by developing the replies to some or all of the questions in Section 1 or it may be easier to deal with them separately and in one section of your reply.)

Section 3 – Views on the Future

1 What function or functions do you envisage for your organisation

during the period of the next 25 years in the light of the general
trends which you expect? (It will be helpful if your evidence here
can cover the same functions as you have mentioned in your replies
to Section 2.)

2   In trying to fulfil these functions what problems do you expect to
encounter?

    (i)   financial
    (ii)   administrative
    (iii)   membership
    (iv)   paid staff, including those professionally qualified
    (v)   legal
    (vi)   relationships with statutory bodies
    (vii) relationships with other bodies
    (viii) any other?

3   What changes would you like to see which might make the work of
your organisation easier in the next 25 years?

List of Northern Ireland Organisations which gave evidence in response to a special questionnaire prepared by the Northern Ireland Council of Social Service

Armagh Citizens' Advice Bureau
Armagh Credit Union

Ballymoney Community Service Committee
Belfast Charitable Society
Belfast Hard of Hearing Club
Belfast Simon Community
Benevolent Fund for Nurses
Boys Brigade in Northern Ireland
British Association for Early Childhood Education (Northern Ireland
    Committee)
British and Foreign Bible Society (Northern Ireland Area)
British Rheumatism and Arthritis Association

Cancer Research Campaign
Christian Aid Irish Office
Churches Central Committee for Community Work
Church of Ireland Social and Family Welfare Association

Coleraine Citizens' Advice Bureau
Community Shop Association
Cystic Fibrosis Research Trust

Federation of Women's Institutes of Northern Ireland

Glendhu Children's Hotel

Home for the Blind, Cliftonville

Irish Temperance League

Methodist Orphan Society
Missions to Seamen
Multiple Sclerosis Society

National Council for the Single Woman and her Dependants (Belfast)
National Society for the Prevention of Cruelty to Children
National Trust Committee Northern Ireland
Newhill Youth and Community Association
Newry and District Community Social Council
Northern Ireland Association for the Care and Resettlement of
    Offenders
Northern Ireland Association for Mental Health
Northern Ireland Branch Muscular Dystrophy Group of Great Britain
Northern Ireland Chest and Heart Association
Northern Ireland Council for Orthopaedic Development
Northern Ireland Marriage Guidance Council
Northern Ireland Preschool Playgroup Association
Northern Ireland Scout Council

Order of Malta Ambulance Corps

Presbyterian Church in Ireland Old Age Fund
Protestant/Catholic Encounter

Rathcoole Citizens' Advice Bureau
Retirement Association of Northern Ireland

Samaritans
Save the Children Fund Northern Ireland

Shankill Road Mission (Presbyterian Church in Ireland)

Ulster Archaeological Heritage Society
Ulster Cancer Foundation
Ulster Girl Guides
Ulster Institute for the Deaf
Ulster Society for the Prevention of Cruelty to Animals

Victoria Homes

War on Want
Workshops for the Blind

Young Farmers' Club
Youth Hostel Association of Northern Ireland
Young Men's Christian Association (Belfast)
Young Women's Christian Association for Ireland

Appendix 2

Research carried out for the Committee

Research was carried out for the Committee under the supervision of Stephen Hatch, the Senior Research Officer. Four Research Assistants were employed for shorter or longer periods – Susan Cooper, Rosalind Howell, Ian Mocroft and Paul Unsworth. A considerable amount of general fact-finding and analysis was undertaken, much of which has found its way in a more or less distilled form into the pages of the Report. A number of specific enquiries were also initiated. These are listed below, together with indications of what further publications arising from the research are likely. Some of the research projects had not been finished by the time the Committee's Report was completed, and the Joseph Rowntree Memorial Trust has made further funds available for the continuation of the research by what will be known as the Voluntary Organisations Research Unit.

1 Locality Studies

These are described in Chapter 3. In addition to work carried out by the staff of the Committee, Philip Bryers of Glasgow University was commissioned to design and supervise studies made in Glasgow, Alison Chipendale carried out lengthy interviews with consumers of services in the three main towns studied and Jill Cohen did much of the field-work in one town. It is hoped that a much fuller report will be published at a later date.

2 Participation in Voluntary Work: The National Opinion Poll Survey

A short account of the findings was published in *New Society* for 7 April 1977, under the title 'Voluntary workers' by Stephen Hatch and Ian Mocroft. It is hoped that a fuller account of the findings will be made available through the Volunteer Centre before the end of 1977.

3 Survey of Family Fund Applicants

A survey of applicants to the Family Fund enquiring into their involvement in voluntary organisations for handicapped children was carried out in cooperation with the Family Fund Research Team. The findings of this study are to be published in *Child Care, Health and Development* as an article entitled 'Voluntary organisations for handicapped children and their families: the meaning of membership' by Jonathan Bradshaw, Caroline Glendinning and Stephen Hatch.

4 Cost-Effectiveness

Three main sets of comparisons were made. First, Serge Lourie was commissioned to examine available evidence about the relative costs of housing associations and local authorities. Second, analysis of the costs of six statutory and two voluntary hostels in London was made by the staff of the Committee. Third, a more extensive analysis of the costs of the children's homes run by three large voluntary agencies and three local authorities was undertaken. Further work on the children's homes has still to be carried out, leading it is hoped to a separate publication.

5 Finance

The results of the Committee's enquiries are presented in Appendix 6, including in Appendix 6D the results of the one specific research project carried out in this field.

6 The Location of Branches

This study examined the location of the branches of 22 national voluntary organisations in towns in England and Wales, excluding London, with a population in 1971 of over 50,000. The presence or absence of branches was related to 27 indicators of economic and social conditions. Some of the findings are reported in Chapter 3. A fuller account is being prepared with a view to publication.

APPENDIX 3

List of Works Mentioned in the Text and of Other Works Consulted in the Preparation of the Report

Calouste Gulbenkian Foundation, *Current Issues in Community Work,* Routledge & Kegan Paul, London 1973

Geraldine M. Aves, *The Voluntary Worker in the Social Services,* Bedford Square Press and Allen & Unwin, London, 1969

Geraldine M. Aves, *Pivot,* Report of a Working Party on the National Association of Voluntary Help Organisers, The Volunteer Centre, Berkhamstead, 1976

Michael Bayley, *Mental Handicap and Community Care,* Routledge, London, 1973

Lord Beveridge and A. F. Wells (eds), *The Evidence for Voluntary Action,* Allen & Unwin, London, 1949

Lord Beveridge, *Voluntary Action: a report on methods of social advance,* Allen & Unwin, London, 1948

Charles Booth, *Life and Labour of the People of London,* London, 1891-1903

William Booth, *The Salvation Army and Poor Law Reform,* Salvation Army, 1909

A. F. C. Bourdillon, *Voluntary Social Services, Their Place in the Modern State,* Methuen, London, 1945

Jonathan Bradshaw, Caroline Glendinning and Stephen Hatch, 'Voluntary organisations for handicapped children and their families: the meaning of membership', *Child Care, Health and Development,* forthcoming

Margaret Brasnett, *Voluntary Social Action,* National Council of Social Service, London, 1969

Maurice Bruce, *The Coming of the Welfare State,* Batsford, London, 1961

Civic Trust, *The Local Amenity Movement,* London, 1976

Raymond Clarke and Richard Davies, *A Chance to Share,* PEP Broadsheet no. 552, June 1975

Alice H. Collins and D. L. Pancoast, *Natural Helping Networks: A Strategy for Prevention,* National Association of Social Workers, Washington, 1976

Commission on Private Philanthropy and Public Needs, *Giving in America* (the Filer Report), Washington, 1975

P. F. Cousins, 'Voluntary organisations and local government in three south London boroughs', *Public Administration*, vol. 54, spring 1976

Giles Darvill, *Bargain or Barricade?*, The Volunteer Centre, Berkhamstead, 1975

Peter Falush, 'Trends in the Finance of British Charities', *National Westminster Bank Quarterly Review*, May 1977

J. H. Goldthorpe *et al.*, *The Affluent Worker in the Class Structure*, Cambridge University Press, 1969

The Goodman Committee, *Charity Law and Voluntary Organisations*, Bedford Square Press, London, 1976

Roger Hadley *et al.*, *Across the Generations*, Allen & Unwin, 1975

Stephen Hatch and Ian Mocroft, 'Voluntary workers', *New Society*, 7 April 1977

J. R. Hay, *The Origins of the Liberal Welfare Reforms 1904–1914*, Macmillan, London, 1975

Ralph M. Kramer, 'Future of the voluntary service organisations', *Social Worker*, November 1973

Ralph M. Kramer, *The Voluntary Agency in the Welfare State*, forthcoming

John Lansley, *Voluntary Organisations Facing Change*, Calouste Gulbenkian Foundation, London, 1976

J. D. Livingston Booth and M. Redmond Mullin, *Report on Foundation Activity*, Charities Aid Foundation, Tonbridge, 1976

Gordon Manser and Rosemary Higgins Cass, *Voluntarism at the Crossroads*, Family Service Association of America, New York, 1976

Christine D. McKee, *Charitable Organisations*, University of Birmingham Centre for Urban and Regional Studies, 1974

Henry A. Mess *et al.*, *Voluntary Social Services Since 1918*, Routledge, London, 1948

Caroline Moorehead, *Helping*, Macdonald and Jane's, London, 1975

Sheila Moore, *Working for Free*, Pan Books, London, 1977

Mary Morris, *Social Enterprise*, National Council of Social Service, London, 1962

Mary Morris, *Voluntary Work in the Welfare State*, Routledge, London, 1969

John Moyle and David J. Reid, 'Private non-profit-making bodies serving persons', *Economic Trends*, No. 259, May 1975

George J. Murray, *Voluntary Organisations and Social Welfare*, Oliver and Boyd, Edinburgh, 1969

George J. Murray in W. F. Maunder (ed.), *Review of UK Statistical Sources, Vol. 1*, Heinemann Educational Books, London, 1974

Kenneth Newton, *Second City Politics: Democratic Processes and Decision-Making in Birmingham*, Clarendon Press, Oxford, 1976

Benedict Nightingale, *Charities*, Allen Lane, London, 1973

Harold Perkin, *The Origins of Modern English Society: 1780-1880*, Routledge, London, 1969

Madeleine Rooff, *Voluntary Societies and Social Policy*, Routledge, London, 1957

Michael E. Rose, *The Relief of Poverty, 1834-1914*, Macmillan, London, 1972.

Andrew Rowe, *Democracy Renewed*, Sheldon Press, London, 1975

B. Seebohm Rowntree, *Poverty: A Study of Town Life*, Macmillan, London, 1901

Sally Sainsbury, *Measuring Disability*, Bell, London, 1974

Ethel Shanas *et al.*, *Old People in Three Industrial Societies*, Routledge, London, 1968

T. S. Simey, *Principles of Social Administration*, Oxford University Press, London, 1937

Adrian Webb *et al.*, *Voluntary Social Service Manpower Resources*, Personal Social Services Council, London, 1976

Sidney and Beatrice Webb (eds), *The Break-up of the Poor Law*, Being Part I of the Minority Report of the Poor Law Commission, Longmans, London 1909

Wells Collection, (1973 supplemental edition), Wells Group of Fund-Raising Companies, London, 1975

Lord Windlesham, *Politics in Practice*, Jonathan Cape, London, 1975

Government Publications

Central Statistical Office, *National Income and Expenditure 1965-1975*, HMSO, 1976

Central Statistical Office *Social Trends*, HMSO, annual

Charity Commissioners, *Report of the Charity Commissioners for England and Wales*, HMSO, annual

Department of the Environment, *50 Million Volunteers*, HMSO, 1972

House of Commons Expenditure Committee, Session 1974-75, *Charity Commissioners and their Accountability*, HMSO, 1975

Report of the Committee of Enquiry on Local Government Finance (Layfield Report), Cmnd. 6453, HMSO, 1976

Report of the Committee on Local Authority and Allied Personal Social Services (Seebohm Report), Cmnd. 3703, HMSO, 1968

Report of the Royal Commission on the Poor Laws and Relief of Distress, HMSO, 1909

Social Insurance and Allied Services, Report by Sir William Beveridge, HMSO, 1942

APPENDIX 4

Government Departments and Voluntary Organisations
Note for the Wolfenden Committee

The following paper has been prepared by the Home Office Voluntary
Services Unit on the basis of information provided by all government
departments about the nature of their relationships with voluntary
organisations working in the United Kingdom. It was considered that
the Committee would probably find it more helpful to have one composite paper attempting to give an overall view of the relationship
between government departments and the voluntary sector than a series
of individual papers by different departments. General points made in
the paper can, however, be expanded in relation to particular departments and the Voluntary Services Unit will gladly provide more detailed
information on request.

General Policy

2. The general attitude of the government towards voluntary organisations was set out in a speech in the House of Lords on 25 June 1975
(O.R. 25.6.76 Cols 1410-1418) by Lord Harris, the Minister of State at
the Home Office with special responsibility for voluntary services. He
denied the view that the development of the welfare state reduced the
need for voluntary service, pointing out that the statutory services were
under more pressure than at any time since the last war and that if the
lifeline provided by many dedicated volunteers were cut, many of the
most under-privileged in society would be the first to suffer. In this and
other Ministerial speeches it has been stressed that there is a need for
voluntary services complementary to those provided by the State and
that a society in which all needs were met by the State would be a less
civilised and humane one. References have been made to the importance
of the pioneering role of voluntary organisations, identifying needs and
demonstrating how to meet them; to the need for greater involvement
in the community and more emphasis on mutual help; and to the increased opportunity for self-fulfilment open to individuals concerned
with voluntary work. It has been made clear that all these aspects of
voluntary work are highly valued by government and that the general
government policy is to encourage the use of volunteers and the involvement of voluntary organisations wherever this is practicable.

3. The belief that voluntary organisations have an important role to

play in the United Kingdom is demonstrated by the setting up under a Conservative government and the continuation under a Labour one of the Voluntary Services Unit. The Unit has four main functions. First of all, it is intended to act as a link between voluntary organisations and government departments, giving advice to the former as to their best points of contact within departments and alerting the latter to the possible effects upon voluntary organisations of certain major policy proposals, legislation, or government directives. Secondly, it provides a useful focal point for the diverse departmental interests within Whitehall relating to the voluntary sector. For this purpose, the Unit has within each major government department a Liaison Officer at Assistant Secretary level who is responsible for keeping the Unit informed on matters relevant to its work and who attends quarterly meetings with the Unit and all the other Liaison Officers at which information and advice can be exchanged and matters of general interest to the voluntary sector can be discussed.

4. The third function of the Unit is to stimulate the use of volunteers where this can appropriately be done by central government and to encourage voluntary organisations to cooperate with each other and to coordinate their activities in an effort to avoid unnecessary duplication of effort. Finally, the Unit functions as a financier of last resort within Whitehall, with limited funds available to assist national organisations or projects whose work spans the interests of several different departments or which are not the direct responsibility of any single department. Its funds are also used in exceptional cases to support innovatory local projects from which lessons of national relevance can be learned, and to maintain organisations working in areas of high social priority where alternative funds will definitely be available within a short time.

5. The creation of the Voluntary Services Unit did not in any way interfere with the working relations already established between most government departments and the voluntary organisations concerned with the services for which the departments are responsible. Nor did it lead to any overall decisions as to the optimum level of government expenditure on voluntary organisations. Each department still decides, in relation to its own priorities and resources, which organisations it will support and the extent to which such support will be given. The only general policy, which is a direct result of the current restraints on spending, is that departments should at present give priority to meeting existing commitments to voluntary organisations, should then assist, where possible, existing organisations whose work is of high social

priority but likely to fail for lack of finance, and should only then
encourage new services or the extension of existing ones, again where
the work is of high social priority.

Departmental Policies

6. Generally, voluntary organisations deal within departments with
whatever division or branch is relevant to their work. Some departments, notably the Department of Health and Social Security and the
health divisions of the Scottish Home and Health Department, have a
central point of reference – a group of officials who act as a point of
coordination within the Department and, in the case of the group of
officials in the Department of Health and Social Security, a point of
origin for general policy formulation. This point of reference is particularly useful for organisations which, within the department's overall
sphere of activity, span the interests of more than one branch or division, but such arrangements are not common and are probably only
necessary in the larger and more complex departments. In the Health
and Social Services Department in Northern Ireland there is also one
designated branch responsible for voluntary organisations. Policy
towards voluntary organisations in the Social Work Services Group in
the Scottish Office is decided at a meeting of heads of division, chaired
by the Under Secretary and with senior professional advisers present.

7. Responsibility for dealing with voluntary organisations generally
rests therefore at divisional or branch level and in consequence a variety
of Ministers may theoretically be concerned with voluntary organisations from time to time. Generally, no one Minister within any one
department has a specific responsibility for matters concerning voluntary organisations, except in the Department of Health and Social
Security, where the Minister of State (Health) has a responsibility for
the voluntary sector in so far as it relates to DHSS responsibilities, and
in the Home Office where the Home Secretary has a general coordinating interest in government policy towards voluntary organisations, and
one Minister of State has a particular concern for those voluntary
organisations which fall within the terms of reference of the Voluntary
Services Unit.

8. Broadly speaking, government support to voluntary organisations
may be divided into three main categories. These are where it is considered that voluntary provision is preferable to a statutory service;
where the voluntary organisation can provide an alternative to existing
statutory provision, providing an element of choice for users of the
service concerned; or where a statutory service can be supplemented or

extended by voluntary means. These categories are not mutually exclusive; it is often difficult to place a grant clearly in one or other of them but taken together they account for the great majority of government grants to voluntary organisations.

9. There are various reasons why voluntary provision might be considered preferable to statutory provision in relation to particular services. The most obvious is where there is clearly a need to be met but the government is not satisfied that statutory provision is either necessary or desirable. The decision not to provide a statutory service may be made on grounds of finance or lack of manpower or, more commonly, because the number in need is not great enough to justify special statutory provision (e.g. specialist provision for unusual physical handicap), or for any of the reasons for preferring voluntary effort which are mentioned below. Over time, changes in circumstances or in the climate of public opinion may lead to a change in priorities or opinions which will means that the voluntary provision is overtaken by a statutory service. The existing health and education services and to a large extent the child care and social welfare services all emerged from this pattern of a pioneering voluntary effort, at first unaided by government, then assisted with government funds, and finally leading to a comparable statutory service.

10. One of the main reasons for preferring voluntary to statutory services in certain instances is the 'non-establishment" image of the voluntary sector. This is particularly useful in providing services for those who might generally be anti-authoritarian or afraid of people who are assumed to be on the side of the establishment, e.g. ex-offenders, alcoholics, drug addicts, or down-and-outs. Another reason is that voluntary organisations can often respond more flexibly to people with a wide range of social needs than a statutory body which is usually geared to the provision of one particular service. The provision by voluntary bodies of general welfare services such as help and advice to young people, e.g. Release, West End Coordinated Voluntary Services, and Girls Alone in London, or to problem families, e.g. Family Service Units, is assisted by government for both the above-mentioned reasons.

11. Sometimes there is a feeling that, particularly where advice on personal problems or on difficulties with statutory bodies is concerned, there may be some advantage in the person giving the advice not being part of a statutory service. In the marriage guidance field, for instance, the final report of the Committee on Procedure in Matrimonial Causes (Command Paper 7024, January 1947) and the report of the Departmental Committee on Grants for the Development of Marriage Guidance

(Command Paper 7566, October 1948) issued by Parliament recommended that there should be a marriage guidance service sponsored by the State but achieved by giving encouragement and financial assistance to voluntary organisations already operating in this field. The development of the Citizens' Advice Bureaux, as non-statutory offices although supported nearly 100 per cent by the State, is another case in point as are the Law Centres funded at local level by the Lord Chancellor's Office.

12. Finally, there may be areas where lack of popular appeal may inhibit the provision of statutory services and equally make it difficult for voluntary oganisations to raise funds yet both government and the voluntary sector recognise a need and wish to provide for it. Grants made by the VSU in respect of counselling on sexual problems and by the Department of Health and Social Security in the fields of drugs and alcoholism fall within this category. In all the above examples, voluntary provision is generally acknowledged as preferable to statutory provision.

13. An area in which a preference for voluntary provision overlaps with the desirability of providing voluntary alternatives is in the field of the after-care of offenders. There is clearly an important statutory task in providing assistance to ex-offenders but there is also much scope for voluntary help, partly for the 'image' reasons previously mentioned and partly because of the belief that an ex-offender has more chance of rehabilitation if he has the sympathy and understanding of his local community. It is for reasons of this kind that the work of, for instance, the National Association for the Care and Resettlement of Offenders is given government assistance, the Northern Ireland Office and the Scottish Social Work Services Group encourage and support voluntary work amongst ex-offenders, and the Home Office has a grant scheme specifically to encourage voluntary effort to expand the provision of after-care accommodation for ex-offenders.

14. The provision of desirable alternatives to statutory services is clearly seen in the area of housing, where the Department of the Environment, the Welsh Office, the Scottish Development Department, and the Department of Housing, Local Government and Planning in Northern Ireland have given considerable encouragement to housing associations. This does not mean that housing associations are considered to be better placed to be able to build, convert and provide accommodation than the relevant statutory authorities, but that they are able to offer housing to people who would prefer not to depend on statutory provision but cannot meet the requirements of ordinary

private sector housing. It is, however, increasingly recognised that what
housing associations have to offer in the area of housing management –
in particular their ability effectively to encourage tenant participation
in management – is both valuable and unique and can provide useful
experience for statutory bodies.

15. The extension and supplementation of statutory services by
voluntary effort is most evident in the social services field where the
outstanding example is the Women's Royal Voluntary Service. The
WRVS is funded mainly by the VSU and has a specific role in helping
local authorities to perform their statutory duties. The work done by
the WRVS demonstrates how the mobilisation of hundreds of volunteers, who would probably be unable or unwilling to take full-time
or part-time jobs with local authorities, can enable the provision of
services which would be far beyond the resources of local government
in terms of either money or manpower. The Department of Health and
Social Security similarly encourages the use of volunteers in the health
service as do the Home Office in the probation and after-care services
and the Department of the Environment in the carrying out of conservation measures. These are all labour-intensive services where flexibility of
volunteers who can be available for short periods of time when needed
instead of, like employees, being constantly available whether needed or
not, is a great asset. The dividing line between using voluntary services
to supplement statutory ones and using voluntary organisations as
agents to provide statutory services is a very narrow one and it is doubtful whether, in practice, the distinction is worth making. The WRVS,
for instance, sometimes works alongside statutory employees and is
sometimes wholly responsible for the provision of a particular service.

16. It is perhaps relevant to mention at this point that departmental
policy is not always implemented directly by the department but sometimes by way of a statutory agency. Where statutory agencies have been
set up to pursue particular government policies, they usually have power
to make grants to voluntary organisations in pursuance of these policies
and they sometimes have considerable funds available for this purpose.
Within broad guidelines established by the departments, agencies such
as the Housing Corporation, the Development Commission, and to a
lesser extent, the Community Relations Commission have considerable
discretion to make grants and although the grants made require the
approval of the relevant responsible department it would be extremely
unusual for such approval to be withheld.

17. The fact that policy towards voluntary organisations is generally
decided in the context of the particular area in which they work means

inevitably that it would be difficult to have a more specific overall government policy towards them than that described in the opening paragraphs of this paper. The lack of specific overall policies is on the whole probably advantageous to voluntary organisations because it allows for a more flexible and pragmatic response to the needs of the voluntary sector than would be possible if there were general rules about the kind of organisation which could be helped and the type of situation in which voluntary effort should be encouraged. One of the functions of the Voluntary Services Unit, which it is only just beginning to fulfil, is to identify situations where consistency of approach might be beneficial to all concerned, and where appropriate, to encourage departments to work towards a common policy. The number of situations in which policy towards voluntary organisations might be standardised, e.g. by agreeing that coordinating organisations should be funded, by agreeing to encourage joint (i.e. statutory/voluntary or multi-organisational) projects in preference to single organisation ones, or to press for the sharing of premises and equipment is undoubtedly limited by the different approaches of individual departments, and although there may well be room for more consistency in the process-ing of applications, the criteria for funding, the methods of control, and the arrangements for review, all of which, as the following para-graphs indicate, vary considerably from department to department, relatively few organisations deal with more than one department so differences in procedure are unlikely to cause undue difficulty.

Finance

18. All government departments operate within the strict principles and rules for the provision and expenditure of public money, including central government decisions for allocation to various services and Parliamentary approval of departments' estimates year by year. Within the resources made available to them, departments proceed in accord-ance with their recognised functions and responsibilities. When a department decides, as a matter of policy, that government funds should be made available for certain voluntary activities, authority to make payments may be provided under a specific statute. Annex A to this note lists the Acts of Parliament which give specific powers to make grants to voluntary organisations as well as some of those which refer to voluntary organisations or require consultations with them without making any provision for funding. The existence of specific statutory powers does not necessarily mean that grants will be made and, con-versely, the lack of statutory powers does not mean that grants cannot

be made; but if the assistance is substantial and continuing it is expected that covering legislation would be obtained.

19. As might be expected, given the fact that most voluntary organisations are dealt with by the division or branch of particular departments which is most relevant to their work, composite departmental 'bids' or 'estimates' are not common, excepting only in those departments which have one central point of contact or policy-formulating group of officials concerned with voluntary organisations – namely, those departments in Whitehall, Scotland and Northern Ireland which are responsible for health and social services. The group of heads of divisions and professional advisers chaired by the Under-Secretary in the Social Work Services Group in the Scottish Office also considers in a composite fashion the estimates put forward by each division so that the final composite estimate put forward reflects the policies and priorities agreed by the group, but the lack of general policy decisions in departments about the use and encouragement of voluntary organisations is reflected in the fact that few departments set aside sums for voluntary organisations in a composite way

20. The implication of the preceding paragraphs is that if departments decided, as a matter of general policy, to support voluntary rather than statutory services there would, in theory, be nothing to prevent them from doing so. In practice, of course, where departments have certain statutory responsibilities which must be met from the total amount of money made available to them, only limited funds are left over for help to voluntary organisations which are not simply acting on an agency basis to fulfil statutory duties. This is why, contrary to the impression given above, it is more often financial restraints which determine specific departmental policies than general departmental policies which determine the availability of funds. The powers of the Department of Education and Science, for instance, are so wide that it would be possible for them to fund almost any voluntary organisation concerned with education in its broadest sense but limited funds mean that grants are in practice restricted. They go mainly to national voluntary youth organisations in the form of recurrent grants towards the cost of HQ administration and to local voluntary youth organisations for capital building projects. There is, in addition, a small programme of grant-aided experimental work with youth and a few grants are made to voluntary bodies providing services in the sphere of special education. The availability of funds is, therefore, the decisive factor after applying the normal stringent criteria of merit and need which must be met before a grant can be made.

Duration of Grants

21. The availability of funds also obviously has a considerable influence on the duration of grants. Except where a grant is made for a specific non-renewable period, usually for a particular project or piece of research which has a clear termination date, grants are usually made for a year at a time and are subject to annual review. Strictly speaking, grants can be made only on an annual basis because they are always subject to Parliament voting the necessary funds, but many organisations are offered slightly more security by being offered three-year grants, subject to Parliament voting the necessary funds and to the satisfactory fulfilment of any conditions of grant.

22. Generally speaking, it is recognised that where the need for an organisation's services continues, renewal of annual grants is bound to be more or less automatic. The annual review therefore normally assumes continuation of a grant and is primarily for the purpose of altering the amounts needed, perhaps increasing them to allow for inflation or improvement of services or because of an increase in the scale of the organisation, or decreasing them because, for instance, of greater self-sufficiency, reductions in staff, or changes in the services offered. In the course of the annual review all departments are prepared to consider increases for inflation but in many cases shortage of funds or the current policy of minimum expansion excludes increases for any other reason.

23. The difficulty about this general policy is of course that departmental funds are in danger of becoming totally and automatically committed to on-going grants year after year with the effect that new organisations with useful and coherent aims or new projects put up by organisations cannot be funded. For this reason, more thorough reviews are often held at periodic intervals when, although sympathetic consideration is given to renewal of grant, departments will need to satisfy themselves that serious attempts have been made to find money from alternative sources, that the need still exists, that the work is still in line with government policy, and that the service given is still of value to it or to the client group. In the light of the strict limitations on public expenditure over the next few years departments may eventually have to decline to continue grants, even where a need still clearly exists, because other needs must be given priority, but this is not known to have happened to date.

Applications for Grant

24. Generally speaking, the attitude of most departments to voluntary

organisations is responsive rather than positive, i.e. reacting to demand rather than actively planning for the involvement of voluntary organisations in the pursuance of any particular policy. Some departments, e.g. the Scottish Social Work Services Group, may very occasionally ask an organisation to undertake a particular project, but these are exceptions. The Department of Employment has actively sought the involvement of the voluntary sector in the Job Creation Scheme but this is also an exception to the general rule, mainly because the funds available are large enough to enable applications to be invited without selecting certain voluntary organisations to approach.

25. Where only limited funds are available, there is an obvious difficulty in inviting applications from all comers. There is, however, even greater difficulty in selecting particular organisations to undertake work for government departments on an agency basis. Departments which have taken initiatives have found that they can be open to embarrassment and criticism when adopting positive rather than responsive stances. Even though there are certain national organisations such as NACRO, and national coordinating agencies such as the National Council of Voluntary Youth Services, which are positively approached by government departments as part of their departmental policy, it cannot be assumed that the existence of a national body solves this particular difficulty, for these agencies may not be universally accepted by nor representative of all voluntary organisations operating in similar fields. Most departments therefore take the view that it is only in the area of research, where the requirements and their fulfilment can be very specific that it is practicable to commission work from voluntary organisations.

26. Although, therefore, government departments usually wait to receive applications for grant from voluntary organisations rather than actively offering grants to individual organisations, advice on the availability of funds and how applications can be made is given by a variety of means, many of which are very positive in their approach. The Department of the Environment has published a booklet which sets out clearly what powers exist, which divisions are responsible for each particular area of activity, which officials are responsible, and where they can be contacted. Many departments in both Scotland and Northern Ireland issue circulars from time to time, either direct to voluntary organisations or, where appropriate, indirectly through local authorities, area boards, or national coordinating organisations. A good example is Circular HSS 15(OS) 1/74, issued by the Department of Health and Social Services in Northern Ireland, which sets out the

Department's policy and powers in a most clear and encouraging form.
Other departments choose to publicise information about the availability of funds or changes in arrangements through the national coordinating agencies. Under the Urban Programme, periodic circulars are
used to invite applications for Urban Programme funds, and these are
sent for information to national voluntary organisations at the time of
issue to local authorities, which are simultaneously reminded of the role
which can be played by voluntary organisations. Circulars and all other
forms of what might be called 'positive' steps both to inform and
encourage, can, however, fairly be used only when funds are available
and, as has been noted frequently already, this is very often not the
case. Hence, rather than actively publicise the availability of funds and
powers, or the nature of current policies, many departments rely on the
fact that they are 'generally well-known already' (two departments used
these exact words) and therefore prefer to adopt a responsive stance.

27. In order to help voluntary organisations make their applications,
most departments either issue forms or guidance notes or allow officials
or advisers to meet organisations to offer personal help and advice. Most
applications necessitate, sooner or later, meetings between the organisations concerned and officials or advisers. The information requested by
departments varies considerably. Most will either ask an applicant
organisation to supply certain background financial details, e.g. what
other sources of support it has and what other applications for funds
have been made, or will make enquiries on such questions so that it can
be ascertained whether other sources of funding would be more appropriate. Some departments ask formally for copies of the organisation's
constitution or for the composition of the board of trustees or management committee; others specify that this information must be included
in the grant application; and others make enquiries about the structure,
standing and constitution of the organisation only if informal enquiries
raise doubts or questions.

28. Because the VSU is concerned primarily with applications which
either span the interest of several departments or fall between them all,
it is necessary for all departments likely to have an interest to be consulted on every VSU application, either to establish whether any single
department feels that the application falls within its own responsibilities
or to determine that no department has the power to deal with it. Other
departments do not automatically consult each other unless it is clear
that an application does overlap departmental responsibilities. The pro-
cessing and consideration of applications generally takes place entirely
internally, though in the case of local projects the relevant local

authority would normally be consulted. Advisers and the Inspectorate (in the case of education and probation services) would also normally be consulted, particularly in the case of new or experimental projects. External consultation is very rare, on a formal basis at least, but the consideration given to an application would normally be affected by informal external consultations of a non-specific nature carried out by advisers and inspectors. In this way individual applications are not considered in isolation but in a total context.

Criteria for Funding

29. Against the broad general policies described above, departments apply a large variety of criteria to determine which voluntary organisations should be supported. The primary determinant must obviously be that the organisation is working to a policy which is in accordance with the department's own policy. Most departments stress that the services provided must be cost-effective, and managerial competence and the avoidance of duplication and overlap are also regarded as important criteria. A government-funded organisation is also generally expected to be clear in its objectives and to be able to demonstrate an ability to carry out successfully the work for which it is being funded. If the organisation is being funded because it works in one of the areas already mentioned where the voluntary image or style is valued *per se*, criteria based on that valuation are applied, e.g. the extent to which community participation is encouraged in the running of hostels for ex-offenders. The Department of Education in Northern Ireland, which funds community groups, specifically investigates, for instance, how representative of their local community applicants for grants are. The need to establish whether these criteria are, and continue to be met, raises fundamental questions to which reference will be made later about the extent of control involved in government funding.

30. Because departmental funding is usually related to the provision of specific services, organisations basically orientated to research, to campaigning, or to pressure activities are generally less likely to obtain government funds for these activities. However, most of the major departments do have limited funds available for research and although applications would normally be received from or commissions given to, academic bodies, voluntary organisations may also be considered.

31. Central government departments are more likely to support national than local organisations. This is partly a question of powers, but mostly a question of policy, because central government does not wish to intervene at local level where government funding might upset

local priorities. Exceptions to this general rule are where a policy deci-
sion is made at central government level about the general desirability
of funding certain types of voluntary work which are local by nature.
Examples of this are the funding of local law centres by the Lord
Chancellor's Office, of local hostels for ex-offenders by the Home
Office, and of local sheltered workshops by the Department of Employ-
ment. Another exception is where departments such as the Home Office
(Voluntary Services Unit), the Department of Health and Social
Security, the Welsh Office and the Scottish Office (Social Work Services
Group) are prepared exceptionally to fund local projects for a specified
period if they are innovatory and of national significance. With the
above exceptions, however, central government does not usually fund
local work. Although the Urban Programme administered by the Home
Office is often regarded as a method of central government funding of
local voluntary projects, the grants are made to, and on application by,
local authorities and not direct to voluntary organisations.

32. The emphasis on funding national rather than local work is
reflected in the purposes to which government grants can be put. In
general, central departments give money for the administration of
national voluntary organisations and, to the limited extent described
earlier, for the administration of local work (e.g. staff of hostels,
sheltered workshops and law centres). Their ability, as a matter of
powers, and their willingness, as a matter of policy, to fund project
work (that is for project workers and project expenses, as distinct from
purely administrative workers and administrative expenses) is more
limited, though most departments do not rule out this type of funding
entirely. In the case of historic buildings, countryside and tourism work,
grants are normally for projects and, as has been mentioned already,
certain departments may fund project work if it is innovatory or if it is
in keeping with general policy decisions, e.g. the funding by the Department of the Environment of Keep Britain Tidy allows for project as
well as administrative expenditure.

33. In a sense it is quite logical for project work to be a relatively
minor area of government funding, as this is traditionally the area in
which trusts and foundations have operated. Similarly, it is quite logical
for government to be tending to make grants for 'unattractive' items of
expenditure, such as administrative staffing costs and telephone and
postage bills. The funding policy of the Voluntary Services Unit has
taken this to its logical conclusion. Many organisations are multi-pur-
pose in their activities, and in the past these have often not been able to
secure funds for central administrative expenditure, though in many

cases departments have been able to make grants for specific aspects of their work which are related to that department's sphere of interest. Now the Voluntary Services Unit is able to make grants towards central administrative expenditure, whilst individual departments continue to provide funds for specific purposes.

34. The generalisations made above about the reluctance of government departments to fund local work do not necessarily apply to the statutory agencies which make grants to voluntary organisations in pursuance of government policies. Although some agencies, such as the Development Commission and the Sports Council, keep their grants to national or regional or, at the lowest, county level, others such as the Housing Corporation and the Community Relations Commission must, because of the nature of their remit, make grants at local level.

Conditions of Grant

35. The extent to which departments keep a check on organisations to which a grant has been made depends largely on the nature of the grant. If it represents only a small percentage of the income of the organisation, it is quite likely that the only conditions of grant will be that some form of annual report and audited accounts should be submitted to the department and that any grant unspent at the end of the year should be returned. These are the most common conditions of grant. The annual review described in the section on the duration of grants would then in general be considered to provide a sufficient opportunity to confirm that the organisation was still doing satisfactorily the work in respect of which the government grant was being made.

36. Where a particular project is being funded rather than the central administration of an organisation, the project, e.g. a hostel or a workshop, is sometimes made subject to inspection by government inspectors but this would often be the case for premises of this kind whether or not in receipt of a government grant. There is an increasing recognition among departments of the need to establish some valid way of assessing the effectiveness and value of projects supported by public money and a number of grants for specific projects are now made on condition that some form of independent monitoring or evaluation is undertaken. The Department of Employment arranged for the Community Industry Scheme, during its experimental period, to be evaluated by university researchers and the Voluntary Services Unit has required several of the organisations to which it makes grants to include monitoring in the project work. In some cases, e.g. the Family Day

Centre Project and the various Area Resource Centre projects, one of the conditions of grant is that the individual organisations concerned should cooperate with each other in a coordinated monitoring exercise to ensure that the experience gained and the lessons learned are shared with other projects doing similar work. Where an independent assessment is not a condition of grant organisations themselves and their user bodies may be asked to provide an evaluation at the end of a given period but this is not generally considered satisfactory. The most common situation is for departments to assess the project themselves by informal contacts, reliance on professional advisers who may make fairly regular visits, and taking the views, usually informally, of those with whom the project has the closest contact.

37. If the grant made to a voluntary organisation represents a substantial proportion of its income it is regarded as a 'controlled fringe body' and becomes subject to government location policy and must have government approval to the levels of pay proposed and the conditions under which staff are employed. Where, in particular, income from government amounts to fifty per cent or more, there would be embarrassment if the pay and conditions of service of the staff could not be reconciled with civil service or other appropriate public sector standards. The implications of these controls are set out more fully in subsequent paragraphs.

Influence and Control

38. It is very difficult to generalise about the extent to which the receipt of a government grant by a voluntary organisation means that it becomes subject to government influence and control. Clearly, the very fact that government money may be available if an organisation pursues one activity rather than another may have an influence upon the organisation's decisions but this would presumably be only at the margin. It is unlikely that any voluntary organisation would change its activities simply in order to obtain government funding and if it did so the department to which it made a grant application would probably be very doubtful of its ability to carry out the work in question. Nevertheless, an organisation which has been given a government grant on the understanding that it will continue to follow a certain line of action may well be influenced, if only indirectly, in the extent to which it modifies or alters that action, particularly if it is frequently reminded, either by informal contacts with the department or by having a departmental observer on its management or executive committee, that the continuance of the government grant depends on the maintenance of the

government-approved work.

39. As just mentioned, departments will sometimes have an observer or assessor, who may be either an administrative or a professional civil servant, attached to the management or executive committee of a voluntary organisation in receipt of a grant. This is not usually a condition of grant but is done by agreement between the voluntary organisation and the department, often at the request of the former. In the voluntary after-care hostel field, however, it is a condition of grant-aid that a senior member of the local probation and after-care service become a member of the voluntary management committee. Although individual observers/assessors may influence the relevant committee simply by the advice and information they can provide, there is not question of them being there in order to exercise control; the arrangement is intended to be of mutual benefit and to increase understanding between the voluntary and statutory bodies.

40. When a grant is made to a large voluntary organisation operating in a clearly defined area, there is likely to be the same kind of informal contact and consultation between officials of the organisation and the relevant department as between departments. The element of control becomes obtrusive only when, because the organisation is a controlled fringe body, the department has to approve its pay and grading structure, with subsequent monitoring of grading standards, and agree its salary levels and conditions of service. It is inevitable that this should be seen by some voluntary organisations as an unwelcome interference with their managerial discretion.

41. Generally speaking, the need to approve salaries and grading should not affect a voluntary organisation's policy but may be regarded as beneficial both to the management, who are provided with a rational basis for settling the pay and conditions of staff and with access to a body of expertise not available within their own organisation, and to the staff, who are ensured comparability of pay and conditions with people doing equivalent work elsewhere. On the other hand, it is well-known that voluntary organisations do not always pay their staff as well as their equivalents in statutory or commercial jobs and if the government presses for salaries to be raised, the financial effect on the organisation can be serious, particularly if the government grant is made on a percentage basis and the organisation must therefore meet some of the increased cost itself. This is, in effect, a direct interference with managerial control because it prejudges whether money from other than government sources should be spent on salaries or on other items or work which the organisation may consider more important.

42. In practice, apart from the control over location, salaries and grading to which fringe bodies are subject and the help and advice given on request to some new and experimental projects, the amount of influence or control exercised by government departments over the voluntary organisations to which grants are made is on the whole remarkably small. Once the decision to make a grant has been made it is assumed that the organisation will spend the government money in accordance with its application. Provided that there are sufficient checks when making and reviewing the grant to satisfy the requirements of public accountability there are clearly good reasons for lack of interference other than in relation to the grading, pay and conditions of service of the staff. Where a voluntary organisation is funded to provide a particular service for image-related reasons or because it is more able to be flexible than its statutory counterpart it would clearly be counter-productive to exercise any real degree of control over its activities. In those cases where a fair measure of control is exercised experience confirms that on-going contact can take up a considerable amount of time which is usually just not available. There are many anomalies and variations in this area, both between departments and in the way in which the same department treats different organisations funded by it. It is in consequence difficult to make any valid generalisations and perhaps the best that can be said is that most departments make every effort to ensure than a voluntary organisation retains its essential individuality and independence however great the degree of government funding.

43. In spite of this, the increasing extent to which voluntary organisations seem to be turning to statutory sources, both central and local, for funding does have implications for their independence which cannot be ignored. Although it is at present the case that most departments do not exercise important control over voluntary organisations even where there is substantial funding, such funding is bound to give organisations what might be termed a semi-statutory image in the eyes of both those they deal with and the public as a whole. Once gained, an establishment image is extremely hard to change and as, for instance, the Scouting Association has found, makes it very difficult to branch out into new areas. The more crucial effect is perhaps that when a voluntary organisation is funded largely from government sources its income from voluntary sources is likely to decrease and its ability to experiment and follow separate policies is correspondingly diminished. Moreover, if the public at large increasingly sees government as a proper source of funds for voluntary effort it is questionable whether it will be possible for voluntary organisations to maintain their traditional pioneering image

and functions. There is therefore a very real dilemma between the need
to obtain an assured income and the need to maintain a separate
identity independent of government.

Consultation

44. The whole emphasis of this paper so far has been on the relationship between government departments and voluntary organisations in so
far as the latter are dependent on the former for funds. The amount of
money made available to voluntary organisations by government departments, (see Appendix 6B) shows the extent of that dependence and
indicates why the financial relationship may be considered a significant one. But given that voluntary organisations are generally funded,
as stated previously, to provide services in much the same areas as
statutory bodies, their experience and their views are obviously
relevant to the formation of government policy and practice, and liaison
and consultation between departments and voluntary organisations is
therefore also extremely important.

45. Almost all departments liaise and consult with voluntary organisations as part of the process of policy formation on particular issues.
A good recent example of this has been the widespread consultation
carried out by the Working Party on Young People and Work which was
set up by the Manpower Services Commission. Voluntary organisations
were consulted on an individual as well as a collective basis, and they
were also encouraged to submit papers and convene meetings both
nationally and locally. The result has been highly productive. Where
departments and organisations have a relationship through funding, contact between them on an informal basis may be, as mentioned earlier,
almost as close and continuous as between departments themselves and
this kind of exchange obviously has a considerable influence on both
policy and practice.

46. While informal consultations are undoubtedly more common
than formal ones, formal arrangements do exist in a number of cases.
Officials from the Department of Housing, Local Government and
Planning sit as observers on the Northern Ireland Committee of the
National Federation of Housing Associations and this is regarded as an
important formal link with housing associations and an opportunity to
consult formally on policy matters. In Scotland the Standing Consultative Council on Youth and Community Service is appointed by the
Secretary of State and it includes people from both the statutory and
voluntary sides and represents a similar forum to the one described
above in which consultation on a formal level can take place. There are

other Standing Conferences or Committees and Advisory Councils of a similar nature, e.g. the Standing Conference on Legal Services.

47. Where such formal consultative mechanisms exist there are no problems attached to formal consultation but where they do not the business of formal consultation becomes more difficult. In some fields there are large national organisations whose standing, knowledge and experience are accepted in both the statutory and voluntary world. But in most cases the situation is not so clear and a department may lay itself open to embarrassment and criticism where it enters into formal consultations with one or a group of organisations and appears to exclude other organisations who feel that they too have a right to be involved. It is in consequence of this that informal consultations tend to be preferred to formal ones.

48. In some areas and fields of work there are coordinating agencies of which departments may make use as a way of carrying out formal consultations with all organisations operating in a particular field of work. However many departments point out there are disadvantages in this approach. The coordinating agencies' claim to be representative may not necessarily be valid – it may be representing no more than its own opinions or it may represent the majority opinion to the exclusion of equally valid minority views or further it may not be universally accepted by the voluntary organisations it claims to represent. In many areas there is such a proliferation of coordinating agencies, standing conferences, working parties and advisory committees that it is very easy to offend even when painstaking and time-consuming attempts are made to involve all parties. Often the situation is exacerbated when some of the parties forcefully demand consultation with officials. Such demands cannot fairly be refused even though the consequences can very often be embarrassing.

49. In spite of the difficulties described above, it is generally true to say that where departments and voluntary organisations are operating in the same field of work there is a fair degree of liaison and consultation. This is not so true where problems common to all voluntary organisations are concerned. This kind of problem, e.g. the introduction of Value Added Tax, the effects on charities of the Community Land Bill, the effect on voluntary organisations of EEC regulations controlling the use of minibuses, is likely to arise in the context of a general government policy in which the interest of voluntary organisations may not be immediately apparent to the department concerned. One of the Voluntary Services Unit's functions is to try to identify such issues and ensure that the voluntary sector's interest is taken into account. It is however

virtually impossible for information about all policy changes which might be relevant to the voluntary sector to be channelled through one department and it is not easy either to pick up the significance for the voluntary sector of certain legislative proposals before they have progressed too far for consultation to serve much useful purpose or to identify the best way of consulting the voluntary sector on this type of general issue. The National Council of Social Service is generally recognised as the major coordinating agency for the views of the voluntary sector in England but it is not entirely exempt from the difficulties described in the preceding paragraph and cannot always be considered as the appropriate body to speak exclusively for voluntary organisations. This is an area where there is considerable room for improvement but equally considerable difficulty in seeing how such an improvement could be effected.

Conclusion

50. In attempting to generalise about relationships between government departments and voluntary organisations, this paper inevitably oversimplifies and excludes a great deal of detail which would probably be of interest to the Committee. The object has been, however, to give an overall impression of the way in which departments react to voluntary organisations and the extent to which statutory and voluntary bodies can and do work together to a common end. The paper is intended to be informative rather than philosophical, but it indicates a number of areas in which thought needs to be given to the relationship between voluntary organisations and the government, particularly at a time of economic restraint involving a standstill in expenditure on many statutory services.

Annex A

The following Acts of Parliament give statutory power for government departments to make grants to various recipients including voluntary organisations:

Department of Education and Science

Education Act 1944
    Section 100(1)(b):   empowers the Secretary of State to make provision by regulation for the payment of grants

towards expenses incurred (other than by local education authorities) in the provision of educational services or for the purposes of educational research.

Department of the Environment

Historic Buildings and Ancient Monuments Act 1953

enable grants to be made for urban conservation and the upkeep of historic buildings. to voluntary organisations who are the owners of such buildings.

Ancient Monuments Act 1931

enables grants to be made to owners to assist in preserving ancient monuments and acknowledgement payments to occupiers to protect field monuments. Also permits grants for carrying out emergency excavation in advance of the destruction of a monument by new developments.

Housing Act 1974

Sections 29 to 32: grants payable for housing projects approved by the Secretary of State. These are made to housing associations who provide housing for rents, and who must be registered as a charity or Friendly Society.

Development and Road Improvement Fund Act 1909

Section 1(1): empowers the Development Commission to make advances for schemes which may be calculated to benefit, directly or indirectly the rural economy of Great Britain provided no other statutory provision for helping them exists.

Local Government Act 1974

Section 9: empowers the Countryside Commission to provide financial assistance to organisations which, in the Commission's opinion, further any of the purposes of the National Parks and Access to the Countryside Act 1949 or the Countryside Act 1968 — i.e. the conservation and enhancement of the natural beauty of the countryside of England and Wales and the improvement of

facilities for the enjoyment of the countryside
and for open-air recreation.

National Parks and Access to the Countryside Act 1949 (Section 86) &
Countryside Act 1968 (Section 2)

empower the Countryside Commission to contribute to the provision of information services
about those countryside issues which relate to
the Commission's principal functions.

Nature Conservancy Council Act 1973

Section 3:   the Nature Conservancy Council has power to
give financial assistance by way of grant to any
person or persons carrying on or proposing to
carry on, any project which the Council would
have powers to carry on (i.e. in the area of
nature conservation).

Road Traffic Act 1972

Section 39:   grants can be made to promote road safety by
disseminating information and advice relating
to the use of roads or to give practical training
to road users. (The grant to ROSPA is given
under these powers.)

Town and Country Planning Act 1971

Section 253:   provides for grants to be made to promote or
assist research and education with respect to the
planning and design of the physical environment.

Town and Country Planning (Amendment) Act 1972

grants may be made towards schemes for enhancing the character and appearance of outstanding Conservation Areas (this can include
grants to Amenity Societies).

Department of Employment

Employment and Training Act 1973

Section 2:   enables payments to be made to organisations
providing facilities for people to select, train
for, obtain and retain employment

Section 5:   enables grants to be given, subject to Treasury
approval, to organisations providing people with
temporary employment, and to organisations
undertaking research into matters relating to

employment, unemployment or training.

Disabled Persons (Employment) Act 1944

Section 15:   enables payments to be made to organisations
                       providing sheltered employment for severely
                       disabled people.

Department of Health and Social Security

Children and Young Persons Act 1969

Section 65:   powers to give grants to voluntary organisations
                       in connection with the establishment, mainte-
                       nance or improvement of voluntary homes
                       which are, or are becoming, assisted community
                       homes under part II of the same Act.

Health Services and Public Health Act 1968

Section 64:   empowers the Secretary of State to help volun-
                       tary organisations in the health and social ser-
                       vices field if they are providing a service similar
                       to a relevant service — that is, a service which
                       she or a local authority must or may provide, or
                       are promoting or publicising such a service or a
                       similar one, or giving advice on how such a ser-
                       vice or a similar one can best be provided. (In
                       addition, since 1 April 1974, this power has
                       been delegated to the regional and area health
                       authorities set up under the National Health
                       Service Reorganisation Act 1973.)

Supplementary Benefits Act 1976

Schedule 5:   powers to give grants to voluntary organisations,
                       towards the cost of maintaining centres for pur-
                       poses similar to those of the re-establishment
                       centres or reception centres maintained by the
                       Supplementary Benefits Commission.

Home Office

Criminal Courts Act 1973

Section 51(3)(c):   enables funds to be paid to any society or
                       person engaged in establishing or carrying on
                       bail hostels or approved probation hostels or
                       homes

Section 51(3)(f):   enables grants to be paid to any society or
                       person engaged in supervising or assisting

persons convicted of offences with a view to
their rehabilitation.

Section 51(3)(g):   enables funds to be paid to any body or persons
approved by the Secretary of State in the con-
duct of research into the causes of delinquency
and the treatment of offenders.

Local Government Grants (Social Need) Act 1969

This is the statutory authority for the Urban
Programme. The Act empowers the Secretary of
State to pay grants to local authorities which in
his opinion are required to incur expenditure by
reason of the existence in any urban area of
special social need. The ability to channel assistance to voluntary organisations through the
Urban Programme derives from the various
powers which local authorities have to pay
grants to voluntary organisations, and from the
fact that such expenditure by local authorities
may be grant-aided by central government within the terms of the 1969 Act.

Race Relations Act 1976

Section 44:   enables the Commission for Racial Equality to
give financial or other assistance to any organ-
isation appearing to the Commission to be concerned with the promotion of equality of
opportunity and good relations between persons
of different racial groups. Government money
may not be used for this purpose without the
consent of the Secretary of State.

*Department of Trade, Welsh Office and Scottish Economic Planning
Department*

Development of Tourism Act 1969

Gives the English, Wales and Scottish Tourist
Boards discretionary powers under Section 4 to
offer financial assistance for schemes to improve or provide tourist amenities and facilities
in certain areas; and under Section 5 to contribute to or reimburse expenditure by other
organisations in promoting or undertaking publicity, providing advisory and information

services and promoting or undertaking research.

Welsh Office

Children and Young Persons Act 1969
    Section 65:   see under Department of Health and Social
                           Security
Health Services and Public Health Act 1968
    Section 64:   see under Department of Health and Social
                           Security

Scottish Office

Scottish Development Department

Countryside (Scotland) Act 1967
    Section 7:   empowers the Countryside Commission for
                           Scotland to provide financial assistance to any
                           person, other than a public body, carrying on a
                           project which in the Commission's opinion is
                           conducive to the attainment of the purposes of
                           the Act, viz the provision, development and
                           improvement of facilities for the enjoyment of
                           the Scottish Countryside, and for the conserva-
                           tion and enhancement of the natural beauty
                           and amenity thereof.
Historic Buildings and Ancient Monuments Act 1953
                           enables grants to be made, for urban conserva-
                           tion and the upkeep of historic buildings, to
                           voluntary organisations who are in fact the
                           owners of such buildings.

Housing Act 1974
    Sections 29 to 32:   See under Department of the Environment
Housing (Scotland) Act 1966
    Section 158:   Grants payable, in aid of expenses, to any
                           central association or other body established
                           for the purposes of promoting the formation
                           and extension of housing associations and of
                           giving them advice and assistance.
Road Traffic Act 1972
    Section 39:   See under Department of Transport.
Town and Country Planning (Scotland) Act 1972
    Section 240:   Provides for grants to be made to promote or

assist research and education with respect to
the planning and design of the physical
environment.

Town and Country Planning (Amendment) Act 1972

Grants may be made (including grants to
Amenity Societies) towards schemes for
enhancing the character and appearance of
outstanding Conservation Areas.

Scottish Economic Planning Department

Highlands and Islands Development (Scotland) Acts 1965 and 1971

Section 8:   Enables the Highlands and Islands Development
Board, subject to arrangements approved by the
Secretary of State and Treasury, to make
financial assistance available by way of grant
and/or loan to any person (including organisation) carrying on any activity which in the
opinion of the Board will contribute to the
economic or social development of the Highlands and Islands.

Scottish Education Department

Education (Scotland) Act 1962 (Section 75) as amended by Education
(Scotland) Act 1969 (Section 12) and also Further Education (Scotland)
Regulations 1959

Section 75 of the 1962 Act enables grants to be
made to persons providing education or educational services and the 1959 Regulations enable
grants to be given to an organised body of
persons whose objects include the provision of
further education provided that the Secretary
of State is satisfied as to its constitution,
financial stability and fitness to receive grants
and that it is not conducted for private profit.

Social Work Services Group of the SED

Social Work (Scotland) Act 1968

Section 8:   enables the Secretary of State to pay grants for
research into matters connected with his func-
tions, the functions of local authorities or the
activities of voluntary organisations in the field

Section 9(3): of social welfare.
enables the Secretary of State to pay grants to 'any body of persons' providing training on social work.

Section 10(1): empowers the Secretary of State to make grants or loans to voluntary organisations or other persons engaged in any activity connected with his functions or the functions of local authorities under the Act. ['Voluntary organisations' is defined in Section 94(1) as a body the activities of which are carried on otherwise than for profit.]

Scottish Home and Health Department

Health Services and Public Health Act 1968

Section 64: empowers the Secretary of State to help voluntary organisations in the health field if they are providing a service similar to a relevant service — that is, a service which he or a local authority must or may provide or are promoting or publicising such a service or a similar one or giving advice on how such a service or a similar one can best be provided. (The power has, in addition, been delegated to Health Boards set up under the National Health Service (Scotland) Act 1972.) [Originally, as in England, this power also related to the social work field but was superseded in that respect by Section 10(1) of the Social Work (Scotland) Act 1968.]

Northern Ireland

Department of Education

Social Need (Grants) Act (Northern Ireland) 1970
Under this act the department must pay grants 'to local authorities, statutory authorities or other persons whomsoever in respect of expenditure incurred by them by reasons of the existence in any urban area of special social need'.

Recreation and Youth Service (Northern Ireland) Order 1973 (as amended by the Recreation (Northern Ireland) Order 1975) enables the department to make grants towards the approved expenses of a voluntary organisation in providing facilities for recreation, sport or the youth service or for social physical or cultural activities.

Community Relations (Amendment) (Northern Ireland) Order 1975
enables the department to give grants to organisations which appear to the department to be concerned with community relations, or with research in that area.

Department of Health and Social Services

Health and Personal Social Services (Northern Ireland) Order 1972

Article 71(2):   enables grants or loans to be made to voluntary organisations providing services similar or related to any of the health or personal social services.

Article 71(3):   provides for assistance to voluntary organisations by permitting them to use premises or equipment belonging to the Ministry by gift, loan, etc.

Children and Young Persons Act (Northern Ireland) 1968

Section 151:   enables grants to be made (subject to approval of Finance Ministry) to enable staff of voluntary organisations to undertake training, and to enable such training to be provided.

Section 152:   grants for voluntary homes for improvement of premises, maintenance of equipment, and securing of qualified staff. Also provides for grants to any voluntary organisation whose primary object is to promote the welfare of children or young persons.

Department of Housing, Local Government and Planning

Housing Act 1945 (Section 1) applies to housing associations by virtue of Housing and Local Government (Miscellaneous provisions Act (Northern Ireland) 1948 (Section 12))
subsidies for new building work.

Housing Act (Northern Ireland) 1963

Section 15:   subsidies for the provision of hostel accommodation by the conversion of existing buildings.

Housing (Northern Ireland) Order 1976

Articles 27 to 31:   grants payable for housing projects approved by
the department. These are made to Housing
Associations who provide housing for letting
and who must be registered as a Friendly
Society and registered with the department.
This Order enables the department not only to
assist established Housing Associations but also
to provide financial assistance to emergent
Associations.

Northern Ireland Office

Prison Act (Northern Ireland) 1953

Section 41(2):   the Secretary of State may make grants towards
the expenditure of any society approved by
him or any individual, who is engaging in super-
vising or assisting persons convicted of offences
with a view to their rehabilitation.

Children and Young Persons Act (Northern Ireland) 1968

Section 150(1):   grants, subject to Treasury approval, towards
expenditure incurred by managers of approved
training schools.

Section 169:   grants to promote or assist research or investi-
gation into any matter connected with the
functions of the department or of a local
education authority under the Act.

Probation Act (Northern Ireland) 1950

Section 11(1)(a):   the Secretary of State, may, with the approval
of Treasury, enter into arrangements with
voluntary societies for the reception and care
of persons required to reside on their premises
by a probation order.

APPENDIX 5A

Local Voluntary Councils in England and Wales

This appendix seeks to present a more detailed summary than was possible in Chapter 6 of the work and resources of local voluntary councils (LVCs) by providing information on the numbers, location, income, grant-aid and paid staff of Councils for Voluntary Service (CVSs) and Rural Community Councils (RCCs). We continue the use of the terminology of Chapter 6 and discuss separately RCCs and CVSs. One must, however, remember that the actual titles of the 200 or so local voluntary councils in England are as varied as their size and activities, and hence in many cases, the formal title of an organisation may conceal its real sphere of activity: for example, many RCCs now omit the word 'rural' in their titles; some RCCs prefer to be known as councils for voluntary service, e.g. Buckinghamshire; and many CVSs are known as community councils (e.g. St Helens Community Council) but are not necessarily related in activity or funding to either RCCs or the statutory Scottish Community Councils.

Rural Community Councils

RCCs now exist in all the 39 non-metropolitan counties in England except Norfolk and the Isle of Wight. There are 36 of these county-based bodies. East and West Sussex are covered by one RCC and the Yorkshire RCC continues to serve the rural areas of the South and West Yorkshire metropolitan counties and does not confine its activities to North Yorkshire. In Chapter 6 we discussed their major activities and finance. A further guide to their sizes and scope of activity is the employment of paid staff. This is the largest single item of expenditure for most LVCs. Table 1 gives summary details of employment of paid staff by the 36 rural community councils in England.

These 36 RCCs together employ over 260 staff. The number of staff for each RCC is drawn from activity sheets maintained by the Community Work Division of the NCSS; part-time staff are counted as half, i.e. the approximate full-time equivalent. Not all RCCs confine themselves exclusively to work in rural areas, hence there is no clear-cut separation of the roles of CVSs and RCCs. Several RCCs are active in urban areas in addition to their rural work, and are providing services which are more characteristic of CVSs. For this reason, 10 RCCs are affiliated both to the Standing Conference of CVSs and the Standing

242

Table 5A:1. Numbers of RCCs according
to size of paid staff

Number of paid staff	Number of RCCs
2– 4	3
4– 6	13
6– 8	12
8–10	3
over 10	5
TOTAL	36

Conference of RCCs. They are: Buckinghamshire, Cheshire, Cumbria, Durham, Hertfordshire, Humberside, Kent, Lancashire, Shropshire and Surrey.

The 6 Welsh Rural Community Councils have their own conference which was newly constituted in 1977 concurrent with the change from Development Commission to Welsh Office funding. At the time of writing there is no organisation which separately services and supports the Welsh RCCs' conference as the NCSS does the Standing Conference of English RCCs, though Welsh RCCs still maintain contact with NCSS. All 6 receive grants from the Welsh Office plus grant aid from their county councils and many of their constituent district councils. Powys, Dyfed and Gwynedd RCCs each employ between 7 and 9 staff; Clwyd, Gwent and Glamorgan each employ between 5 and 2. The total number of staff employed by RCCs in Wales is 33 (full-time equivalent).

Councils for Voluntary Service

There are over 160 CVSs in England. Scotland has 41 CVSs and the Scottish Council of Social Service. Wales has 3 CVSs and the Council of Social Service for Wales. Most CVSs are active in an entire district local authority (metropolitan or non-metropolitan) or London Borough. A minority cover only a part of a single authority, e.g. Sale (part of Trafford MD) and Ashton-in-Makerfield (part of Wigan MD). A second minority of districts are covered by several CVSs, e.g. Wirral MD has 5 CVSs in its area and the London Borough of Merton has two. Most of these decided not to amalgamate or wished to remain 'local' on local government reorganisation.

The CVSs in England and Wales are distributed between different types of local authorities as shown below. The number affiliated to the Standing Conference of CVSs (SCCVS) is indicated in brackets.

London Boroughs

23 CVSs (18) covering 22 boroughs out of 32.

Metropolitan Districts

48 CVSs (34) covering in part or whole 33 districts out of 36.

Non-metropolitan Districts

92 CVSs (49) covering in part or whole over 90 districts out of 333 non-metropolitan districts.

In addition the London Council of Social Service covers the whole of Greater London and there are two CVSs covering entire metropolitan counties (Merseyside and Manchester) and two CVSs covering non-metropolitan counties (Northampton and Oxford). The latter two counties also have RCCs which confine themselves to work in rural areas. Some two thirds of the CVSs are affiliated to the standing conference; non-affiliates tend to be the smaller organisations. There are two reliable indices of the size of CVSs — number of paid staff and income.

Employment of paid staff

The most up-to-date and comprehensive information on CVSs size is available from data on staff collected by the SCCVS covering most of their affiliated members: 93 replied, that is, just over half the CVSs in England and Wales. These 93 are probably relatively well established when compared with the 58 CVSs not affiliated to the Standing Conferences. Citizens' Advice Bureaux and Age Concern organisers are excluded from these totals as only some CVSs have CABx and Age Concern within the organisation. Staff employed under the Job Creation Programme by four CVSs and a few staff seconded by other organisations, e.g. National Westminster Bank, local authority social services departments, are included in the totals.

There is a tendency for towns with a large population to have CVSs with large staff, but there are some notable exceptions, e.g. Worthing CVS has over 10 staff; while Bradford CVS has fewer than 5.

Altogether these 93 CVSs employ 89 'General Secretaries' or 'Directors' and over 300 other staff. Half are designated 'administrators' or 'general office staff'. The remainder are involved in a variety of activities. Twenty-four CVSs employ a total of 30 staff in organising volunteer bureaux. Otherwise no clearly defined pattern emerges from the data available to us. The description of some posts clearly indicates

Table 5A:2. Staffing of CVSs in different types of local authority

CVS in:	Number of paid staff (full-time equivalent)				
	None	*1*	*1–5*	*5–10*	*Over 10*
Metropolitan districts	6	7	13	3	5
London boroughs	—	2	10	1	3
Non-metropolitan districts	—	8	26	6	3
Total Replying	6	17	49	10	11

a developmental, intermediary role, while that of others suggests direct service giving of one kind or another.

Income

We have gathered information on CVSs' income and local authority grant-aid from CVS annual reports. Most of these reports refer to the financial year 1974/75, and in a few cases to the calendar years 1974 or 1975. Not all the reports are readily available; we have therefore concentrated solely on the 71 CVSs in metropolitan districts and London boroughs. In Figure 1 the total income of 64 CVSs is plotted on the vertical axis and on the horizontal axis the percentage of its income received as local authority grant aid. Data on the remaining 7 CVSs was not available.

In the metropolitan districts in 1974/75, CVSs varied in income between the £445 p.a. of Ashton-in-Makerfield and nearly £150,000 for Birmingham. Most of the CVSs had an income of over £4,000 p.a. but only two had incomes above £100,000 p.a. Another way of considering the resources deployed in the community by CVSs is to divide their individual incomes by the population of the authority; the figures for CVSs' income then represent a spending between the extremes of ½p per head in Gateshead and 25p per head in Liverpool. Most CVSs in metropolitan districts in fact only spend between 3p and 5p a head. This level of expenditure can be compared with the average of £13 a head spent on local authority personal social services in metropolitan districts. All these CVSs received local authority grants in 1974/75 with the exception of Sale (Trafford MD). Rochdale has withdrawn its grant-aid since 1974/75 and the new Merseyside County CVS currently receives no grant.

In the London boroughs, CVSs varied in income in 1974/75 between the £4,000 of Hillingdon and Havering and £268,000 in Camden. This represents a spending of between a fraction of a penny per head in

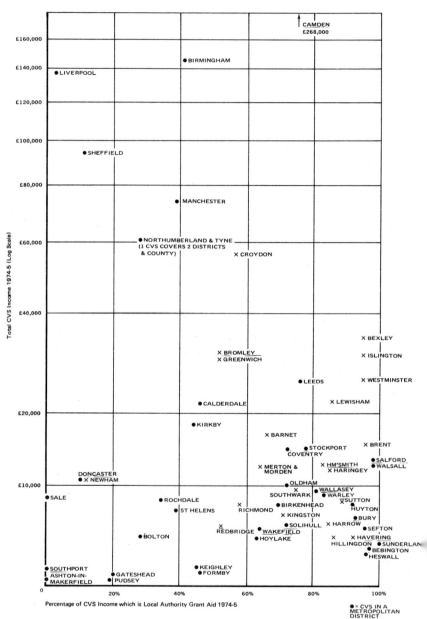

Figure 1. CVS in Metropolitan Districts and London Boroughs:
Income and Grant Aid

Hillingdon and Havering, to £1.33 per head in Camden. Most London boroughs spent between 4p and 16p a head. This can be compared with an average spending on personal social services of over £21 a head by London Boroughs. In 1974/75 all CVSs in London Boroughs received grant-aid; since then Greenwich CVS has ceased to function. A majority of all the CVSs in these metropolitan areas are highly dependent on local authority grant-aid and receive over 50 per cent of their income from their local authority. The CVSs in London boroughs are particularly dependent on such grant-aid; and altogether 12 CVSs have negligible income (less than 10 per cent) from other sources.

The 92 CVSs scattered throughout the non-metropolitan counties vary widely in size between those of large urban areas, e.g. Bristol and Leicester, employing over 10 staff, and smaller bodies such as the CVSs of Sidmouth and Redditch. We have not been able to collect detailed information on their incomes; however the Standing Conference have informed us that most are in receipt of some form of grant-aid from local government.

Table 5A:3. CVSs in non-metropolitan districts: sources of local government grant-aid 1976/77

Source of grant	No. of CVSs
District & County	38
District only	15
County only	12
District & New Town Development Corporation	1
None[a]	1
No reply to SCCVS questionnaire	24

[a]This CVS relies heavily on money from the Job Creation Programme.

The Effects of Inflation and Local Authority Grant-Aid Policy on CVSs

The Standing Conference of CVSs circularised all English and Welsh CVSs in August 1976 and again in February 1977 with a questionnaire which asked whether their current level of local authority grant aid had risen or fallen, they have been obliged to make cuts in staff or services, or retrench in other ways, and what are their expectations of grant aid for 1977/78. The Standing Conference has kindly made the results of this survey available to the Committee. Taken together the answers give some indication of CVSs' current fortunes and future needs. 116 CVSs replied out of 168: 28 in metropolitan districts (including

Table 5A:4. Grant aid compared with previous year and expected grant next year

(a) 1976/77		*(b) 1977/78*	
The current grant represents	*No. of CVSs*	*Next year's grant is expected to be:*	*No. of CVSs*
Increase (in money terms)	67		7
No change	25		49
Cut	11		25
Don't know	8		30
Receiving no grant	5		5
Total Replies	116		116
No Reply	52		52

2 metropolitan counties), 20 London borough CVSs, and 68 in non-metropolitan districts. Nearly all the London borough CVSs replied; the metropolitan and non-metropolitan district CVSs which replied are fairly representative of all CVSs in these types of authority according to the numbers of population which they serve. The replies did not suggest that there were any significant differences between the position of CVSs in different types of authority.

All replies referred to grants in money terms. In 1976/77 60 per cent of the CVSs who responded had received an increase over the previous year's grant. However, many pointed out in their replies that the percentage increase was less than inflation over the year. Another 22 per cent of the respondents received the same amount and 10 per cent have received a smaller sum than the previous year's grant. Very few CVSs (5) in this sample received no grant aid from the local authority.

The second question asked whether retrenchment in services and number of CVSs staff had taken place during 1976/77. The replies suggest that despite the fact that many of the increased sums in grant were less than sufficient to maintain the real value of the grants, about two thirds of the CVSs have been able to maintain staff and services at their current level. However only one CVS was in the process of expanding and 29 per cent of the respondents (32) mentioned retrenchment. The 32 are of all sizes, from the large organisations of Bristol and Manchester employing many staff, down to those with only one paid worker in Friern Barnet and none in Sidmouth. Whilst some admit that their grant aid has been cut in cash terms, many of the 32 state that they received a cash increase over the previous year's figure.

When we consider the replies to the third question on expectations

Table 5A:5. Retrenchment by CVSs in 1976/77

Changes in staff and services	*No. of CVSs*
Expansion	1
Same	70
Retrenchment	32
Don't know	8
Receiving no grant	5
Total replies	116
No reply	52

for aid for 1977/78, it seems likely that even more CVSs will be obliged to retrench in 1977/78. The replies refer to CVSs negotiations with their local authorities for grant-aid in the new financial year. Again all CVSs replying to this third question talked in cash terms while realising that 'the same grant' really implied a cut in resources. These replies suggest a radical change from the position of the last two years; whereas in 1976/77, 67 CVSs could record some increase in grant-aid, in 1977/78 only 7 CVSs expected any increase; 30 CVSs did not know what level of aid they would receive; and if the expectations of the remainder are fulfilled, they will experience real cuts in their income ranging from perhaps a few per cent to the majority of their income in some cases. Havering Council of Social Service stated that closure is a real possibility in 1977/78. Lancaster and Morecambe CVSs expected a complete cut of all grant-aid from the County Council in 1977/78.

The overall picture of the work and resources of the CVS is more complex than the replies to the three questions suggest. The level of services in any one area does not solely depend on the local authority grant aid; CVS may be able to seek assistance from their member organisations or may be dependent on volunteers as their main resource; a few have proportionally large incomes from investments; many CVS stated that they are having to devote more resources to fund raising and appeals. This would explain the replies to the first two questions which suggest that many CVS were able to maintain their existing level of activity despite the fact that probably only a few received a grant which maintained its real value. Nevertheless, the replies to the third question suggested poor prospects for the year 1977/78. A quarter of the CVSs were in the insecure position of not knowing what their level of grant will be. Very few expected an increase in aid, even in cash terms, and the existence of some CVS may be in jeopardy.

APPENDIX 5B

Some Organisations Set Up Originally By the NCSS and Now Independent

(Date of becoming independent in brackets)

National Association of Boys Clubs (1925)
Youth Hostels Association (1930)
National Federation of Young Farmers Clubs (1932)
Rural Industries Loan Fund (1940)
Social Workers Pension Fund (1946)
World Assembly of Youth (1948)
National Association of Parish Councils (1951)
National Television Advisory Group (1956)
National Children's Bureau (National Bureau for Cooperation in Child
    Care) (1963)
Pre-Retirement Association (1964)
Age Concern (National Old Peoples Welfare Council) (1969)
Charities Aid Foundation (1975)
National Association of Women's Clubs (1976)
National Association of Citizen's Advice Bureaux (1977)

Constituent Bodies of NCSS (1977)

National Association of Citizen's Advice Bureaux
London Council of Social Service
Standing Conference of Rural Community Councils
Standing Conference of Councils for Voluntary Service
National Federation of Community Associations
National Council for Voluntary Youth Services
Women's Forum
National Drama Conference
Standing Conference for Amateur Music
Standing Conference for Local History
Standing Conference for the Advancement of Counselling

APPENDIX 6A

The Income of Voluntary Organisations in 1975

Two estimates have been published quite recently of the total income of charities. These must be the starting point for an examination of the income of voluntary organisations. In the May 1975 issue of *Economic Trends* Moyle and Reid suggested that in 1970 charities received £970 million, or £1009 million if one takes the figures for 'charities and other non-profit bodies' used in their tables. This work was the result of an attempt by the Central Statistical Office to improve the data available about households by separating non-profit bodies from the personal sector of the national accounts. The CSO is now updating its figures, but in the end was unable to let us see its results before the completion of this report. The other recent estimate was published by Falush in the May 1977 issue of the *National Westminster Bank Quarterly Review*. He produced a figure of £999 million for 1975. Since retail prices nearly doubled between 1970 and 1975 these two estimates are much more discrepant than might appear at first sight. Indeed if one adjusts the CSO figure upwards in proportion to the rise in retail prices, and like Falush includes legacies, one emerges with a figure for 1975 of £2000 million, or double that of Falush.

The actual figures are shown by source of income in Table 6A:1. In seeking to reconcile the figures the following points are relevant. The figure of £186 million given by Falush for charities' income from public authorities includes £96 million attributed to central government. However the £96 million referred to by Falush relates simply to education (see Table 7:1, *National Income and Expenditure 1965-75*). The data in Appendix 6B indicate that about £24 million was provided by central government under other headings, not counting expenditure by such bodies as the Arts and Sports Councils. On the other hand, if one counts simply grants and excludes fees and charges and assumes that the national average for grants by local authorities was little more than £1 per capita, his figure for local authorities seems unduly high; so the total figure may not be far out. It is giving by individuals that shows the widest discrepancy. Falush bases his estimate on giving recorded by the Family Expenditure Survey: he makes a small upward adjustment for the under-representation in the FES of better-off households, but even if one makes a further allowance for unrecorded gifts and assumes that only a half of all private giving is caught in the FES net, one is still left

Table 6A:1. Alternative estimates of the income of charities, by source of income

	Moyle and Reid 1970 £m	Falush 1975 £m
Rent	57	Not estimated
Dividends & interest	203	336
Central government	50	} 186
Local government	40	
Companies	8	42
Individuals (excl. legacies)	490	200
Overseas	9	Not estimated separately
Sales of publications	12	
Other sales of goods	82	} 70
Other fees & charges	58	
	1,009	834
Legacies	102	165
	1,111	999

with a figure of only £330 million. If the CSO figure for 1970 is multiplied by the increase in giving between then and 1975 recorded by the FES one emerges with a figure of about £620 million. Evidently there are differences of interpretation and coverage here. Falush allows £70 million for what he describes as 'other income (net)'. In arriving at a total figure for the income of charities it makes sense to count only trading profits, not all receipts from trade when these are subsidiary fund-raising activities, but to include all fees and charges when these are in respect of the main activity of the organisation, e.g. providing residential care. If one does this, Falush's £70 million is clearly too small. In 1975/76 local authority social service departments in England and Wales paid £62 million to voluntary organisations and private concerns in the form of agency payments, fees and charges, mostly in respect of children and elderly people in residential homes. Some of these payments may have been what we would call grants rather than fees, and others went to what we would consider commercial bodies. On the other hand, Scotland and Northern Ireland are not included. Equivalent payments by local education authorities in England and Wales in 1975/76 amounted to £34 million, mostly in respect of direct grant and special schools (source: DOE Revenue Out-

turn forms). To these should be added all the fees paid for pupils in
independent schools and various private health establishments with
charitable status. In 1975 there were 329,000 pupils in independent
schools recognised as efficient. More than 120,000 were boarders. Not
all these schools had charitable status, but account should also be taken
of schools in Scotland and Northern Ireland. According to the Independent Schools Information Service fees for boarders at Headmasters
Conference independent schools had reached an average of £1,500 per
annum by September 1975. Pupils of younger age and day pupils of all
ages will have paid considerably less than this. But a minimum figure can
be derived from the sum £750 × 300,000, which equals £225 million.
Altogether, it seems that the income of charities from fees and charges
and profits from trade cannot have been less than £400 million.
Accepting Falush's figures for companies, dividends and legacies (which
are based on CSO data) and adding £100 million for rent received (the
CSO estimate), one arrives at the revised figures for the total income of
charities in 1975 shown in Table 6A:2.

Table 6A:2. Revised estimates for the income of
charities 1975

	£m
Dividends interest and rent	436
Central government grants	120
Local government grants	70
Companies	42
Individuals	330
Legacies	165
Fees, charges and profits	400
	1,563

The total of £1,563 million refers to charities. Certain additions and
subtractions must be made in order to relate this figure to voluntary
organisations as we have defined them. To begin with, some voluntary
organisations like Gingerbread and Friends of the Earth do not have
charitable status, but the amount that should be added on in respect of
such bodies is probably small. On the other hand the income of organisations predominantly dependent on private fee paying needs to be
deducted. If one makes a guesstimate of £375 million for this, the
resulting figure for voluntary organisations as a whole is over £1,200m.

A further set of calculations is required in order to narrow the figure
down to fields with which the Committee was concerned. It should be

remembered that none of the estimates that have been discussed in this appendix include universities and colleges, trades unions and friendly societies or housing associations. But they do include churches and other religious organisations and charities which are intended to promote sport, recreation, the arts, the armed services and animal welfare, none of which could be described as social or environmental services. The Wells Collection gives a figure of £128 million for the income of religious bodies in 1973, which allowing for inflation might have risen to £150 million in 1975. One can make an alternative calculation by taking the number of priests and ministers of religions recorded in the 1971 Census – 41,000 (not counting those working as teachers, etc.): if one assumes that their average income in 1975 plus the associated expenses of running their churches was between £3,000 and £4,000 one again emerges with a total in the region of £150 million. The other charities that fall outside the social and environmental services are more difficult to isolate. However, the annual report of the Charity Commissioners for 1970 gives a breakdown of charities according to their objects. This information, interpreted in the light of the Charity Commissions's 'Classified or Objects Code', suggests that in addition to religion not more than about 10 per cent of all charities fell outside the field of the social and environmental services. If one assumes that they had an income proportionate to their numbers and deducts the income thus estimated and that of the religious bodies one ends up with a figure of about £1,000 million.

Within the social and environmental services the Committee excluded education from its deliberations. About a quarter of all charities registered with the Charity Commission have educational objects. These range from the independent schools already discussed through direct grant grammar schools and various agricultural colleges to such public bodies as the Schools Council. They also include a host of small scholarship or prize funds. To disentangle all these from the other social and environmental services would, in view of the lack of relevant data, be a very difficult task, and it is not attempted here.

Most of the figures presented in this note are to a greater or lesser extent imprecise. They do, however, indicate the orders of magnitude involved and they will we hope, act as an incentive for the collection of more precise information.

APPENDIX 6B

Grants to Voluntary Organisations by Public Authorities

The data on grants made by central government departments and other centrally administered services have as far as possible been confined to fields covered by the Committee's research. For example the Arts Council, the Sports Council and payments to direct grant schools have been omitted. The grants made by the Department of Employment refer to training for handicapped people and to Community Industry which seeks to help young people with special problems. The information available about local authority grant giving is much more patchy, and the nature of data presented is explained below.

	£m 1974/75	£m 1975/76	£m 1976/77
CENTRAL GOVERNMENT DEPARTMENTS			
DES	5.2	6.5	7.2
DHSS	1.8	2.2	2.8
VSU (incl. WRVS)	2.4	3.4	4.5
Home Office (excl. VSU)	0.9	1.5	1.8
Dept. of Employment	3.4	5.8	8.6
DOE	1.6	1.7	2.5
Scottish Office	1.2	1.7	1.7
N. Ireland Office	2.0	4.0	4.6
Welsh Office	0.1	0.2	0.2
Dept. of Prices & Consumer Protection	0.4	0.8	1.2
Other Depts.	0.2	0.2	0.3
Total	19.2	28.0	35.4

Note: In 1976/77 £1.9m reached voluntary organisations under the auspices of the Urban Programme, but this is counted under local authority expenditure

OTHER CENTRALLY ADMINISTERED SERVICES			
Supplementary Benefits Commission	0.05	0.07	0.11
Community Relations Commission	0.54	0.88	1.12
Development Commission	0.6	0.91	1.0
Countryside Commission	0.2	0.35	0.4
Nature Conservancy Council	0.04	0.02	0.03
Total	1.43	2.23	2.66
Health Authorities (England & Wales)	0.17	Not Yet Available	

The above tables do not include the following:

(a) *The Job Creation Programme* began in October 1975. Between then and the end of March 1977 grants totalling £31.2 million had been made by it to voluntary organisations.

(b) *Housing associations.* In 1975/76 housing associations received in all some £240 million from central government, most of it channelled through the Housing Corporation.

(c) *The Equal Opportunities Commission* began making grants to voluntary organisations in 1976/77, when it awarded altogether over £22,000 to organisations concerned with the position of women in society.

Local Government

Data on grants made to voluntary organisations by local authorities in England and Wales is collected in the DOE Revenue Out-turn forms that relate to personal social services and education. The quality of this information suffers from the different interpretations and practices of different local authorities. What in one authority is a grant from the Social Services Committee may in another be a grant by the Policy Committee or counted as payment for services provided. Nevertheless this is the best aggregate data available within these two fields. It includes Urban Aid. The same forms also provide data on payments for services provided by voluntary organisations. Payments to private enterprises are also included, but probably amount to less than 10 per cent of the total.

Payments to Voluntary Organisations by Local Authorities in England and Wales

		£m 1974/75	£m 1975/76
Personal Social Services:	Grants	5.2	7.9
	Fees, charges, etc. (mainly for residential care)	45.0	61.5
Education:	Grants	8.0	no longer collected
	Fees, charges, etc. (mainly for special education)	20.1	33.9

Source: DOE: Local Authority Out-turn figures

Few local authorities seem to collect together information on all the grants they give to voluntary organisations. However we have received full data on the grants given by a small number of authorities. This was not gathered in a systematic way but it does illustrate well the very wide differences between authorities in per capita expenditure.

Grants made by Local Authorities to Voluntary Organisations — some illustrations. (1976/77 unless otherwise stated)

	SOCIAL SERVICES		ALL GRANTS	
METROPOLITAN *DISTRICTS*	*Total* *£000s*	*£ per* *cap*	*Total* *£000s*	*£ per* *cap*
Newcastle-upon-Tyne	305.9	1.03	424.1	1.43
Sunderland	122.9	0.42	387.5	1.32
S. Tyneside	3.6	0.02	82.4	0.48
Manchester	304.1	0.60	940.3	1.82
Solihull	7.4	0.04	10.0	0.05
Sheffield (1977/78 estimates)	80.3	0.14	209.8	0.37
Wirral	not shown separately		67.0	0.19
NON-MET. COUNTIES				
Humberside				
The County Council	28.5	0.03	202.0	0.24
Total for 8 Districts	20.0 approx	0.03	55.5	0.06
Grand Total Humberside	48.5	0.06	257.5	0.30
East Sussex				
The County Council	123.3	0.19	255.0	0.39
Total for 7 Districts	59.1	0.09	110.1	0.17
Grand Total	182.4	0.28	365.1	0.56
Avon				
The County Council	302.5	0.33	549.3	0.60
Districts	not available		not available	
Hampshire				
The County Council	192.2	0.13	476.4	0.33
Districts	not available		not available	
GREATER LONDON				
Inner London Boroughs				
Islington	805.5	4.69	1,239.0	7.22
Wandsworth	not shown separately		494.0	1.74
Hammersmith	not shown separately		206.0	1.21
Camden	not shown separately		1,200.0	6.46
ILEA (1977/78 estimates)	not a social services authority		3,244.0	1.30
Outer London Boroughs				
Brent	101.0	0.39	258.1	1.00
Croydon	not shown separately		161.6	0.49
London Boroughs Assoc.	not shown separately		440.0	0.06
GLC:	Not a social services authority		1,960.0	0.28

These figures are intended as a guide to the level of local authority grant-aid and have limitations. Some authorities may have omitted smaller budgets such as support for the arts, and it should be recognised that some of the grants were made in support of activities outside our field of interest.

If per capita grant-aid is plotted on a graph against per capita social
services expenditure, there is a noticeable positive correlation of high
social services expenditure with per capita grant-aid to voluntary
organisations. It would appear that those authorities which maintain a
high level of per capita social services expenditure also give propor-
tionately large sums in grants to voluntary organisations. On examination we find that this relationship is established mainly by the London
boroughs, (particularly the inner London boroughs which have very
high levels of social services expenditure) and the larger metropolitan
districts: Newcastle, Manchester, Liverpool, Birmingham, Sheffield and
Leeds. A similar graphical comparison of per capita social services
expenditure with per capita grant-aid to CVSs shows the same relationship. There are very few authorities where one might suspect that grant-
aid to voluntary organisations was used as a substitute for local
authority social services department expenditure. However the majority
of local authorities combine a low level of per capita grants with a low
level of per capita expenditure on the personal social services.

APPENDIX 6C

Trends in Voluntary Giving

The volume of the services voluntary organisations can provide and their independence from statutory authorities is much affected by the amount of money they can raise from the general public. This appendix brings together data from various sources on trends in voluntary giving since 1970.

There are limitations to the generalisations that can safely be made on the basis of each individual source of data. These are indicated below. Also it is essential to take price changes into account. As explained in Chapter 9, the choice of which index of prices is used makes a considerable difference: the index of retail prices, which rose by 84 per cent between 1970 and 1975, is an indicator of changes in what donors could buy for themselves if they had not given the money away; while the index of personal social services costs, which rose by 124 per cent between 1970 and 1975, is an indicator of changes in what the receiving organisations could purchase with the money donated. In adjusting the figures below to show the effect of price changes the index of retail prices, as published in *Social Trends*, has been used: it should be recognised that this substantially underestimates the effect of inflation on the costs of many voluntary organisations.

Donations by individuals to charities (including covenants)
Source: Family Expenditure Survey

	1969	1970	1971	1972	1973	1974	1975
Average £ per household per week	0.103	0.130	0.115	0.119	0.137	0.157	0.164
Adjusted for change in retail prices	84	100	80	79	82	81	68

Covenanted gifts by persons and companies to charities.
Source: Inland Revenue

	1970	1971	1972	1973	1974	1975	1976
£m total	40.9	49.9	54.0	63.1	62.8	71.9	81.7
Adjusted for change in retail prices	100	110	113	121	103	95	97

Top 50 Fund Raising Charities: Income from Voluntary Giving

	1970	1975
£m	44.6	85.1
Adjusted for change in retail prices	100	103

COMPARISONS	1970	1975
Real income per person	100	117.5
Public expenditure on personal social services adjusted for change in index of pss expenditure	100	170

It is clear that the deterioration of the economic situation since 1974 has been accompanied by a sharp decline in voluntary giving. Whether this is part of a long-term decline, and the extent to which voluntary giving will recover when the economic situation improves is more difficult to tell. Since 1970 public expenditure on the social and environmental services has been rising much faster than voluntary giving: in this respect the relative deterioration of the position of the voluntary sector is indisputable.

The Family Expenditure Survey is a large national survey. Households participating in the survey keep a detailed record of their expenditure over a period of two weeks: when these are analysed donations of all kinds, expenditure at bazaars, etc. are added up and annually covenanted payments are apportioned over the whole year. When the average of weekly donations per household derived thereby is grossed up to produce an estimate for the amount given each year by the whole population the resulting total for 1975 is between £150 million and £200 million. This is well below other estimates and suggests that a lot of gifts are not covered by the survey. Better-off people are thought to be underrepresented in the FES, and this may account for some of the missing millions, as may seasonal fluctuations in giving. However there is no evidence that the coverage of the survey varies substantially from one year to another, so there is little reason to think that the evidence on trends is invalid.

Covenants The Inland Revenue records the sums it pays to charities in respect of tax relief on covenants made by individuals and companies. The total amount covenanted can be calculated in the light of the standard rate of income tax. However the interval between receipt of the covenanted money and repayment of tax may vary, and it is thought that the proportion of voluntary giving made through the medium of covenants may be rising. It is not possible to distinguish sums covenanted by individuals from those covenanted by companies.

The Top Fifty Fund-Raising Charities Our own study (see Appendix

6D) provides evidence of the total amount received by these large organisations from voluntary giving (including trusts) in 1970 and 1975.

APPENDIX 6D

The Income of the Largest Fifty Fund-Raising Charities in 1970 and 1975

Rosalind Howell

Introduction

In 1975 the total income of the 50 organisations in our study came to £134 million; perhaps some 10 per cent of the income of all charities in the country. These 50 organisations are taken from the *Wells Collection* (1973 edition) list of the '100 largest fund-raising charities in the UK'. We excluded from this list five missionary societies and one organisation concerned with animal welfare as being outside the Committee's field of interest; and then took the largest 50 organisations all of which had incomes of £0.5 million or over in 1973. There are a number of charities of this size which do not occur in the Wells list, among them at least a dozen grant-giving trusts, various learned societies, research institutes and some housing associations, public schools and private health organisations. With the exception of the housing associations, nearly all the charities omitted from the Wells list fall outside the voluntary social and environmental services. Within this field we are reasonably confident that, apart from the housing associations and two or three exceptions like the NCSS, all the organisations with incomes over £0.5 million in 1973 and £0.75 million in 1975 are included.

In this report we discuss first the overall performance of the 50 organisations in the light of inflation between 1970 and 1975. We then examine the different sources of their income and changes in the importance of these separate sources between each of the two years, before concluding with some general observations. Information about the income of these charities was elicited from the published accounts for their accounting years ending in 1970 and 1975. The organisations were contacted directly where it was necessary to clarify aspects of their accounting procedure, and sometimes accounts lodged with the Charity Commissioners were consulted. For our purposes income means all income received by the voluntary organisation and shown in its income and expenditure account plus money raised for additions to capital shown in the balance sheet. We also included any income derived from special funds. We did not, however, include gains or losses from the sale of assets. The accounting practices of the organisations studied are far from uniform. The task of adding together data from 50 organisations has not been easy, and it must be recognised that in relation to particular organisations alternative interpretations of the accounts might present a different picture.

Overall Performance

The Retail Price Index rose between 1970 and 1975 by 84 per cent; but this does not reflect at all closely the prices of goods and services to which expenditure on the social services is devoted. An alternative index is that calculated for PESC (the Public Expenditure Survey Committee) in order to provide data on public expenditure on the personal social services at constant prices. This shows a price rise of 124 per cent. The total income of our fifty organisations rose from £65.0 million in 1970 to £133.7 million in 1975, a rise of 106 per cent. Thus their rate of growth falls between the two indices of inflation. In the light of the data presented in Appendix 6C they seem to have been doing well, relative to smaller voluntary organisations.

It should be noted at this point that some of the organisations, particularly those with large numbers of local branches, have not presented consolidated accounts. This is true of the Scout Association for example, where affiliation fees and a per capita levy are noted in the HQ account; this represents the contribution of local organisations to the HQ not their locally-derived income. The British Red Cross has only since 1976 decided to assemble a consolidated account; the performance of the HQ may not bear a close resemblance, in the years we have studied, to the financial position of local branches which have a range of undertakings of their own such as the running of homes. It has not been possible to overcome this limitation on our findings in the time available to us.

Differences between organisations

Table 6D:1 demonstrates the great variation in the fortunes of the 50 organisations during the five years. They are a very disparate group. The National Association of Youth Clubs has become the instrument for the Government's Community Industry Programme and this accounts for its position at the top of the table. Even when it is excluded, the incomes of the organisations still range from an increase of nearly six times their 1970 income achieved by Help the Aged, to a decrease of 49 per cent represented by Shelter. We have indicated in the table those organisations which experienced an increase of more than double the 106 per cent average of the group. It will be noticed that all those organisations

Table 6D:1. Change Between 1970 and 1975 by Source of Income (1970 = 100)

Organisation	Legacies	Voluntary Giving (incl. legacies)	Fees and Charges	Central Govt. grants	Invest-ment	Total	Total Income '75 £m
All 50 combined	228	191	263	238	204	206	133.7
National Association of Youth Clubs	*	120	164	2713	108	738	2.1
Help the Aged	3566	570	—		2382	572	5.6
Royal Hospital and Home for Incurables	425	353	495	—	161	395	1.4
Nightingale House	194	496	329	—	232	376	1.0
RSPB	772	367	265	—	460	360	1.1
Cheshire Homes	?	243	375	—	375	325	5.4
. . . . . Increase of double the average							
Jewish Welfare Board	194	320	240	—	423	285	1.6
Multiple Sclerosis	301	266	—	—	378	275	1.1
Royal National Mission for Deep Sea Fishermen	290	253	—	—	396	262	0.7
National Trust	179 ↓	337	227	252	186	259	9.3
National Children's Home	140	161	623	47	227	251	6.2
National Society for Cancer Relief	264	235	—	—	405	247	1.5
Arthritis & Rheumatism RC	296	234	456	—	423	246	1.3
C of E Children's Society	234	215	230	—	214	245	4.5
Methodist Homes for the Aged		222		—	294	228	1.2
Institute Cancer Research and Royal Cancer Hospital	246	238	—	210	206	223	2.7
Marie Curie Memorial Fund	309	221	209	**	190	221	2.0

Table 6D:1. (continued)

Organisation	Legacies	Voluntary Giving (incl. legacies)	Fees and Charges	Central Govt. Charges	Invest- ment	Total	Total Income '75 £m
NSMHC	301	160	441	—	371	220	1.3
RNLI	212	219	—	—	218	219	5.3
Imperial Cancer Research Fund	234	210	—	—	255	218	6.7
NSPCC	255	190	128	**	140	213	2.5
Cancer Research Campaign	243	211	—	—	220	212	6.1
. . . . Average increase							
Jewish Blind Society	351	169	270	—	267	200	0.7
Barnardos	182	165	305	—	219	198	7.5
RNID	272	199	193	—	196	196	0.7
RNIB	225	206	177	1	337	194	5.3
National Fund for Research into Crippling Diseases	212	209	—	—	131	194	1.2
Royal British Legion	273	180	—	180	192	192	3.1
Heart of Variety	?	197	—	—	26	190	1.0
Shaftesbury Society	175	137	225	*	197	189	0.8
Tenovus	671	144	—	**	1175	188	0.6
SSAFA	385	140	53	276	170	187	1.6
RAF Benevolent Fund	228	193	—	—	180	187	1.9
Salvation Army (Social Work in UK)	171	156	193	—	160	186	4.7
Army Benevolent Fund	161	182	—	—	187	184	0.7
British Heart Foundation	194	176	—	—	246	183	1.1
National Council YMCAs	106	102	195	206	187	183	3.1

King George's Fund for Sailors	339	202	—	—	160	179	0.5
Spastics Society	229	157	224	—	166	175	6.8
British Red Cross HQ	172	166	—	—	107	161	1.4
DGAA	147	144	139	—	244	159	1.2
. . . . . . Increase of half the average							
Save the Children	296	145	—	105	407	146	3.7
Oxfam	↓	149	—	*	154	145	4.8
World Wildlife	2913	130	—	—	899	140	0.9
St Dunstans	?	134	—	—	145	139	2.3
Christian Aid	268	143	—	*	208	139	4.2
RUKBA	117	115	303	—	144	138	1.3
Scout Association	89	133	—	132	225	136	0.7
War on Want	?	70	—	—	1847	74	0.5
Shelter	?	51	?	—	42	51	0.5

KEY

* Receipt in 1970 only

** Receipt in 1975 only

— No receipts under this item

↓ Items undifferentiated from other source

? Item not mentioned but probably included under another source

have managed to attract substantial increases in funds from voluntary
sources and are comfortably off, irrespective of increases in other
sources of income. At the bottom end of the table we have marked off
those organisations with an increase of less than 50 per cent below the
average. It is difficult to discern a common feature in their performance.
St Dunstan's and RUKBA are old organisations whose style of operation may be attracting less popular support than before, while the
relief organisations will have been much affected by the absence of
major disasters in 1975. Shelter's income dropped by 50 per cent in
absolute terms. No doubt this reflects the controversy that has
surrounded its affairs after its early successes. In interpreting this data
it should be remembered that special circumstances may raise or
depress the income of a given organisation out of line with preceding or
following years.

Sources of Income

Table 6D:2 shows the proportion of income coming from different
sources in each of the two years.

Table 6D:2. Sources of Income in 1970 and 1975

Sources of Income	1970 per cent	1975 per cent
Donations, Subscriptions etc. (including income from trusts)	51	44
Legacies	18	20
Fees and Charges	16	21
Central Government Grants	3	4
Rents, Investments, Dividends	11	11
TOTAL INCOME	£65m = 100	£134m = 100

Voluntary Giving

In many sets of accounts, different forms of voluntary giving were
lumped together in a variety of permutations. We found it necessary to
aggregate the sums coming from these sources in order to achieve some
degree of comparability. Thus 'voluntary giving' consists of transfers
from private persons, including legacies, subscriptions and donations;
transfers from companies, transfers from charitable trusts, and
covenants. This information is available from all 50 organisations and is
aggregated in Table 6D:1. In Table 6D:2 the proportion of income

coming from legacies is not included under voluntary giving, except in the case of the eight organisations which did not give a separate figure for legacies.

The income of the top 50 from all voluntary sources has risen from £44.6 million to £85.1 million, an increase over the five years of 91 per cent. This is just over the rise in the Retail Prices Index but it falls far short of the rise in the PESC index. In 1970, 17 organisations depended on voluntary giving for more than 90 per cent of their income, compared to eleven in 1975. The greatest proportionate increases in income from voluntary sources were achieved by Help the Aged and Nightingale House.

Legacies

We have isolated legacies from the voluntary giving in order to assess their importance as a source of income and their impact upon the growth of voluntary contributions received by the top 50. Our information is derived from 42 organisations only since several accounts did not distinguish legacies from donations generally. Income from legacies seems to be more buoyant than voluntary giving as a whole. The total amount received in legacies by these 42 organisations was £11.8 million in 1970 and £26.8 million in 1975, an increase of 128 per cent. This compares with total incomes of those 42 of £55.2 million and £107.7 million in 1970 and 1975 respectively. However, we do not think that the remaining eight organisations were less dependent upon legacies than the 42 and if the total is grossed up on the basis of the percentage of total income derived from legacies to yield a figure for all 50 organisations, this raises legacies to £13.9 million in 1970 and £33.2 million in 1975.

As far as we know, the three organisations which were most dependent upon legacies in 1975 were the Imperial Cancer Research Fund (60 per cent), the Arthritis and Rheumatism Research Council (58 per cent) and the RNLI (54 per cent). Among the least dependent was the Army Benevolent Fund (0.8 per cent), and other organisations for the forces relied little upon legacies: SSAFA (5.0 per cent), Royal British Legion (5.7 per cent). Organisations for youth acquired little from this source — National Association of YMCAs (0.9 per cent), Scouts (5.3 per cent), and it was not a major item for the international relief organisations — Christian Aid (4.5 per cent), Save the Children Fund (7.6 per cent), nor for Salvation Army social work (2.7 per cent).

Profits from Trade

Profits from trade have been included with voluntary giving in the tables, since we felt that it was generally the case that customers bought from charities as one way of making a voluntary contribution to those organisations. Information about this item in the accounts was in many cases difficult to isolate. We have firm information from twelve organisations which gave us a total of £1.1 million in 1970 and £2.1 million in 1975. The actual amounts for all 50 organisations is hard to estimate: we do not known the precise extent to which the temporary withdrawal of rate relief to charity shops in 1974 has affected the net profits of these organisations.

Fees and Charges

We have information from 24 organisations about fees and charges. These 24 represent most voluntary organisations in our group providing services to the aged, children and the handicapped. This includes both local authority paid charges and those paid by clients, since only six of the 24 organisations gave a breakdown showing the contribution of local authorities separately. From our knowledge of the work of the remaining 26 organisations we believe that their income under this heading is small. The 24 organisations received altogether £10.6 million in fees in 1970 and £28.0 million in 1975. This is an increase of 163 per cent overall. The organisations most dependent in 1975 on fees and charges were: National Council of YMCAs (89 per cent), Salvation Army social work (83 per cent), the Shaftesbury Society (69 per cent), Cheshire Homes (68 per cent), the Royal Hospital and Home for Incurables (63 per cent), the National Children's Home (56 per cent). The YMCA is in a special position regarding its income from fees and charges. Our figures refer solely to the National Council's income, a large part of which is derived from their provision of goods and services to the armed forces at home and abroad. They do not include the income of all the local YMCAs.

Although this increase in fees and in the organisations' dependence upon them has been substantial and applies mainly to those organisations which provide residential or day care, we do not know to what extent the number of clients has changed. Although we suspect that the number of clients has not generally increased, we do know that children's organisations are now tending to claim the full current cost of keeping a child in care and not merely a proportion. The local authority paid fees for six organisations amount to £2.2 million in 1970 and £9.9 million in 1975, an increase of 347 per cent in the five years.

For the same six organisations the client contribution by contrast increased by only 120 per cent from £0.7 million to £1.5 million. The increased importance of fees and charges represents the most significant change in the incomes of those voluntary organisations to which they are relevant. This is demonstrated even more strikingly in the concurrent research of Dr Judith Unell of the NCSS. She has been analysing both the incomes and expenditure of 80 national service-giving organisations. For these organisations the proportion of income derived from fees and charges has gone up from 25 per cent to 37 per cent.

Central Government Grants

Sixteen organisations received grants from central government departments in either 1970 or in 1975 if not in both years; we think that most central government funding was mentioned separately in accounts. The central government grants to the 16 organisations amounted to £2.4 million in 1970 and £5.6 million in 1975, an increase of 132 per cent over the period. Part of this central government money consisted of sums paid to international relief organisations: Christian Aid, Oxfam and Save the Children Fund. The first two of these received grants only in 1970 and these were earmarked for special relief programmes for disasters during that year. This is a sharply fluctuating source of income, reflecting government funding of specific projects as well as changes in government policy affecting particular need areas, for example using the National Association of Youth Clubs as a vehicle for Community Industry.

Investment Income

All 50 organisations received income from investments and dividends and from rented property. In 1970 this amounted to £7.3 million and in 1975 £15.0 million, an increase of 104 per cent. Again within this group, growth in investment income varied enormously. The investment income of 35 organisations grew faster than retail prices, and by 1975 14 were receiving three times as much from this source as they were in 1970. However, our evidence does not tell us whether organisations have been increasing the amounts they invest or conversely whether they have been using capital for building projects, for example. The proportion of income derived from investments has changed little between 1970 and 1975. It contributes approximately 11 per cent of the total. In 1975 those organisations which relied most upon their investment income were mainly organisations concerned with the services; RUKBA (49 per cent), King George Fund for Sailors (48 per cent), the RAF Benevolent Fund (44 per cent), St Dunstan's (42 per cent) and the Army Benevolent Fund (35 per cent).

Conclusions

Taken together, the income of the 50 large charities kept up with retail prices between 1970 and 1975, but not with social service costs; and it fell well below the rise in public expenditure on social and environmental services generally. The performance of individual organisations varied immensely. We suspect that no 50 local authority departments would show such a wide range of variation. Whether seen as flexibility or insecurity, voluntary organisations have much more of it!

APPENDIX 6E

Possible Improvements in Statistics

This report has argued for a strengthening of the voluntary sector. The bigger the part it plays the greater the need will be for systematic and reliable information about it. Elsewhere in this report, and particularly in the earlier parts of this appendix, we explain the limitations of the data at present available. Here we outline briefly a number of simple ways in which statistics about the voluntary sector could be improved. The emphasis is on data about the voluntary sector as a whole. As regards particular organisations or need areas there is, with the partial exception of residential care, a dearth of data on the work of voluntary bodies; but the remedy is bound to be specific to the need area and the bodies concerned and the purposes for which data is required. In the field of the personal social services the suggestions made not very long ago by George Murray* are still valid.

There are two possible avenues of advance. One relates to the data on private non-profit-making bodies produced by the Central Statistical Office (Table 4.4, *National Income and Expenditure 1965–75*), the other to the work of the Charity Commission. A breakdown of private non-profit-making bodies into different categories was made by Moyle and Reid in the article in *Economic Trends* discussed in Appendix 6A. Besides 'Charities and other NPBs', the main categories are universities and colleges, trade unions, friendly societies and housing associations. Information about a large proportion of these other categories should be available from the UGC, the Registrar of Friendly Societies and the Housing Corporation respectively, so that it should not be too difficult to present disaggregated data for non-profit-making bodies on a more continuing basis. The main uncertain quantity is 'Charities and others'. In seeking information about it the Central Statistical Office has twice made use of a sample survey, but without going to this trouble some of the items of information could be made more reliable. The Department of the Environment now collects from local authorities through its Revenue Out-turn forms information about payments to voluntary organisations under the headings of education and personal social services. It would not be difficult to gather from local authorities more thorough and more precisely defined information about the support

*In Maunder, W. F. (ed.), *Reviews of UK Statistical Sources*, vol. 1, Heinemann Educational, 1974.

they give to voluntary organisations across all fields of activity. Better
data on company giving would be obtained if the Inland Revenue
distinguished tax repayments made in respect of covenants by individuals from those in respect of companies. On the expenditure side, the
Inland Revenue records wages and salaries paid by non-profit-making
bodies. This is the biggest item of expenditure and a more detailed
breakdown into type of body would not be impossible.

Charities are themselves an extremely diverse group, and it would be
a major task for the CSO to collect a lot more detailed information
about different groups of charities. However, it would be a valuable
improvement if full data on grants and charges paid by public
authorities to voluntary organisations were collected and published in
the DOE's *Local Government Financial Statistics* or the National
Income Blue Book. The recent omission of grants, though not agency
payments, from the Revenue Out-turn form for education is a step
backward in this respect.

As regards the Charity Commission, charities are supposed to lodge
their accounts with the Commission; but anyone who peruses the
Commission's files quickly finds that up-to-date accounts even of quite
large charities are often absent, and that the information contained in
the accounts that are available is inconsistent. In 1970 two thirds of the
registered charities had incomes of under £100, and only 3 per cent had
incomes over £10,000. Little would be gained by seeking more up-to-
date and consistent information about the great mass of small charities.
However there is a case for collecting better information about the
larger charities, say those with an income of over £100,000. They are
not impossibly numerous, and the considerable size of the tax benefits
they receive does entitle the public to information. The Charity
Commission is not at present geared to the production of statistics, but
steps to produce periodically aggregate data about the largest charities
plus sample information about the smaller ones could yield useful
indicators of the progress of charitable organisations and the voluntary
sector generally. The Charities Aid Foundation is now taking steps
which may have this result. But if useful aggregate data is to emerge it
will be essential for the relationship between the data that is collected
and the total population of charities and voluntary organisations to be
exactly known.

The preceding discussion relates entirely to finance, and thus ignores
work done voluntarily. The questions asked for us by the National
Opinion Poll Ltd have enabled us to estimate the size of the voluntary
effort. Comparable questions included in future surveys would make it

possible to refine and update these estimates. The Volunteer Centre is the body with the most direct interest in this topic. It could, as we did, pay for questions to be included in a commercial survey. Alternatively it could seek to persuade the Office of Population Censuses and Surveys that voluntary effort was of sufficient public interest to justify the inclusion of questions in the official General Household Survey.

References

John Moyle and David J. Reid, 'Private non-profit-making bodies serving persons', *Economic Trends*, No. 259, May 1975.

Peter Falush, 'Trends in the finance of British charities', *National Westminster Bank Quarterly Review*, May 1977.

Wells Collection (1973 supplemental edition), published by the Wells Group of Fund-raising Companies, London, autumn 1975.

Report of the Charity Commissioners for England and Wales for the year 1970, HMSO, 1971.

Central Statistical Office, *National Income and Expenditure, 1965-1975*, HMSO, 1976.

J. D. Livingston-Booth and M. Redmond Mullin, *Report on Foundation Activity*, Charities Aid Foundation, 1976.

APPENDIX 7

Report on Visit to the Netherlands

In November 1976 two members of the Committee, Roger Hadley and David Jones, visited the Netherlands, accompanied by our Senior Research Officer, Stephen Hatch. This appendix is an edited version of the report they made to us.

The purpose of the visit was to examine the organisation of social welfare in Holland, where a large proportion of social and health care is provided through the medium of independent non-statutory, non-profit organisations. This form of provision stems from the structure of Dutch society, which has until now been based on three denominational 'pillars' — Protestant, Catholic and 'Humanist' — reflecting the historical religious divisions of the country. Since the Public Assistance Act of 1963, local authorities have been responsible for providing income support to individuals on criteria laid down centrally, but almost all the other social services are provided by the independent agencies. The Ministry for Culture, Recreation and Social Work (CRM) is responsible for three of the various branches of the social services — social casework, 'socio-cultural work' (i.e. youth work, adult education and community work based on neighbourhood centres or settlements) and work with ethnic minorities. We directed most of our attention to the first two of these.

Since the Second World War, government finance has become steadily more important, and now accounts for nearly 100 per cent of the agencies' funds. The number of separate agencies is very large and CRM funds directly between two and three thousand. Originally dependent to a large extent on voluntary effort, the voluntary element has now been almost entirely superseded by paid professional staff, and is confined largely to membership of the governing boards. This proliferation of agencies came about through the practice of groups of individual citizens, who shared a common denominational identity, coming together and on their own initiative arranging for the provision of a service designed to meet local needs. Hence, in a town of any size there have tended to be at least three agencies providing a home help service, three looking after the elderly, three carrying out social casework, probably more than three neighbourhood centres or settlements, acting as bases for youth work, adult education and community work and so on. These organisations are linked together on a vertical rather than a horizontal basis through national federations, which are in turn joined together in the National Council on Social Welfare.

The situation is, however, changing fast and it added greatly to the interest of our visit to find ourselves in the middle of a major controversy about the organisation of social welfare. The main changes giving rise to this controversy seem to be:

(a) The declining salience of denominational divisions in an ever more secular world. This is leading to mergers between different organisations providing the same kind of service in the same area.

(b) Partly for this reason the vitality of the independent agencies has declined at board level: control has shifted towards the professional workers in the absence of any other organised outside constituency.

(c) There is also movement in the Seebohm direction towards the integration of specialised agencies doing different, but related, work.

(d) New needs are being met outside the old denominational framework, e.g. womens' refuges and services for immigrants from Surinam.

(e) There is a growing demand for participation and decentralisation.

(f) Particularly in government circles there is a view that the vast multiplicity of organisations makes the coherent pursuit of social policies of any kind almost impossible. We were told it produced a kind of smokescreen, which inhibited the implementation of adequate levels and standards of provision. There were strong feelings that more effective machinery was needed for monitoring standards, maintaining minimal levels of coverage and ensuring that independent agencies carried out the work for which they were grant-aided. A related point was that often change could only be brought about by the establishment of new agencies.

(g) Since 1973, there has been a socialist-dominated government which has been pursuing the goal of greater equality and promoting social reform under the slogan 'New for Old'.

Decentralisation to the local government level is the solution to these problems which the government is in the process of espousing, together with the development of contractual agreements that would specify more precisely the work to be done and indicators of what had been achieved. The local level, it is felt, is the appropriate one for the pursuit of coordination and accountability. However, in Rotterdam this policy is being interpreted and developed in a way which is causing deep concern to the independent agencies. We were told that the municipality really wanted to take over social services and run them itself, rather on the British pattern. The professional workers from Rotterdam whom we met said that the municipality was endeavouring to impose much tighter control: they felt that the municipality did not understand the nature of the work they were trying to do, and feared that it would prune back their work with unpopular minorities such as drug addicts. However, within Holland the Rotterdam situation is exceptional.

This context provided a favourable opportunity in which to ask questions about the value, actual or potential, of independent voluntary organisations in the social welfare field. One response to these questions was to say that the independent voluntary agencies were so deeply entrenched in Dutch society that their nationalisation or municipalisation was not politically possible. In contrast the General Secretary of the National Council on Social Welfare gave forceful expression to the principle of pluralism: that not all of society could or should be comprehended within and subjected to the political system, which itself should be seen as only one facet of a much larger social whole. Other points in favour of the present system were the choice it offered the consumer (though the exercise of choice depended on understanding its complexities), the ease with which new initiatives could be undertaken and the low level of bureaucracy.

What particularly interested us was the view that the independent agencies were potentially, if not always in practice, a bridge between the individual and the state. It was suggested that a major problem of modern European society was the alienation of the individual from the large scale, often incomprehensible and inflexible bureaucratic apparatus. The independent agencies would be worth preserving if they could overcome this 'us and them' dichotomy, if they provided choice and a countervailing power, if acting on a small-scale local basis they constituted a channel for public involvement and a source of independent initiatives. At the moment they were not adequately fulfilling these functions because their way of working provided inadequately for public involvement and accountability. However, there is evidently growing interest in developing greater accountability, and we were told of experiments and plans for recruiting consumers and neighbourhood representatives onto the boards of certain agencies. It seemed to us that the independent agencies would only be able to maintain their role in the long run if they were successful in widening their constituency by measures such as these.

Another topic we discussed was volunteers. As already stated the voluntary element in the independent welfare agencies has declined and it was our impression that the level of voluntary work is probably lower than in Britain, but steps are being taken to reverse the decline. Experiments in the use of TV to recruit volunteers are well beyond the stage that has been reached in this country, and steps are now afoot to establish a chain of local bureaux which would match the supply of volunteers with the demand for help.

We concluded that the Dutch model is not one that could be transplanted in this country. But equally our visit led us to the view that the present distribution of responsibility and resources between voluntary and statutory sectors in this country should not be taken for granted. A much greater role for the voluntary sector was conceivable and would have certain advantages.

INDEX OF SUBJECTS

INDEX OF NAMES